Praise for *Cos*

"Maum's slender, intelligent *Costalegre* is about many things: art as spectacle and art as discipline; life as joke and life as tragedy; the role of unreason in paintings and politics."   —*The Boston Globe*

"Wounded by her mother's inattention, infatuated with a sculptor, burdened by her femaleness, and increasingly serious about making art, Lara is extraordinarily poignant. By internalizing and then transcending her sources, Maum has created a brilliantly arch and haunting novel of privilege and deprivation."   —*Booklist*

"With both humor and criticality, Maum's coming-of-age novel probes the hypocrisy of the art world, the challenges of being a child of artists, and the dangers of not being loved."   —*Ploughshares*

"A young girl follows her mother and a wayward group of artists into the Mexican jungle on the eve of World War II in this spare, enchanting novel . . . A lush chronicle of wealth, art, adventure, loneliness, love, and folly told by a narrator you won't be able to forget."
                                    —*Kirkus Reviews* (starred review)

"When young Lara finds herself in Costalegre, living with her mother and a gaggle of nineteenth-century surrealist artists, wonder and mayhem ensues. With this slim novel, Courtney Maum has gifted her readers with a breathtaking meditation on youth, art, and the ever-mysterious bonds between mothers and daughters. *Costalegre* is a spectacular high-wire act that dazzles and devastates."   —LAURA VAN DEN BERG,
                                    author of *The Third Hotel*

"Mesmerizing and unsettling, *Costalegre* is a wonder, and Courtney Maum shows herself once again to be a writer of many gifts. This is a book for anyone who's ever loved and not felt sufficiently loved in return; and for anyone who's had to try to grow up; for, that is, everyone."
                                    —R. O. KWON, author of *The Incendiaries*

"This story of a daughter searching for connection all around her has a sharp cutting edge, a world that changes its mood in an instant; bleak as the dregs of a wine-soaked dinner, then bullish as a house of hapless surrealists attempting to boil an egg. Memorable and meaningful, Maum's work remains with me as a reminder of love in the agony of teenage years and art in the terror of war." —AMELIA GRAY, author of *Isadora*

"Here is war, and here is art. And here is a child trying to become an adult in the midst of a Mexican exile. Maum's stirred a brew of careless Bohemians, führers and failed art students, negligent mothers and missing museums. *Costalegre* is as heady, delirious, and heartbreaking as a young girl just beginning to fall in love with our world." —SAMANTHA HUNT, author of *The Dark Dark*

Praise for *Touch*

"Exuberant . . . Maum's writing is easy, eager and colloquial, as oxygenated as ad copy." —*The New York Times Book Review*

"At the heart of Maum's smart, playful, satirical novel is the clash between technology and human interaction . . . As she demonstrated so well in her previous novel, [Maum] brings astute social observations to relationships, whether workplace or romantic." —*The National Book Review*, 1 of 5 Hot Books

"Maum's incisive, charming, and funny novel ebulliently champions the healing powers of touch, the living world, and love in all its crazy risks, surprises, and sustaining radiance." —*Booklist* (starred review)

"Maum . . . has such an incisive grasp of where tech and culture meet that she could add sociologist to her resume." —*Publishers Weekly* (starred review)

Praise for
I Am Having So Much Fun Here Without You

"Here we have the literary beach read—a book that pleases people who read two books a month and people who read two books a year . . . [Maum] is abundantly gifted—funny, open-hearted, adept at bringing global issues into the personal sphere . . . eventually creating that rare thing: a book for everyone."   —*The Washington Post*

"Maum is funny: the kind of funny that is mean and dirty, with some good bad words thrown in. And she has a satiric eye for artsy pretension . . . Enticing."   —*The New York Times Book Review*

"Courtney Maum bursts onto the scene with a hilarious and wise novel . . . Richard Haddon is one of the more lovable male characters we've encountered this season . . . You'll find yourself agog at Maum's masterful storytelling and dead-on descriptions."   —*Glamour*

"Antic, sexy, satirically deft, and of course funny, this novel is also, on both the personal and political levels, smart about the bottomlessness of our capacities for self-sabotage, and moving about the fierceness of our yearning to make good."   —JIM SHEPARD, author of *You Think That's Bad* and *Like You'd Understand, Anyway*

BEFORE AND AFTER THE BOOK DEAL

A Writer's Guide to

- ☑ FINISHING
- ☑ PUBLISHING
- ☑ PROMOTING
- ☑ and SURVIVING

Your First Book

COURTNEY MAUM

Catapult  New York

Before and After the Book Deal

Copyright © 2020 by Courtney Maum

ISBN: 978-1-948226-40-0

Cover design by Sarahmay Wilkinson
Book design by Jordan Koluch
Illustration by Amy Kurzweil and Courtney Maum

Library of Congress Control Number: 2019941065

Printed in the United States of America
10 9 8 7 6 5 4

For the dreamers who sat down to tell a story
that no one asked them to write

Contents

Contents

Contents

Book Two: After the Book Deal

Contents

Contents

Contents

Introduction

The first time I realized publishing a book would be a different experience from writing one was when my publisher asked me to send an email blast to my personal contacts with a preorder link for my debut. Although I'd received such emails in the past from other writers and was familiar with the enterprise, it felt anything but comfortable to write one for myself.

"I've always wanted to be a writer, and now I've finally done it!" I typed before hitting delete. "Twenty-six dollars might seem like a lot of money for a book, but when you divide this sum by the years that I spent writing it . . ." Delete. "Preorders are actually a really important way to . . ." Delete.

As I tried and tried again to find the right tone for this email, I felt a clench of nausea where before there'd been only pride. Up until that moment, I had been my book's author. Now I was its publicist. It wasn't a job that I'd applied for, and yet, the job was mine.

The professionalization of creativity is a by-product of the digital age, and nowhere is this trend more apparent than in publishing, where contemporary authors are expected to be the brand ambassadors for everything they write, taking to their social media feeds, favor banks, and Gmail to shape their book's reception. It can give you a sense of purpose and control to be your own book's champion. But spending too much time promoting our work can change our writing process, and that's a scary thing. Doubts seep in. We consider the marketability of what we are creating. We start comparing ourselves with others—an act that's far too easy now that most authors are online.

I had a really good run with my first novel. Great cover, supportive editor, ride-or-die agent, the whole deal. There was actual cash money put behind the marketing of my debut, and I still came out of that experience a shaking, anxious mess. There were just so many *things* that no one told me. About jealousy. About competition. About the seasonal best-of book lists that come in to ruin your life. About how hard it would be to write something new when your inner multitasker wants you to be on social media all the time. There are a lot of craft books that tell you how to write a book, but I couldn't find any that covered what it feels and looks like when you actually publish one.

And so I sat down to write the crowdsourced turducken of a self-help craft book that I couldn't find. In addition to giving writers the information they need to feel in control of their publication journey, *Before and After the Book Deal* is a safe house for the publishing questions many authors are too afraid to ask.

Do you need to go to book parties? Should you hire an outside publicist? What kind of advance is everyone *else* getting? Should you send trinkets of affection along with blurb requests? Our contributors' advice on these and other matters reflects the time that their interviews took place: writers here might be fretting about debuts that went on to be successes, editors might be referencing new titles that were commercial flops, first-time authors who never thought they'd write again will have managed to turn in their second book projects.

Things change in publishing. Sales go up and down. The muse comes, and then the muse plays hide-and-seek. But if there is one constant I have learned in writing this, it's that everyone is freaking out about their work. From the veteran bestsellers down to the writers who are preparing their manuscript for agent queries, everyone approaches their workspace wondering how the hell they managed to get something good onto the page the day before, because today it feels impossible. Until they start to write.

Whether you are a writer who wants to become an author, or an author who wants to remember how to be a writer once again, I hope that you find comfort here for whatever creative project you are tackling. And if you have picked up this book because you know and love a writer and you're curious about their process, you are a modern hero. Please leave a five-star review on every platform known to readers and say nice things about our books.

With gratitude,
Courtney

Book One

Before
and After
the
Book
Deal

I did not say that writing ought to make everything clearer, but instead makes everything worse; what I said was that writing makes everything clearer *and* worse.

—FRANZ KAFKA

I
....

Getting it right

It is a common misperception that writers write. What a quaint idea! Writers don't write, they fight for time to write. And when they get this time, they dismantle the procrastination traps scattered 'round their desks, and then they write, a little . . . or rather, they *revise,* and then the doorbell rings, and at the door is someone with a fire that only the writer can put out, and by the time the writer has got the fire somewhat under control, the forty-five minutes they had allotted to their writing is up, and they have to go out in the world to teach, edit, read, child-mind, blurb, review, and write for other people so that they can afford to find another forty-five minutes in their week to write for themselves.

If you want to see your work published, all of the craft stuff is important: developing a unique voice, learning how to tell a story, learning through trial and error which stories you are best positioned to tell. But if you lack the skills to create, protect, and wisely use your writing time, you won't have time to write.

Making time to write (and then actually writing)
....

In 2012, I edited a series for *Tin House* called the Super Sad True Habits of Highly Effective Writers. (I borrowed the title from Gary Shteyngart's third novel, but he was a contributor, so, fairsies?) The series ended up revealing that a lot of writers have compulsions they indulge in before they can actually write. I drink tea out of the same mug every morning; Matt Bell uses a secret drafting font that is only for his eyes; Jim Shepard has to have an even number of unanswered emails in his inbox before he can write well. But creating the optimal conditions for writing doesn't mean a writer is going to *write*. You can light a candle, do some push-ups, and say a couple writing prayers, and still find yourself on Clickhole for two hours. Most writers write on computers, and the only thing between their unfinished manuscript and the World Wide Web is willpower.

Even if the Internet isn't your procrastination go-to, there are always a hundred other things to do than write. So how do you stay focused when your dirty dishes have taken up long-term residence in your kitchen sink? How do you *force* yourself to write?

Seek pressure from your peers

Most humans have an innate desire to please people, which is why I shaved off all my arm hair as a ten-year-old when my best friend told me to.

Peer pressure doesn't always have positive outcomes, but it *can* help if you need accountability. The author and critic Michele Filgate used to host a Friday writing group called Get Your Ass on the Bench and Write that helped her generate new work because other people were expecting it, and author Tony Tulathimutte credits much of his professional success to the writing group he has been a part of for fifteen years. Writers such as Lisa Ko find parallel work motivational ("It's hard to go do something else to procrastinate or avoid your work when your friends are busy writing in front of you"), which is why coworking spaces are an attractive option for those who put laundry first and writing seventh when they "work" from home.

There are coworking spaces that exist exclusively for writers that give you access to caffeine, a desk, and a printer for a certain price each month. The downsides are that the printer might not work and you must get into the creative zone alongside a stranger who wants to be published in the exact same places you do; the upside is that you don't have to bring your computer with you every time you go to the restroom.

Monetize your writing

When author Mira Jacob was unexpectedly laid off from a corporate job she'd held in different capacities for over a decade, her husband convinced her to pretend that her two months of severance pay was an advance for her first novel. Almost immediately, though, Mira started receiving sympathy job offers from professionals who knew she had been the only parent working at a parenting website. "I don't think I would have had the courage to turn those opportunities down if I hadn't had an awesome agent who begged me not to take another job," Mira explains. "She told me, 'Don't go back and work for any assholes; this book is going to sell. It will sell for real money. It's going to change your life.' I'd been writing that book for almost ten years," Mira says, "and I finished it in a month."

Mira wasn't setting out to get fired, and she certainly doesn't recommend tacking LAYOFFS! onto your vision board, but it's true that Mira made advances in her writing when she decided to monetize her work. Regardless of what it is—a novel, a collection of short stories, a book of poetry, or essays—most writers will not be getting paid for their first book before it actually becomes one, so you are going to have to trick yourself into believing in its value while you're writing it.

Maybe you divert part of your salary to pay yourself a writing wage—an unnecessary visit to Instagram will feel more lamentable if you're on the clock. If you have the budget, some writers find it useful to rent a separate office or a desk in the kind of communal workspaces we've mentioned. Heck, maybe you need to rent a computer by the hour at an old-school Internet café—whatever it takes to shame your inner procrastinator into actually writing.

DIY your own writing retreat

Customized residencies are a godsend because you don't have to apply for them; you don't even need to leave your couch to participate in one. If you need a weekend to turbospeed ahead in a writing project, put up an out-of-office reminder, change your social media avatars to a note saying "Gone writing," and lock yourself inside your dwelling. (Or have someone lock you up in theirs: when the aforementioned Michele Filgate was trying to finish a difficult personal essay, a friend agreed to keep Michele locked inside their apartment until she finished it, and Lisa Ko has done some of her best writing while pet-sitting for friends.)

Airbnb has homeowners attuned to people's space needs, and savvy hosts have realized how far writers will travel for solid peace and quiet. Formerly private residences like The Porches in Virginia, Patchwork Farm in Massachusetts, or Spruceton Inn in the Catskills have transitioned into retreat centers with customized residencies for writers, and nothing stops you from contacting a hotel to see if they'll offer you a discounted rate if you bring your writing group. For writers looking to pack a little vacation into their retreat, Shaw Guides has a titillating list of conferences in destinations like Peru, Greece, and Mexico, as well as a variety of lesser-known retreats and conferences throughout the United States.

Because writers aren't the only species craving stillness, DIY re-treaters should take note of the meditation resources in their communities. Poet Aaron Belz enjoyed many a writing weekend at the Vision of

Peace Hermitages in Missouri, where twenty-five dollars a night would get him a private cabin or trailer, with meals delivered by a monk in a golf cart for a pittance more. Cameron Dezen Hammon used to do silent retreats at the Villa de Matel convent in Houston, Texas: it was completely free for day use, and the donation for an overnight stay was up to the retreater's discretion. Author Samantha Hunt favors the Holy Cross Monastery in upstate New York, where seventy dollars gets her a room, three square meals, and all the silence she can write through. An added benefit of religious and/or mindfulness programs is that alcohol isn't allowed, which can certainly aid focus.

Know when you work best (and try to write during those times)

When I'm deep into a project, I'm not an easy person to live with. I'm snippy, distracted, disheveled: you interrupt me at my writing desk, I will actually snarl. I have a spouse who also works at home and a young child, and although they're willing to share space with my wild boar–ness sometimes, every day's not cool.

After fits, starts, and therapy, I discovered that planning the work week around my energy levels is the only way that I can show up for all my roles. Mondays and Tuesdays I'm at my most energetic, so I reserve these days exclusively for my creative writing. The other days of the week, I eke out life stuff (email, freelance work, groceries, parenting, attempts at human kindness), and I feel calmer about that eking because of my hyperconcentrated work at the beginning of the week. You can't write all day during a weekday if you have a nine-to-five, but you can learn to honor your energy patterns when you make a writing schedule. If you're not a morning person, it's unlikely that you are going to be able to sustain an existence in which you write before your day job. Likewise, if you have responsibilities that leave you exhausted in the evenings, maybe writing after midnight isn't the best choice. To the extent that you can control for this, try to plan your writing time when you have energy to write.

Setting writing goals

In order to maximize the time they have for writing, the most successful of our brethren decide what they want to accomplish before they start to work. Writing goals often fall into the three following categories:

Quantity

People balk at the idea that a novel can be written in a month, but National Novel Writing Month (better known as NaNoWriMo) exists to prove the contrary. Participants set ambitious word-count goals per day in order to write the entirety of a novel draft during the month of November, and the website offers fun tools to track your progress and to connect with writing friends.

Although NaNoWriMo has created unnecessary stress for literary agents whose inboxes are flooded with half-baked manuscripts each December, it proves that you can make ambitious writing projects manageable by breaking them down into small parts. A ninety-thousand-word novel, for example, can be written over a year by writing three hundred fifty words on each day of the workweek (reward yourself for your productivity and take the weekend off!). For people who have a hard time visualizing word-count amounts, three hundred fifty words is roughly the length of the desperate, run-on email you just sent to your best friend. So to reach your writing goals, stop writing long emails, and work on your book instead.

Most writers who use the word-count method feel productive if they write one thousand words a day. Regardless of the number you pick, remember that hitting your word-count goal doesn't perfect the project; revision does. So leave time to revise!

Butt-in-the-chair time

"I am for consistency," says author Gina Sorell. "There have been times in my life I've been able to write for a few hours every day, and times when I can only write for a few hours on Saturday mornings. But I find that the consistency of the routine, whatever that may be, is key. Right now, five days a week, I'm at my desk by 5:30 a.m. for two hours, before family life and work life wake up. I'm not bragging about the time of day that I get up," Gina adds. "I'm a terrible morning person, but dawn is the only time I can feel free of other responsibilities to write."

You have to be a particular kind of person with a particular work schedule to maintain a daily writing habit. For writers whose day jobs already require that they think, edit, and write all day for the benefit of others, it can be virtually impossible to find the reserves during the week to write creatively for themselves. And, of course, for someone who is responsible for other people in their household (offspring, aging parents), maintaining a daily writing habit is a pipe dream that bursts open during cold and flu season.

Be wary of the people who say that you have to write every day to be a writer: they're projecting their inadequacies onto you. *Think* every day about the things that you want to write, and when you have time to get to your desk, honor your intentions. You wouldn't go grocery shopping during a dermatologist appointment: don't organize your closet during your writing time.

If your current schedule makes it impossible to carve out windows of writing time each week, try the bingeing route. Pick one day somewhere in your schedule where everything can go to hell except your writing, and write the hell out of that day. The author Cheryl Strayed is a notable binger—in interviews, she's admitted that she goes for months without writing a word only to "write like a motherf*cker" at artist residencies. An editor I know, who is also a writer, sets aside Saturdays to nest with her own projects: she'll lock herself away and write for up to ten hours at a time.

Content goals

For the author Miranda Beverly-Whittemore, content goals are the only way she has been able to seesaw between her writing and other responsibilities (of which parenting is one). To make her writing time more effective, she works from an outline and concentrates on completing a certain number of beats. "I focus on plot points," Miranda says. "Sometimes it's a whole scene, sometimes there are three or four beats in a scene. Working this way means I can always feel like I've accomplished something even when I've only had fifteen minutes to write."

I find content objectives gratifying, too. The first thing I do on my writing days is assess my energy and the amount of time I have to write, and then I give myself a content-related task: I'm going to write the sex scene today; I'm going to work through the father section in this essay; I'm going to get through my research on American-made automobiles in the 1930s for this thing I want to write. It's easy to identify your manuscript's trickiest parts: they're the ones you're not writing. Tackle those bits first. Start your week by writing those scenes terribly. At least they're written! If they're written, you can move on to making them better and more realistic, which is a far more nuanced and interesting job than getting words onto the page. If you do the hardest work first, the rest of the writing can feel like a reward.

Stay off of social media

Social media is the great enabler of procrastinators, so a lot of people protect their writing time by making the Internet difficult to surf. Some writers swear by web-blocking services such as Freedom; others write in cafés where they don't know the Wi-Fi password; the truly desperate ask their roommates to change the Wi-Fi code in their apartment and to keep the code from them. During a short-lived steampunk phase, I used an old-timey hourglass to regulate my social media use: I couldn't go online until the sand had transferred from one bulb to another. This was diverting until my cat—who has no respect for whimsy—knocked it to the floor.

These days, I use guilt and old-fashioned self-loathing to regulate my Internet use, and when that fails, I hide my computer and write longhand, which results in meditative, restorative, and completely illegible work.

Whatever your strategy is for getting words onto the page, don't forget to give yourself a break from all the goal-making and the typing and the writing notes by hand. If you don't hit your word count, if you take a phone call from a friend during your writing time, if you have a hangover and your soul needs you to watch reruns of *Dynasty* on your allotted writing day, you are still a writer and you'll find another time to write.

Killing your inner perfectionist

For reasons we will not get into here, I once attended clown school. We had to do an exercise where we walked around the room in circles at our normal pace. Then we did the exercise walking at "the speed of fun." "The speed of fun," explained the instructor, as people started bumping into one another, "is when you're going too fast to hear your inner critic."

I've never met a writer who doesn't have an internal naysayer second-guessing all she does. The problem is so common, some psychologists advise giving your self-critic a name and an identity: mindfulness blogger Wendy de Jong refers to hers as "Perf," and in a *Psychology Today* article on the same subject, an anonymous client calls hers a "hungry wolf."

Perfectionism can be a good trait in a writer: it drives you to deliver work that is spell-checked, fact-checked, and free of glitchy formatting, while also including such essentials as nice sentences and plot. To this end, your editors will appreciate your perfectionism because it saves them time.

But perfectionism can hold you back. So many people are afraid of writing badly, when the truth is that bad writing is the only way you're going to start writing well. "I'm unable to write that really shitty first draft," says the writer Hallie Goodman, who admits to being stunted by her "perfectionist bullshit." "I'm unable to suspend judgment, I line edit as I'm writing. For me, it's a scarcity-of-time issue. I feel like nothing can be wasted. I'm afraid of wasting time."

Hallie has been able to indulge this fear because she *does* lack time. In addition to writing and freelancing for magazines, she also runs a successful reading and workshop series called Volume, which keeps her in constant contact with authors and their publicists, students, and local commerce owners, troubleshooting and event managing to keep everything on track. But recently, Hallie was awarded a monthlong fellowship at the MacDowell Colony, and her excuses didn't hold water anymore. "All of a sudden, I couldn't tell myself I didn't have time to write," she says, "because time was all I had."

One thing that comforted Hallie, and ultimately got her writing, was realizing that so many other writers had the exact same problem. She met people who had affirmations tacked up all over their studios, writers who forced themselves to write two thousand words a day without a single concern for quality—the idea was just to write.

"I had to do all these infantilizing tricks," Hallie admits. "I put up notes like, 'There is no bypass. You must write that shitty first draft.' And god, I made myself a star chart," she laughs, recounting how she walked to CVS to get herself some puffy glitter star stickers that she would put up when she allowed herself to write atrociously.

Perfectionism can negatively affect not just how you write, but *what* you write, as well. Author Amy Brill spent fifteen years working on her first novel about a female astronomer in 1845 Nantucket, and her perfectionist drive to incorporate all her research nearly derailed the book. "I was so sure I had to adhere to every minute fact, every turn of phrase, every one-hundred-sixty-year-old date," Amy admits, "that I ended up with hundreds of pages of deadly boring epistolary junk. Its verisimilitude was admirable, but as a novel, not so much."

When Amy lost an entire crop of research in a backpack she misplaced, what at first felt like a tragedy turned into a liberation. "The original questions—what would make a teenaged girl spend the entire night on her roof, in every season, searching for something in the night sky that would change her life—had been engulfed by *thee* and *thou* and other things that barely belong in a novel, much less on every page. I had to start over, and I did. The next version kept some of the facts about the inspiration for my character, but dispensed with most of them. If I wanted to tell the story of that girl on the roof, I had to make it up. That's the book that became my first published novel, *The Movement of Stars*."

If you're into disassociation, hire your inner critic to be your copy editor. But do not let her write. And take heed if you're paralyzed by the idea of a bad draft: a good book usually takes about seven shitty versions, not one.

Developing your voice

Narrative voice is your literary aura, your essence, the thing that allows writers the world over to write about the same topics in thrillingly different ways. Even though it's yours, your voice can take a long, long time to find.

Postcollege, I spent two years trying to write like Raymond Carver. Raymond Carver I am not. But I got it into my head that this is what serious writing sounded like: alcoholic, importantly mundane. It was depressing to try to write like this, but the shorter my sentences got, the more I felt like I was approaching publication somewhere really big. It took me hundreds of rejections to give myself permission to dance like no one was watching—clearly, no one was. I embraced my inner freak and incorporated humor into my writing. And I started getting published.

I think a lot of young writers make similar detours—they start out writing a certain way for a specific audience, before eventually coming to the realization that they don't like this kind of writing—or these people!—very much. In a popular lecture the author Claire Vaye Watkins delivered at the Tin House Summer Workshop called "On Pandering," she admitted that she herself spent much of her early career writing for old white men. "Countless decisions I've made about what to write and how to write it have been in acquiescence to the opinions of the white male literati," Claire said in the lecture, which was published as an essay in issue 66 of the magazine. "Not only acquiescence but a beseeching, approval seeking, people pleasing. More staggering is the question of why I am trying to prove myself to writers whose work, in many cases, I don't particularly admire?"

Purists argue that once you've found your voice, you need to keep it isolated in order to protect it: don't read work by any other writer while you're working on a project; live inside your words. IMHO, these people are wrong (and also maybe need to be checked on? It sounds like they haven't left their house in quite some time). If you want to be a writer, you need to *engage* with the writing world. You need to purchase, read, and celebrate the work of other writers, editors, and translators. There will come a time when you might need to protect the slant or tonality of a project by isolating yourself, aesthetically, but that point is not at the beginning of your career.

Much is said about the merits of reading other writers, but it's important to go out and hear them, too. Something instructive happens at live readings. You will hear people who are merely reading from their writing, and you will also see people *perform*. You'll see jokes land, and you will also watch them fall so flat that people have to step around them where they lie, cowering, on the floor.

Having a piece bomb at a live reading is a form of rejection, but rejections can be way finders. As your confidence builds, you'll come to learn the difference between bad-faith rejections (rejections that come because the rejecter is prejudiced against you or what you stand for in some way) and useful rejections, which indicate whether you are close (hot!) to or far (cold!) from finding your own voice.

When you do find your voice, you'll still encounter rejection, but it won't sting as much: you have fuel now, you have water in the desert, you have found your core. So write. Submit. Get on stage and bomb. Get excited by your rejections. They are road maps toward the kind of work that you were born to write.

Making the most of your writing workshop

Writing workshops take many forms. They might be a compulsory part of your MFA program, they might take place during a summer conference you've signed up for, or you might be in a homegrown workshop comprising writers you have been working alongside for many years.

In case you're not familiar with the workshop scenario: each participant gets to have a piece of writing "workshopped" by the other writers in the class. You'll usually have about a half hour to hear what your fellow writers thought of your piece, starting with positive feedback, and working, gradually, as your heart rate rises, to the "constructive feedback" portion: i.e., what you're doing wrong.

In my experience, workshops are an invaluable tool if you know what to do with the feedback you are given, some of which will be insightful and beneficial, some of which will be biased or dead wrong. Follow me for a moment on a tangent to the supermarket. Let's say you have gone there to gather ingredients to make a chicken curry. For this chicken curry, you need some chicken, but you don't see any there. There is a man working in this supermarket; you ask him about the lack of poultry products in the store. He says not to worry, and he hands you five eggplants, a bottle of laundry detergent, and a mini horse. Don't worry, he repeats, when he registers your surprise. These items are free. You will need them on your journey. You should take them from the store.

You have been raised to be polite; you don't want to hurt this man's feelings, especially if these items are gratis. So you take the eggplants and the detergent and the horse and you try to make the curry when you get to your apartment, but you don't have what you need to make it; instead you have a horse. He's cute, certainly, but you can't help but feel like your life has taken a direction that you did not want it to go in. You feed the curry, which isn't very good, to the horse, who poops on your rug.

Is it possible to get what you actually need out of a workshop, instead of the desire to never write again? Can you make a curry with some detergent and a horse?

Ask for what you need

Now that I've been writing and publishing for a while, it's mind-altering to realize that workshops do not have to be a vomitorium of disgruntlements from your workshop peers. Did you know that you can ask for specific feedback? Did you know that you can challenge people to give you more than *meh*?

"I think it's a nice idea to tell people what you specifically want help with when your piece goes up for workshop," says author Julia Fierro, who founded the Sackett Street Writers' Workshop in 2002. "Pacing, plot, the narrative structure, the pace of dialogue . . . If you don't ask for what you need, you can have this out-of-body experience during the workshop; I'm here, but I'm not here."

To protect yourself against the tepid feedback that the author and founder of the workshop program CRIT, Tony Tulathimutte, calls "the bland reading the bland," encourage specificity from your peers when your piece is on the chopping block. If someone says that they don't like one of your characters, ask if there is a technical choice that impacted the way they feel. And as a workshopper, you should challenge yourself to the same standards. Saying that you "liked" or "didn't like" something isn't helpful: offering ideas the writer can use to solve a problem or improve a passage is.

Learn what to let go of

You'll encounter different personality types in workshop, and if you take all of their advice to heart, the only thing you're going to want to write at the end of workshop is an SOS.

"You can get wounded in a way in workshop that you will eventually figure out is time wasting and pointless," says Tony on the topic of bad feedback. "There are pernicious aspects to it: the tacit pressure to pander, to people please, to impress either the teacher or the people you are sharing a room with. This is inevitable, I don't know a way to work around this: the group gaze of a workshop only heightens this pressure. You just have to stick with it long enough that the participants learn to workshop the manuscript, not the author."

You also have to learn where your peers are coming from so that you don't get wounded. People have preferences and biases: if you're in a workshop with the same people long enough, you'll start to understand *why* they say the things they do. Maybe that one dude just doesn't "do" science fiction; the teacher secretly yearns to write erotica; nothing resonates with that one student unless you're writing about her.

Nevertheless, during your initial critiques, you are going to have a dozen people throwing feedback balls at you and you only have so many hands. First-time workshoppers have a tendency to incorporate *all* the recommendations they were given into their revision, resulting in what Julia calls a "Frankenstein." This happened to me: after workshopping an unruly piece during a summer conference, I spent four dismal months revising a draft honoring each of my classmate's opinions: *This one will make Sonia happy because no one's using foreign words; this one will please Jeremy because the narrator's motivations are clearer.* I ended up with nineteen drafts of that short story, each one of them further from the kernel of magic I'd had in the first. It took me a year to let the useful feedback rise to the top of my brain (and to let go of everything else) so that I could actually think, with agency, through what I needed to do to make the story stronger in a way that preserved its weirdness. That story, "Notes from Mexico," won an award in a chapbook contest, and it's closer to the original first draft than not.

This is not to say that I think that I, or you, or any writer, should be above constructive criticism, or that other writers (and readers) don't have the ability to help us with our work. (They do. I would be incomprehensible without my editors.) What I want to emphasize is that workshops can't actually help your writing until you understand how to preserve your special sauce. Protecting what is odd and tender about your voice is not you saying that you write better than anyone else, so screw all of their opinions . . . it's about knowing where your creative boundaries are and getting to the point where you can distinguish useful feedback from biased criticism. The former will actually serve your manuscript. The latter usually comes from a writer who prefers you write like them.

This level of awareness takes time to come by, and in order to get there, you're going to have to ruin a few pieces by incorporating bad advice. Once you know how to sieve good advice from the extraneous, you can workshop to the high heavens, with your armor intact.

Find positive in the negative. Even in the comments of [name redacted] That Person You Can't Stand

There are going to be asshats in your workshop, and if you can't find a way to transform their tomfoolery into something positive, animus will poison your writing time. "Even with the reader who doesn't like your work, who doesn't read it correctly, who 100 percent isn't your ideal reader and is giving you the kind of feedback you absolutely don't want," says Catapult's writing programs assistant, Stella Cabot Wilson, "even this person's feedback might still be helpful in some way—either as something to strike against, or for giving you a new idea or opening up how you think about your work."

Also remember that the workshop is a crash course in what it feels like to have other people read and publicly comment on your private writing. If you can maintain your dignity and confidence when a wind-bag calls your content "navel-gazing," you'll be better prepared for the faceless online commenter who gives your debut two stars because he doesn't like the shirt you're wearing in your author photograph.

If there's someone in workshop that you just can't make the positivity leap with, use your interactions with them as a character study: at least you'll have material to draw from when it comes time to write a jerk.

Learning to revise

It is a truth known but little spoken that the secret to great writing is revision. After putting countless failed manuscripts out to pasture, I've come to see writing as the pleasurable—even hedonistic—part of the writing process, and revision as the work.

In revision, you improve the places in your manuscript that can be deepened, tightened, or clarified, and you cut . . . a *lot*. In Stephen King's craft book, *On Writing: A Memoir of the Craft*, he suggests that a good second draft is the first draft minus 10 percent. In the movie *Neruda*, the actor playing the Chilean poet Pablo Neruda says, "To write well, delete." Did Pablo Neruda actually say this? Let's pretend he did!

Like a lot of baby writers, I started out attached to every word I wrote. My sentences defined me! Each one advanced not just the narrative of my story, but my personal one as well. I valued baroqueness over efficiency, circuitous reasoning over candidness, the em dash over the period. My writing was overlong and hyperactive, in need of scissors and sedation, both.

If I'm proud of anything in my writing process, it's that I have become a Herculean deleter, callous and unfeeling, my only queen the work. On a Thursday many years ago, three days before my agent was going to send my first novel out on submission, she called to tell me how excited she was about it, how absolutely positive she was that this was going to be my debut book, and that P.S., it needed to be twenty thousand words shorter by Monday morning. Twenty thousand words less!! I didn't waste time fighting her on this or asking why. I reread the manuscript (quickly) and answered those questions for myself. Then I went for a run with angry music on. And spent the weekend deleting, down to the exact number, twenty thousand words.

The difference between a published writer and an unpublished one might be their ability to revise. Even if an agent or an editor sees promise in a manuscript, they might pass because they don't have the stamina for the amount of revision the work needs. If you can train yourself to revise well, you're pushing your manuscript thirty steps closer to a publication yes.

At the beginning of the revision process, you might be so close to the material that you can't see your project's flaws. Happily, there are a lot of talented professionals who can. Online writing programs across the country have manuscript consultants for hire, and many of these offer intensive revision workshops such as the Novel Incubator program at GrubStreet, the Novel Year program at The Writer's Center in Washington, D.C., the Novel in a Year: Revise and Launch Class at StoryStudio Chicago, the twelve-week Novel Generator Program at Catapult, or the Writing by Writers Manuscript Boot Camp in Lake Tahoe, just to name a few.

If you want to improve the way that you revise, you should use a manuscript consultant as a bellwether, not a crutch. Don't just read their notes, *decode* what they are saying for your writing as a whole. Identify any negative patterns that crop up in your writing and keep a list of what they are so that you can start to edit them out yourself. Learn your narrative weaknesses and devise a shorthand for dealing with them. If you're terrible at landscape descriptions, for example, rather than spending a dark day trying to ace a paragraph about Bolivian salt flats, why not put a line in parentheses about what you want to go there and highlight it in yellow, then come back to it on a day where you have the energy to write a challenging paragraph.

Revision is about editing out the parts of a narrative that take you away from the story's truth. Belabored points, repetitions, opaqueness, narrative indulgences, all these are examples of nonessentials that can slow a story down, but it's equally important to learn how to identify subject matter that can belittle or offend.

Using sensitivity readers

Writing is about storytelling, and every time we come to the page, we're taking a certain risk with the stories that we share. Maybe we're using valuable free time for an uncompensated activity that doesn't make sense to the people that we love. Maybe we're telling a true story whose publication might damage relationships we value. Or maybe we're venturing into territory that we haven't lived firsthand. If you're writing from a viewpoint that is vastly different from your own, delving into a culture that isn't native to you, writing about a historical experience you didn't live through, or venturing out of your comfort zone in other important ways, your manuscript might benefit from a sensitivity reader who will vet your work for stereotypes, internalized bias, negatively charged language, sexism, and other content that readers could find offensive.

We Need Diverse Books is a great resource for writers and readers questioning the representation of diverse experiences and characters in children's literature, and until recently, Writing in the Margins maintained a database of sensitivity readers that was pulled down after the writer (and site administrator), Justina Ireland, saw many of their readers being mistreated or not being paid for the work that they took on. In an article on Medium about her decision to stop maintaining the database, Justina writes, "I still believe that Sensitivity Reading can be a valuable tool for those authors who have done the due diligence and have worked hard to analyze their own place within systems of oppression. But for those who see diversity as a way to make a quick buck, it is one more tool to keep the voices of centered identities the loudest in publishing." The writer and advocate Jennifer N. Baker runs a podcast called *Minorities in Publishing* in which she discusses the lack of diversity in literature with book publishing professionals. It's an indispensable resource both for people writing outside of their own identities and for emerging writers from marginalized communities seeking industry advice.

The Children's Book Council also has a helpful list of resources for people interested in representing (or reading about) experiences outside their own backgrounds, and an Internet search will bring you the writers and editors offering sensitivity-reading services online.

Am I wasting my time and money in this MFA program?

A simple Internet search will prove that there's a lot of hand-wringing over the value of a Master of Fine Arts degree. I personally didn't get one, but most of my colleagues did, or are in the process of earning one now. In addition to the trove of online articles devoted to an MFA's pros and cons, there's also the informative book, *MFA vs NYC*, edited by Chad Harbach (a writer and one of the founders of *n + 1*), which is a great resource for those questioning life with (or without) an MFA.

In my own non-MFA-having opinion, whether you go for this advanced degree or not should depend on your budget and your long-term career goals. Can you afford not only to attend an MFA program, but to go without income while you're studying? If you intend to teach, can you survive on an adjunct's salary for several years? (Really? Are you sure?) If you already know that you want to teach in some capacity, it's wise to pursue an MFA because most academic employers will require that you have one. If you want an MFA because of the prestige attached to it and the certainty that this particular degree will land you a book deal, let's have a come-to-Jesus talk.

"I really do try to disabuse my students of the notion that the MFA is this magic bullet," says author Saïd Sayrafiezadeh, who teaches at both the graduate and undergrad level, although he doesn't have an MFA himself. "It's not the MFA that's going to get your book published or bring you teaching opportunities, it's also the publications. You have to write, hustle, submit, network, go to readings, make contacts, be a nice person who people want to help. In a way, you're always going to have your own self-directed MFA."

Although Saïd isn't self-conscious about not having an advanced degree, it does trouble him how often he is asked by his own students— MFA candidates—whether they're wasting their time with one. Usually, Saïd responds that an MFA is useful, but it's not a one-way ticket to anything: not only does it not guarantee a book deal, it doesn't even mean you'll write a book.

"There's this idea that people have that they're going to write a book during their MFA program," Saïd says. "But you're probably not going to write a book in two years. At some point, you're going to have to have a day job. You're going to have to learn how to carve out time to write," a skill that Saïd feels should be discussed and privileged over the inspiration model of writing, which he once subscribed to himself.

"I had no discipline," Saïd remembers of his years as a young writer. "I didn't know that you needed some kind of schedule. No one ever said to me, it's not about inspiration; you have to sit down. You have to write. I spent a long time just walking around thinking, Well! I'm uninspired."

At the end of the day, Saïd believes a solid work ethic is the thing that will allow you to write a book and/or acquire teaching experience, not an MFA. This is something that the writer Cara Blue Adams agrees with, a self-described "cautious" person who "always has a backup plan behind the backup plan."

Although Cara does have an MFA (from the University of Arizona), after college she worked at a law firm, an experience she credits with helping her understand that she could—nay, *deserved*—to earn a healthy wage. "I considered adjuncting at various points," says Cara, "but then I looked at what it paid." Cara optioned to pursue a career as an editor instead, accepting a position at *The Southern Review*, where she worked for five years. This decision was deliberate; Cara felt certain it would serve her to be skilled across multiple disciplines, instead of just an MFA graduate who wanted to write a book. "Even during my MFA program, I tried to do as much as I could to gain professional skills in a range of areas," Cara explains. "I was thinking of my career more holistically: How could I be part of the creative and intellectual community without necessarily teaching? I edited the literary magazine, I ran a reading series, I started a professional development series."

Cara was publishing short stories during all of this, and by the time she joined *The Southern Review,* agents were knocking at her inbox. But she managed the unthinkable: she didn't sign with an agent right away.

For starters, Cara didn't have a complete manuscript yet, but she also felt nourished by her job at the magazine. "One thing an editorial position afforded me was the luxury to not have a hard deadline and to be able to write the book that I wanted to write," she says.

In short, an MFA—even at the most prestigious program—is a privilege you must rise to meet. It isn't going to do the work for you, it isn't going to write the book for you, it isn't even going to make the contacts you'll need professionally unless you organize yourself into becoming the empathetic, curious, and supportive literary citizen that people want to see succeed.

If you feel confident enough in your savings (or someone else's savings) to see yourself through the limited job market that greets most MFA graduates, you're a lucky person. Take that acceptance letter, and go. But if you can't afford a life off salary while you're in grad school, if you would need a loan to attend, and/or you're not in a position to be accepted to a fully funded program, it's not super wise to pursue an MFA. Or at least, not a traditional one. Or at least, not right now.

It's worth noting here that teaching experience is crucial to your success on the academic market, so if you do apply to MFA programs, consider those that give equal teaching experience to their students. First-year candidates in such programs will generally find themselves at the head of a freshman composition or creative writing class, while second- and third-year students can tackle subjects further afield such as literary journalism, travel writing, or experimental nonfiction. Some programs will even give their first-year grad students a crash course in assignment and syllabus creation to ready them for the challenges of teaching and time management. Regardless of the size of the class you're leading—or the topic—these early teaching gigs are worth their time and effort. With each semester, you'll be acquiring the confidence you need to craft syllabi and lectures when the stakes are higher (i.e., when you're doing a demo class in front of an academic selection committee during a campus visit). After all, you want to know you can bike before the training wheels come off!

Is there a world in which I can teach without an MFA?

You can debate the pros and cons of MFA programs until the cows come home, but unless you're exceptional enough to prove the exception, you're going to need one if you want an academic teaching job. The good news is that for most creative-writing positions, you can stop at the MFA. "Most programs won't require that you have a PhD in order to get a tenure-track creative writing job," says this book's editor, Julie Buntin, who has been through the academic-market maze herself. "But some that are housed in English departments or that have a theory or comp component to the teaching load might. Pay close attention to the job listing!"

The list of writers who have managed to get teaching jobs without an MFA degree is short on names, but they all have sterling CVs. The aforementioned author Saïd Sayrafiezadeh—who teaches at Hunter College, Columbia University, and NYU—doesn't have an MFA (or a BA for that matter), but he was a finalist for the PEN/Robert W. Bingham Prize, publishes on the regular in *The New Yorker,* has received a Whiting Award as well as a fiction fellowship from the New York Public Library's Cullman Center for Scholars and Writers, and is on the board of directors for the New York Foundation for the Arts. Author Kathleen Alcott—who has taught at Bennington College, the Center for Fiction, and Columbia University—didn't attend an MFA program either, but she has three acclaimed books (one of which was a Kirkus Prize nominee), a short story that made the short list for the prestigious Sunday Times Short Story Award, and bylines in household-name outlets like *The New York Times* and *The Guardian*.

On the other side of the exceptional, Cara Blue Adams—another writer we just met—has an MFA and a tenure-track teaching job, but she doesn't have a book. What she does have, however, is a deeply thoughtful background in both publishing and editing, with awards and fellowships to boot. "People tell me they loved my first book," says Cara, who has published, among other places, in the *Kenyon Review, Narrative Magazine*, and *The Sun*. "They also say they had a great time at my wedding, although neither of these events have happened yet."

In summation, you can get a teaching position without an MFA degree behind you, and you can move up the tenure track without a published book, but you can't do any of these things if you're not busting your butt to create great work on the side. This is easier said than done, of course, and you can't just "decide" to be extraordinary, but what you can do—if you want to circumvent the traditional path to professordom—is acknowledge that you are going to have to work incredibly hard to do so. And then do it: work harder than hard.

Creating (and maintaining) a literary community without an MFA

There are a lot of reasons writers don't attend an MFA program: they're categorically opposed to them; they can't afford them (financially and/or emotionally); they don't know that they exist.

I was in this latter case. I lived in France for most of my twenties, and by the time I moved back to America and woke up to the fact that most authors had MFA programs in their bios, I felt too old, too married, and too financially unstable to pursue an MFA.

I was, however, longing for a literary community, and it wasn't initially clear how I could find one outside of an MFA program. I was living in a really rural part of Massachusetts with very few people—much less *writing* people—around. A serendipitous part-time job offer in New York City gave me the chance to try to find my kinfolk. In order to get as much out of my time in a metropolis as possible, I decided to attend a reading series for each of the four nights that I would be in New York, and to introduce myself—in person—to one stranger at each reading. I did this for four months straight, and although the positive outcomes I experienced were aided by my extraversion, I'm nevertheless convinced that there are solid, actionable, and affordable things you can do to build a literary community without an MFA. Some of these suggestions are free, others require an investment. For the paid options (attending summer conferences or an online writing class), remember to save receipts for tax time so you can deduct these costs as a business expense.

Attend too many reading series

You know the musical expression "playing by ear"? At reading series, you can train your ear to help your writing. Take it from someone who survived a writer's twenty-two-minute "autofiction" revelation about a particular type of oral servicing he once received on a couch: once you hear someone bomb in front of a microphone, you will do anything—*everything*—to avoid terrible writing. In-jokes, tangents, potentially offensive content, narrative indulgences—attend a lot of reading series and you will be only too happy to remove these malignancies from your work.

Volunteer as a reader for a literary magazine

Being a reader for literary magazines allows you to keep your finger on the pulse of what people are writing—and not writing—about, and it can be very useful for your creative writing process to be a gatekeeper for a while. Understanding what makes you want to accept or reject a story will inevitably inform the choices you're making in your own work. Are you trying too hard to be funny? Do you go on tangents? Do your characters do nothing but stare out the window drinking tea? There is just as much to be learned from reading flawed writing as there is from reading polished work, *plus* you'll come away with a new respect for the form rejection letter after you've been exposed to a bog of misspelled, uniquely formatted submissions from misanthropes and misogynists who are only too proud to tell you that they couldn't be bothered with your submission guidelines because this attached thirty-five-thousand-word novella about a man without a girlfriend absolutely needs to be in your poetry journal. NOW.

Attend a summer writing program

The cons of these are that they can be prohibitively expensive (it's nearly four grand to attend the ten-day Bread Loaf Writers' Conference without a scholarship), competitive to get into, and alcohol fuels a great deal of the socializing, but the pros are that you can get nearly a semester's worth of contacts and inspiration in as little as a week. *Poets & Writers* has a solid database of writing conferences that you can navigate by event type, location, even financial aid deadlines.

Although there isn't a writing conference where alcohol is specifically prohibited (yet), the writer Vonetta Young said that the VONA conference (for writers of color) doesn't provide any conference-sponsored alcohol, and writers Caitlin Horrocks and Tara Lindis-Corbell both said the same thing of the Kenyon Review Writers Workshop. Librarian and inn manager Jesica Sweedler DeHart says that food takes center stage at the Orcas Island Literary Festival where most of the events are hosted by a tea or coffee company.

If you need extra support around alcohol, look for programs that have recovery meetings that are relatively easy to get to and attend. "Going somewhere with a strong recovery presence," suggests the writer Hallie Goodman, "can help you connect with other writers who are feeling a little alienlike as they see all of their peers get sloshed."

Take an online writing class

Since the advent of digital technology, there might not be a better boon for writers than the online writing class. Though the classes are online, the students and the teachers are real people, busy ones like you. And with the rising popularity of online writing classes, the standards set for teachers are very (very!) high: as I write, the likes of Arif Anwar, Yahdon Israel, and Leigh Stein are all teaching online, and the talent in the student pool is equally impressive.

Even if you're not meeting in person, online classes offer emerging writers important social benefits: you might make a friend you can go on to workshop with privately; if you have a positive relationship with your teacher, you can ask them for a recommendation letter at some point in the future. Learning to take—and give—feedback from your peers will also help you gain the technical skills you'll need to be more self-reliant when you are revising your own work.

In addition to expanding your personal writing network, online classes can bolster your creativity and imagination, too. Would you try a screenwriting class in an MFA program if you were accepted there for poetry? Maybe not. But with their affordability, convenience, and lower-stakes environment for experimentation, you can try out translation, travel writing, memoir, erotica, and many other genres you might not have had the time—or even the permission—to try in an MFA.

Join (or start) a writing group

If you haven't had any success finding an existing writing group through the common channels (your local library, bookstore, or good old word of mouth), it might be time to start one of your own. You can post flyers in actual brick-and-mortar places, or use social-gathering sites like Meetup to gauge interest in your group. Remember that your group doesn't have to be stylistically homogenous; it will serve you as a writer if your comembers have varied life experiences and are working in different genres than you.

Attend AWP

It's not cheap to get to and it usually takes place in the godforsaken month of February, but AWP (which stands for the Association of Writers & Writing Programs [which should actually be abbreviated as AWWP, but . . . artistic license?]) is an annual conference attended by thousands and thousands of publishing professionals and writers. A conference as large as this one can feel panic-attack-level overwhelming at times, but there's no better one-stop shopping for all your career needs. At the many parties and off-site readings offered throughout the five-day conference, you can hear new work and socialize with like-minded artists; at the book fair, you can spend hours talking with conference and writing-program managers about the different opportunities they offer; you can network for job opportunities in academia and publishing; you can browse everything from quirky chapbooks to door-stopper bestsellers, and enjoy conversations with the editors, publicists, and interns who brought those books to life. If you're feeling up for it, you can even pitch projects to an editor, and you can flick something grody at the editor from [~~name of literary magazine redacted~~] who has rejected every piece you've ever sent.

A word to the wise: AWP lists discount codes on its website for hotel and airline fare. Make sure to use these discounts when you book!

Join a book club if you're not already in one

Learning to read other people's work, to question it, and to praise it in a clear and concise manner are skills essential to any writer, as is the proper handling of oneself around copious amounts of white wine.

Read

Duh, right? Not so fast. If you want to be an active member of the literary community, you have to read beyond the kind of work you normally gravitate toward, in both genre and style. Every fall there are lists about the top ten or twenty books out that year: earmark *Buzz-Feed*'s most-anticipated novels, read the National Book Award poetry finalists, set yourself a goal. Subscribe to literary magazines (and read them), and visit the areas of your local library that you usually avoid. Challenge yourself to leave well-thought-out reviews of these books on social-cataloging sites like Goodreads, so that you learn to speak respectfully about other people's work. In an MFA program, you would be thoughtfully critiquing other people's writing on the regular, so don't slack on this skill set.

A quick tip about book reviews, especially online: Do not leave negative reviews of authors whom you might one day want to beseech or befriend. Early in your career, you might not know who these people are yet, so book-review with caution. As a general rule of thumb, if you have negative thoughts about somebody's creative output, it's best to let them die a silent death inside your mind.

Volunteer at a literary festival

If you can't be invited by them, join 'em. Literary festivals are always in need of volunteers, and they're one of the best ways to stay connected to the writing world. If you offer up your services, make sure to choose a committee that actually suits your career interests: event planning will give you an idea of how panels are organized (with a sneak peak at the kind of topics you can one day hope to talk about yourself), public relations will give you experience writing press releases and interfacing with the media, and hospitality can put you in the same orbit as the authors you admire.

If your volunteer time is limited, festivals, arts organizations, and literary magazines always need extra help during their end-of-the-year fund-raisers.

If you do all these things, or even half of them, while also keeping up a regular writing practice, you're going to find your book people, and they're going to find you. If you still find yourself yearning for a more codified community after all these efforts, start researching part-time and/or low-residency MFA programs. More affordable, less competitive, and more flexible with scheduling than their full-time counterparts, part-time MFA programs will only need you on campus two to three times a week (usually at times that are convenient for nine-to-fivers), and low-res programs offer long-distance education with site-specific meetups one or two times a year.

Am I writing the wrong book?

I cannot tell you how many times I have written a book-length manuscript only to realize that it would perform better as a personal essay or op-ed, and that the novel I actually needed to write was hiding within a sentence on page seventy-three. I'm not exaggerating: I write a book to find a book all the freaking time, and this process is infuriating, and not a little heartbreaking, but it does—eventually—guide me to the thing I'm meant to write.

In case you share my predilection to need to write (and write) your way to the true story, I've come up with a checklist to help you figure out if you are running the wrong race.

Is this book actually a personal essay, and I just don't know it yet?

During the writing of my second novel, I suffered a second-term miscarriage that I wanted to make the topic of book three. There was a lot of mismanagement of my medical information in the wake of the pregnancy loss, and I suffered some bizarre physical repercussions that I'm still navigating today. Accordingly, I felt a deep need to write my way toward a better understanding of what had happened to me and to my body, and I wanted to explore why women's bodies are so little understood and respected in the United States. These are huge topics, and I felt like the appropriate and most exciting place to explore them was in a novel.

So I wrote a manuscript in which a prematurely menopausal thirty-eight-year-old is navigating a world in which her partner has left her in the wake of their lost pregnancy. Infertile in a culture that values fertility, the protagonist feels discarded and unseen. I think these issues are important—this state of being is important—but what I ended up with was three hundred pages of a woman *feeling* things about events that had happened in the past, which is slow-going content for a narrative.

This novel wanted to be a personal essay from the get-go, but I had to write it as fiction—and watch it fail as fiction—to realize this was so. It was a difficult lesson, but an important one: just because something moves us does not mean that it has the engine to power an entire book.

Are you scared?

Of course you're scared. You're a writer! If you're not terrified, I'd like to know what herbal supplements you're on. But all too often, our fear keeps us from writing what we actually need to write. This is especially true for memoirists whose writing can estrange friends or relatives, or even put their careers at risk if they tell the truth.

Unfortunately, the truth is usually the best path to the story. There are two outcomes when you're scared of what you're writing: either you cave in to the fear and you write something superficial that probably won't sell, or you write something brave and vital that might. Your writing can be private for as long as you need it to be. So why not write the thing you're scared of? The worst-case scenario is also the best one: you write something so courageous that an editor wants to pay you to share it with the world. You don't have to say yes.

Does the scope of your project align with the free time that you have?

Let's say you are waking up at five thirty in the morning to adjunct at one college, skipping lunch to teach at another, and traveling to yet a third school to teach an evening class. As an adjunct, you don't have an office, and your shared apartment makes it hard to write at home. Is this the time to be working on your great American novel? Well, sure. Is this the time to be working on your great American novel that features a main character who is a shipbuilder during the Great Depression who falls in love with a migrant farmworker, an epic you plan to write from five different characters' points of view? That sounds like a project that needs a lot of research, and research is tough to do without a desk.

You'll have a lot of story ideas over the course of your career; you don't have to write them all, and you don't have to write them in order. Maybe hold on to the Great American Doorstopper until you have some peace, quiet, and enough time to eat lunch.

Is there a market for your project?

Market trends illuminate what readers are hungry for, which topics are salable, what genres are popular. Knowing that market trends exist can be detrimental to your writing, and you should not account for them if you're feeling good about your project. But it *can* be helpful to gauge the potential interest in your subject if you're feeling uninspired by your work. If you're killing yourself to write a book that is going to receive a hundred "We've published too many memoirs on this topic" notes from agents and editors, maybe it's time to put that project down for a while to either find a new way into it, or to work on something else.

Again—you should only use market trends to provide you with an excuse to pause a project that you're not getting any joy from. If you believe in your book's angle even though everyone is saying that vampires/motherhood memoirs/reproductive dystopias are "done," write on. Market trends make no room for exceptional exceptions. In other words, they're often wrong.

Do you lack experience?

I don't want to use the ageist card, because of course there are twenty-two-year-olds who can write convincingly from the point of a view of an eighty-year-old veteran who has a grandkid with leukemia, but there are also a lot of twenty-two-year-olds who should write delightful, weird, flawed stories about what it's like to be twenty-two.

Obviously, you should write what your heart tells you to write. It is good to be ambitious, and it can be deeply satisfying to undertake projects that require a lot of research. But your writing career will hopefully be a long one, and as you age, you are going to learn so many beautiful and ghastly things about the world; don't feel like you have to rush yourself to a mature voice and an "aching" point of view in order to be taken seriously by others—and yourself. This might feel revolutionary to consider, but you can have fun writing. Enjoying what you're writing is usually proof that you are writing the right thing. (And on this note: if you're "cheating" on your project with something on the sidelines, maybe that passion project should be the main event?)

II

....

Getting it out there

There is a huge difference between writing, and writing to be read. Attempting to get your work published necessitates strategic thinking (where would this piece fit well?), honesty (is the work actually ready yet?), and some seriously thick skin (what does "We have to pass on this" even mean?! It's not a dish of broccoli, for goodness' sake!). These considerations intensify when you start to query agents, and just when you feel you have mastered the revise, submit, and wait game, you'll go through the same process when you and your agent send your manuscript to editors.

So what are the best practices for submitting and for pitching? Are there any residences or fellowships available for writers in the early stages of their careers? It's been twenty-four hours since you submitted a short story to *The Famous Magazine*. Will the editors think you're pushy if you follow up today? (The answer to this last question, dear and hopeful writer, is a resounding yes.)

The logline and the project summary
as (potential) writing tools

....

A logline summarizes your project in a sentence. It comes in handy when someone has the indecency to inquire what you write about. Here's an example of a solid logline:

> Kim Kardashian's *Selfish* is a coffee table book filled with intimate, never-before-seen selfies from one of the most recognizable celebrities in the world.

Depending on whether you're Team Kim or not, this description might not make you want to read this book, but it's pretty clear what it's about.

Another helpful tool is the project summary: This is a rundown of your book's major characters and themes, and the writing of one will force you to acknowledge the places where your manuscript needs work. If you have a great setting but no plot, the summary will shake its head at you; if there's nothing at stake for your characters, the summary will point at a character whose motivations need finessing; if your story lacks a climax, the summary will sigh.

For fun (or at least for the good of your manuscript), try writing a pitch letter for your project well before it's done. If you can summarize, in three sentences or less, what the main themes, conundrums, and character arcs are, stop reading this and get to finishing that book because it's going to be great. If your pitch letter is seven pages long and splattered with disclaimers, defensiveness, and tears, your manuscript needs you to stop writing it and start thinking more strategically about its wants and needs.

Why you should keep submitting work, regardless of rejection

Publishing is an industry that is powered by rejection: regardless of the level that you are playing at, you are going to hear "no" more often than "yes" throughout most of your career.

Accordingly, you must make friends with rejection in order to survive a professional writing life. Rejection is going to be your zany roommate who never does her dishes, has really loud, obnoxious sex, gets drunk and eats your leftovers, and uses strong perfume. Except for that one delightful year that she studied abroad in Cartagena, she's always going to be living with you in one way or another, so make peace with that chick, now.

In addition to conditioning you to the rebuffs coming down the pipeline, submissions start to get your name in front of editors whose support and advice will be so necessary when you have a project to promote. Even if these editors are rejecting you, they're getting to know your work and your aesthetic, they recognize your name in their inbox. And eventually—as long as you aren't writing offensive query letters or disparaging their form rejection emails—from sheer pity alone, they might start to offer you specific feedback. I have a long relationship with the editor of a popular humor magazine that has never published my work. As I kept on sending pieces, it was perversely gratifying to see the rejections move from the standard bouncer fare of "This just isn't right for us" to the validating and/or specific: "This one is actually funny, but we ran a LinkedIn spoof two weeks ago. Glad to see something from you for the third time this week, though!"

Taking part in the submission game is good for your writing: if you're submitting, chances are that you are generating new work and learning how to revise. I have a friend who puts seven dollars in a jar for every piece she submits to a magazine. Every two months, she buys herself something special with the money in the jar, effectively rewarding herself for keeping her skin in the game.

And finally, writing, revising, and trying to publish new work will help train you for the larger, longer process of putting a book out into the world. Regardless of whether you are receiving rejections or acceptances, if you are submitting, you are entering a world where editors and readers matter, you are thinking about the way your work is going to be received, you are considering how it will fit alongside the work of your contemporaries. Submissions are a signal to publishing professionals that you're thinking like a writer.

So where should I submit?

The best thing you can do presubmission is get yourself into an independent bookstore and look through the literary magazines they have to see what they're publishing. Purchase the ones that publish content similar to what you yourself are writing. (A PSA here: if you're freaked out about the price of literary magazines, remember that successful writers put money into the organizations they hope will one day love them back, and also: book and magazine purchases qualify for many writers as a tax-deductible business expense.)

If you live somewhere without a quality bookstore, take to your computer. Duotrope is a solid resource for finding out which magazines are publishing what, when. They list pretty much every online and print magazine in the universe, and you can sort your target magazines by genre, pay, and submission deadlines. Duotrope is five dollars a month, or fifty dollars a year, and it is absolutely worth it. (Save the receipt for this subscription as a business expense, too.)

How should I submit?

Almost every magazine asks that you "familiarize yourself with the work they publish" before submitting anything yourself. And guess what: they mean it. Submissions that are off-tone or don't adhere to the magazine's guidelines will earn your submission a hard pass, plus you will have wasted a potentially helpful editor's time.

Every magazine has submission guidelines: do not disregard them. A lot of magazines these days don't accept attachments, and your work won't even be considered if you send it the wrong way. Use a standard twelve-point typeface, insert page numbers, spell-check. And do not include a copyright page with your submission. In the United States, the minute your work is written in a tangible form (i.e., a submitted manuscript), you and your submission are fully protected by copyright law, so submitting a copyright register is an amateur move that will make editors consider your work with less seriousness than they might have.

Most editors will ask for a cover letter, or a query. These statements should be short, respectful, and look more or less like this:

> Dear [Insert name of editor. You know the name of the editor because you have taken the time to read through the magazine and acquaint yourself with its masthead. And you know you spelled this editor's name right because you checked before you hit SEND.],

> Three sentences max: [Insert a compliment about the magazine. Cite one or two of the pieces that you admired recently, and why this work made you feel like the editor might consider your piece about [insert ultrashort summary of what the piece is about]. If you have met the editor previously, and the interaction was a positive one, remind them of this illustrious time.]

One sentence: [Insert some biographical information: where you live, if you are in or have completed an MFA program, what you do for a living if the MFA bit isn't applicable.]

One sentence: [Thank the editor for his/her/their time.]

[Insert salutation],

[Insert your name]

Can I send multiple submissions?

Can you hear the crickets? This is a tricky question because many journals will tell you that they don't accept multiple submissions, but these same journals might sit on your piece for eight months before rejecting it with a hard pass. The multiple-submissions thing really comes down to careful, methodical submission tracking. Once you receive an acceptance from somewhere, you must quickly inform the other places where you submitted the piece that it's no longer available for consideration because it's being published somewhere else. Note that you don't need to notify editors who have already rejected it, just the ones that haven't yet replied. Note also that you shouldn't get high-horsey in your communication. Sharing the news that a "superior" magazine woke up to your true worth is not the proper way to take your piece out of consideration, unless you don't ever want to publish in any other magazine again.

The aforementioned Duotrope can help you track submissions, but many journals use Submittable, which starts tracking your submission the minute you press SEND. Some writers prefer to create their own spreadsheets to accommodate personalized criteria and miscellanea. The author and editor Matt Bell has created a free submission-tracker template on Google Docs for such writers, which can be found at his website, mattbell.com.

Following up with editors

Most magazines will include an average response time in their submission guidelines. The window of response time varies, but prepare for cold air drafts. As a general rule, agented submissions are responded to faster than nonagented submissions, online magazines are quicker than print magazines, and nonfiction submissions—due to the potential timeliness of their content—are handled faster than fiction.

If you receive a rejection, do not contest it. Never. You may not. The only reason following up to a rejection is ever, ever acceptable (and even then, it isn't), is if the editor is a friend, and you need more feedback than "It just doesn't fit our needs right now" in order to survive.

In all other circumstances, the appropriate response to a rejection is to take the time it takes to write something new, to revise it a hundred times, to spell-check the hell out of it, and to submit this new and sparkling thing to the same magazine again. This is known as the "fail better" approach. Following up a rejection with a "You're all a bunch of losers, anyway" email is subpar human behavior that will get you blacklisted from a lot of magazines.

Once you know what the outlet's average response time is, you can politely follow up once that time period has passed. If it's been a long time (like, the year you submitted it isn't the same year that it is now), the answer is probably no, but there are parallel universes in which your submission was lost or erroneously deleted, so it's worth a try.

Submitting to contests

The process for submitting to contests is much the same as submitting to literary magazines, but contest submissions usually charge a submission fee in the ten- to twenty-five-dollar range, another example of a receipt that should be put directly into your tax accountant's happy hands. (We'll learn why it's worth engaging a professional tax accountant in part three.)

There are all kind of contests: contests for an individual piece of work, for manuscripts in progress, for chapbooks, for collections, for book-length manuscripts. Lots of contests come with publication in the literary magazine in question and prize money: some contests, like the Dzanc Books Prize, award the winner a ten-thousand-dollar advance and book publication.

If you start to win or place in contests (which means you are a finalist or a runner-up), you can mention these achievements in your query letters. Duotrope, *Poets & Writers*, *The Writer* magazine, and *The Writer's Chronicle* are all great places to keep on top of contests, and if you don't place, make sure to read the winning entries to see what made them shine. Turn your letdown into a learning opportunity.

Applying for awards and fellowships
as an emerging writer

So many writers are focused on graduating from their MFA programs and securing a book deal that it becomes easy to overlook the awards that support you before you have an agent, before you have a book deal, before you even know what your potential first book's about. While the United States is certainly not known for its zealous support of writers, research grants, prizes, residencies, and fellowships do exist to help you through the various stages of your career—including the beginning. So how do you find out about these newbie grants?

If you attended an undergraduate or MFA program, these institutions can provide you with fellowship information, both in and outside of the university or college itself. Websites such as ProFellow and Go-Grad can help you customize a database of grants and prizes, the Alliance of Artists Communities has a great selection of residencies, *Poets & Writers* has a solid list of first-book awards, and the magazine *The Writer's Chronicle* has a rotating list of fellowships, awards, and residencies at the back of every issue. For assistance keeping track of deadlines and submissions, Submittable is great—plus they have a customizable database of opportunities in everything from screenwriting to film.

It's worth noting that most fellowship, grant, and residency applications require a nonrefundable application fee of some kind. Sometimes, the organization will throw in a free subscription to a magazine or newsletter if they have one, but usually it's a straight-up payment with no fun swag attached. The more prestigious the opportunity, the higher the price tag can get for the application. The common range is twenty-five dollars to something conspicuously shy of fifty dollars, such as forty-seven dollars.

Is my rejection a rejection?

Most literary magazines have at least two tiers of form rejection letters: "hard" and "soft." You'll know if you received a hard pass because it leaves no room for hope. You'll hear, most likely, that your submission "didn't fit the magazine's needs" or that they "have to pass," which has always sounded vaguely gastroenterological to me. Soft rejections include encouraging sentences like, "We really liked your writing," or, "We'd like to see something else from you in the future." There's a third tier, of course, in which you get a personalized note from one of the editors that says how much they liked your work, with an opaque explanation of why they couldn't use it.

If you are starting to receive soft or personalized rejections, this is cause for celebration: your work is attracting attention, and you are getting close. "Rejection is not only a rite of passage, it's an active, enthusiastic component of your relationship with writing," says author Wayétu Moore, who now sees rejection as a healthy part of her writing process. "Making friends with the word 'no' will diminish the chances that you eventually become resentful of writing and of the literary industry in which it exists. When I became okay with rejection, and stopped taking 'no' so seriously, my writing suddenly felt like it belonged to me again."

Book reviewing and author interviews

If you're chomping at the bit to get some bylines and your magazine pitches aren't landing, reviewing books and conducting author interviews is a nice way to get your foot in the publishing world's door. Magazines, newspapers, and literary journals (both online and in print) have more books that need reviewing than they do reviewers, and publicists are always desperate to have their authors interviewed. The problem is, they need the interviewer to have read their client's book. Reading takes time, and nobody has time, hence the dearth of book reviewers and interviewers doing this good work.

The perks of book reviewing and author interviews are many: there are the free books, of course, and the opportunity to engage with accomplished authors, forge relationships with editors, and see your name in print. The writer Yvonne Conza even credits book reviewing with helping her surmount insecurities around not having an MFA. "Book reviewing teaches you how to read a book," Yvonne says. "Eyeing language more closely, examining structure, seeing what works or doesn't . . . in doing all this my writing has improved."

Unfortunately, most writers can't survive on the pay for these assignments. Especially when you are just starting out, it's going to be difficult to pull in anything over fifty dollars for an interview or a book review, and that's actually a best-case scenario: you're more likely to see a thank-you email with a smiley face than a check. Even when you start playing in the big leagues (glossy magazines, international newspapers), you'll probably experience what a friend of mine calls a "behind-the-curtain-at-Oz moment" when you hear what you're going to be paid. This friend, who I'm not going to name because she would like to write for this particular outlet again, was offered eight hundred dollars to review four books in a thousand-word review for a major newspaper. On paper, that might seem like a good deal: it's eighty cents a word. But what isn't reflected in this writing rate is the fact that the writer had to read *four entire books* quickly with care and consideration, and then find a way to pack each of their themes, strengths, and weaknesses into a pithy and accessible thousand-word review. And this had to be done while the writer was working on her own book, providing blurbs for others, mothering her child, advocating for political causes, and teaching undergrads, plus it meant that she had to put down whatever else she had been reading for actual pleasure. Once you cut off the percentage that goes to taxes and factor in the amount of time such an assignment takes, the per-word rate is more like fifteen cents. Book reviewing can net you bylines in prestigious outlets and it's a good deed for the community, but it's a lot of work.

If you do decide to book review and the pay is paltry, don't agree to review any old thing just because you were asked. In a Facebook group dedicated to questions about writing and money, the author and book reviewer Charles Finch suggested that newbies should be proactive about their preferences, *especially* if they're writing the review for free. "Ask to write about something relevant to your career interests," Charles says. "Not the first thing that they ask you to review."

How to pitch

Merriam-Webster's dictionary defines *pitch* as "a black or dark viscous substance obtained as a residue in the distillation of organic materials," which is pretty much what happens when you ready your personal thoughts and experiences for an editor's inbox.

A pitch is you trying to convince an editor to let you write something for their outlet on a specific topic with a specific angle, and in time, as you start to build up your portfolio, they will become easier, and real, live humans will respond. These pitches usually take place in a succinct and professionally written email—they should never involve you cold-calling an editor unless you enjoy making people incredibly uncomfortable and not getting what you want.

To write a good pitch, follow a simple checklist: Are you sober? Is it the middle of the night? Are you on a sleeping pill? No? Good. Move on to another checklist: Are you familiar with the publication you're pitching to? For successful pitchers, "familiarity" will mean that they read the outlet regularly (or better yet, subscribe), are aware of the content and word counts being published there, and have done their due diligence to understand the different sections in the outlet as well as which editor runs what.

Pitches should go out to the editor of the section (or genre) you are pitching to. Do not write an email that starts "To Whom It May Concern," because it won't concern anyone. Spell the editor's name correctly, identify who you are and where you live, and pitch: Share your story idea and angle on this particular topic, then add why this story is timely and important. Include three relevant bylines with links, as well as an author site if you have one, and thank the editor for their time. Then wait. If you Google "how to pitch" and you come upon a *Guardian* article from 2014 that tells you to call the editor an hour after you've sent your pitch to verify their receipt of it, please do not do that. This was unsound advice in 2014, and it's still suspect now. I think that article might have been hacked.

What makes a good pitch? In short, a good story. But here are some things to consider when you're readying to pitch:

Have you avoided the duh factor?

When he was senior editor at *GQ*, Kevin Nguyen received a lot of pitches from people who wanted to interview Rihanna. "*I'd* like to interview Rihanna," says Kevin. "This is a relatable desire. This is not a pitch."

One way to get around the duh factor is to think niche, not big. We know which books to read before the apocalypse, but do we know which authors secretly *believe* in the apocalypse? Hmmm . . .

Does it pass the so-what test?

Building off of the above, a lot of people would like to interview a celebrity, review a new hotel, critique a hot new book. But "Because I want to" is not the answer to why *you* should write a piece. Since she joined *Electric Literature* as an editor in 2017, Jess Zimmerman attests that pitches usually fail because the only urgency writers convey about the piece is their desire to write it.

Accordingly, Jess uses exigence to judge pitches: "a rhetorical concept that basically means 'the thing that makes this feel urgent and immediately important.'" Says Jess, "Exigence is of crucial importance in a pitch, and yet I get so many that fail to establish it! Don't just tell me what you want to write—tell me why I want to publish it, and why people want to read it, and more to the point why we *urgently need to.*"

When asked for examples of a nonurgent pitch, Jess was rich in precedents: "Anything that's just like 'Here's my personal journey or experience' with no indication of how it might connect to a broader audience," she says. "We get 'Here are the books I read in order to write my book' pitches surprisingly often, which only flies if you're mega-famous (built-in exigence there!). And people love to pitch me some variation on 'I'd like to examine how *x* influences *y*,' to which I always respond, 'Okay, well, how *does x* influence *y*?' In short, it's not enough to have a subject; you also need to have a point."

Are you considering the reader's pleasure?

With so much content migrating online, the reader's reading experience has started to matter just as much as the story itself. For nearly twenty years in her position as the beauty director at *W Magazine*, Jane Larkworthy was the person being pitched. Now she's the pitcher: in addition to having columns for *The Cut* and Covoteur, Jane writes frequently for other high-profile outlets in the food and lifestyle space. "After a while, it's about crying wolf," Jane says. "You know, 'This project will change your life,' or, 'You'll never need to read another interview again.' When I'm thinking about my profiles, I consider what would be a great intro to write, who would make for a funny conversation that would give answers that would make people laugh out loud," she says. "It's less now, for me, about having the hot new intel as it is about providing the reader with a good experience."

Do you sound human in your pitch?

Your pitch should sound professional, but it shouldn't sound like it's coming from a bot. "I get a lot of pitches that are very formal," remembers Kevin Nguyen from his time at *GQ*. " 'Dear Sir,' 'Dear Madame.' If we're going to have a rapport, I want to know that you can write! The pitch is your opportunity to set a scene, set the stakes, say why the story matters, and all this in a way that proves your writing chops."

On the flip side, a pitch that is too casual or familiar can come off as offensive. On the *Minorities in Publishing* podcast, the writer and editor Morgan Jerkins admitted that she gets a lot of pitches from white women using "colloquial black-woman speak and African American slang" in their communications to her. For a hundred reasons: no. Write as if you know the *publication* you are pitching to, not the editor.

Can you be vouched for?

"There's this idea of the perfect pitch making the story," continues Kevin. "I don't buy into that. Fifty percent of it is a great pitch that a writer has thought through, and 50 percent is a working relationship. I have to be able to trust you. Like everyone else, editors are resource-strapped—if you fuck up your reporting or plagiarize, if you don't file on time, if I send someone out and they are really weird to a talent or celebrity, this all reflects badly on me and the magazine."

Although he recognizes that all writers need to start somewhere, Kevin doesn't think a renowned magazine like *GQ* is the place to start pitching when you don't have publications under your belt. "If you've got clips from somewhere I know the editor and the standard is very high, that's a signal for me. I need a certain level of professionalism," Kevin says. "If you file late and you don't let me know ahead of time, I'll never work with you again."

Editors are more likely to give your pitch consideration if they know you, so find a way for them to know you. Lots of magazines host readings and lectures, their editors attend panels, their editors attend AWP. I'm not saying to stalk people (please don't), but if you're in a geographical situation that allows it, it's worth forging cordial relationships with editors before pitching. It's a small world, and people will ask around about you when you start to pitch them. If you've got an editor who can say, "I haven't had the opportunity to work with them, but we had a nice chat at a reading the other day and they're not a megalomaniac," this can convince someone to give your pitch a second look.

What to expect when you're not expecting virality

For writers, "going viral" means that you have a piece of writing (most likely something that was either initially published online, or at least accessible there) that has been rampantly shared in a short amount of time.

If you're expecting an exact number of views that delineates the border between "viral" and "nonviral," we must disappoint you. Virality is relative to different platforms and publications: it means you got a *lot* of reads. If that happens, you will know. The retweets and shares will start a-piling, the comment section will grow. You'll receive both wanted and unwanted comments through your email and various social media platforms. Your article, essay, or op-ed could become a trending topic on Twitter, and part of the cultural conversation at large. In a world in which you go super viral, the literary elite will discuss your publication with insidery succinctness: they'll talk of "Cat Person," "That Op-Ed," your work will be a meme.

Knowing that your writing has been read and shared by thousands of people is exciting, but even more important is the fact that your work has hit a nerve. For *Electric Literature*'s executive director, Halimah Marcus, "*virality* means a piece of writing has crossed a threshold of readership well beyond our regular audience. One person shares, then two, four, sixteen, etc. Sometimes it's because a piece has struck a chord in the zeitgeist, sometimes it's because Iron Maiden shared our list of the 'Eleven Best Metal Songs about Literature' on their Facebook page. Viral pieces on *Electric Literature* have been everything from feminist essays, to Twitter roundups, to book lists. It's always fun to watch those numbers climb, but it's much more satisfying when a substantial essay with challenging ideas catches on, like 'What I Don't Tell My Students About "The Husband Stitch," ' rather than our more playful content."

"Virality has to be taken as its own high point," says the writer Haley Mlotek, former editor of *The Hairpin* and style editor of MTV News. "We don't write in a void. Having proof of a connection to readers in the immediate aftermath of publishing is really valuable. That being said, it's a different commitment on the part of a reader to retweet an essay than it is to buy a book. What happens online matters, but it's hard to know how fair or realistically virality can predict success in publishing."

For writers who encounter the knighthood of virality, it's assumed that a book deal can't be far behind. The article-to-book-deal scenario makes commercial sense: when an author proves that they have a story that is resonating with readers, savvy agents and editors want the writer to keep singing the same song.

Book deals do happen after an article goes viral—in 2017, *The New*

York Times's Modern Love column editor Daniel Jones estimated that sixty book deals had been inked since the column's founding in 2004. But sometimes an article or essay is really popular and absolutely nothing happens. The writer Andrea Jarrell was inspired to pen a *Literary Hub* article called "Can *The New York Times'* Modern Love Column Change a Writer's Life?" when a colleague asked her about the impact of her publication in this iconic column. "I knew what she was asking," Andrea writes in that essay. "Had agents and publishers beaten down my door after the essay appeared?"

If Andrea's essay didn't win her a book deal off the bat, it did give her the confidence to write an actual book. "Having such a committed and discerning editor take an interest in my work at the start of my career made me believe that I had promise and encouraged me to keep going," Andrea writes.

This confidence boost was also experienced by Bethanne Patrick, whose article about her struggles with depression went viral on *Elle* magazine's website. Bethanne received hundreds of comments to her article, virtually all of them positive, and the piece went on to be syndicated in other magazines. Bethanne attests that seeing such a positive response galvanized her as a writer. "The viral component can be really great in supporting you in whatever you're doing," she explains. In Bethanne's case, the thing that she was doing was putting together a book proposal at her agent's request: he was confident about their ability to pitch a memoir because her elle.com piece had been so widely shared. Referring to herself as "the world's slowest emerging writer," Bethanne admits that she wishes the process could have moved quicker—the proposal alone took her six months. ("It's so much work!" she sobs laughs.)

Virality usually comes because of something you yourself have written, but once in a while, writers go viral by association. The author Jess Row received extra attention for his novel *Your Face in Mine*, about a man who undergoes racial reassignment surgery to appropriate the appearance of an African American, when the news story broke about Rachel Dolezal, a Caucasian activist falsely claiming to be black, igniting conversations around the country about cultural appropriation. Although Jess didn't necessarily see an uptick in book sales, the link between this current-events story and his novel did garner more coverage for his book. Jess started publishing more pieces and was frequently interviewed. "As for outcomes," he says, "my book is now definitely associated with Rachel Dolezal, for better or worse."

Dealing with trolls and negative comments

The great thing about publishing online is that your work can be easily shared. If someone likes what they read (or was moved enough to forward it), it's easy for them to bring it to the attention of other readers, which increases your clicks, likes, and page views. But the more attention your work receives online, the more vulnerable you are to public commentary about it. Not all of these comments are going to be pleasant.

Everyone has a different way of engaging (or not engaging) with negative commenters. Personally, I find ignorance works like a charm here, so I don't read the comments section of anything I publish online. But some writers will feel obliged to follow up with readers, perhaps because their piece positions them as an advice-giver or an expert on a topic, or simply because their work now exists in a public space, and as their piece's parent, it's up to them to come to its defense.

Some writers might decide to disable comments: this was the case with Bethanne Patrick, whose essay about depression went viral on elle.com. Others enlist their friends as editors and buffers. The writer Anna Goldfarb has friends scan her comments sections to let her know if there is anything meaningful that requires her attention, while Patty Chang Anker asked friends to come to her defense when her anti-tiger-momming article went viral and attracted the wrath of one particular man who raged on and on about her "lazy" parenting. "They replied to his comments and supported my position," Patty explains about her friends' enlistment. "This was one of my first experiences having my writing read widely, and I was particularly sensitive to what people thought of me and my family. It definitely helped me feel less vulnerable and braver about putting myself out there. Friends are inoculations—you might still get attacked but you feel less pain!"

Over at *The Millions*, staff writer Michael Bourne says he regularly gets called "an idiot or worse" about his published pieces, a line of argument he doesn't pursue unless he "can clear up some obvious misconception that seems to be driving the discussion in a stupid way." This being said, Michael has female colleagues who have felt legitimately threatened by their online trolls. When commentary crosses the line into harassment, Michael suggests asking your editor to either block the commenter or have that same editor reach out privately to the commenter to de-escalate the situation. "Even though comment exchanges are by their nature public," says Michael, "they can feel private to the people involved in them. If you pierce that privacy by sending them a personal message, it sort of helps them see what they're doing—if they're not actually insane, that is."

Some writers fight their trolls with humor—it's worth noting that most people in our fight-back camp are men. When a commenter using the social media handle "NCAA CLACK! Stan" accused author Michael A. Ferro on Twitter of "being a fucking Yankee from Ann Arbor" who knows "nothing" about biscuits in response to satirical commentary about . . . baseball, actually, Michael tweeted back, "Sir, my father worked in the Ann Arbor Biscuit Mines for thirty years. His father founded Ann Arbor with just a divining rod and handful of biscuits. My ancestors came to this country on a giant floating biscuit. I think I know a thing or two about biscuits." According to Michael, these literary flourishes proved too much for NCAA CLACK! Stan, who disappeared into oblivion shortly after this tweet.

In another example of good humor fighting bad, the author Tom Zoellner engaged so vibrantly with a critic of his book about the history of train travel that he got the naysayer to take him out for a steak dinner while he was in Virginia. "Dinner never tasted so good," Tom writes.

Women, and other marginalized writers, aren't often in a position where such humor works, nor would many of them feel safe dining with a troll. Author Kristi Coulter was so bullied by misogynist online commenters after her personal essay about sobriety went viral that she set up a Gmail filter that autodeletes emails with gender-specific slurs (she provided "feminazi" as an example), complete with combine-keyword searches known as Boolean strings. " 'Hope *and* raped,' " wrote Kristi, when asked for an example of such a linked search term, "because an email using ONE of those words could be just fine, but an email using BOTH was likely to be wishing rape on ME, and I only needed to see a couple of those to want them out of my inbox."

Misery loves company, and writers who receive bad reviews deserve companionship. Accordingly, you might enjoy the interview series Thick Skin, in which authors discuss their most negative reviews from critics and strangers alike.

To self-publish or not

In the age of DIY everything and life as a branded experience, the concept of self-publishing as a last resort for desperate writers is outdated and naïve. For writers who are open-eyed to the complexities of traditional publishing and the ever-tightening market, the decision to self-publish can be an empowering and deeply satisfactory move.

In an interview with *The Guardian*, author Maggie Nelson discusses the alternative MFA she earned by moving to New York to participate in a punk-poetry scene catalyzed by the poet and activist Eileen Myles. "I wasn't the kind of writer who was saying, 'Oh if only *The New Yorker* would publish me,'" Maggie remembers in that article. "Self-publishing wasn't what you did because you were rejected by HarperCollins; it was what you did because it was fun to make zines and run around with them."

Speed and affordability are benefits of on-demand publishing, but looking back, a lot of self-published authors fear they clicked PUBLISH far too fast. "One thing I regret is not using an outside editor for content and grammar," says the writer Tony Thompson, who self-published his first memoir *Love, Fate and Afghanistan* with the now-defunct publishing platform CreateSpace. "Some things in the book could have been expanded on, some things could have been shorter, and I see now how an editor could have helped me with these things."

Another frustration Tony had was the amount of energy he put into promoting his books versus the return on his investments. On the advice of a CreateSpace employee, Tony advertised on Facebook, Amazon, and on the listserve of his college graduating class. He created an author website, and he occasionally attended book fairs where he would sell two or three books per fair. "Honestly, I've had more sales come about from taking my own email list and writing people about my book than I have through advertising," Tony says. Disenchanted with the lack of success from the promotional tools he was spending money on, Tony left Facebook and let his author website lapse. With the disappearance of the publishing platform he was used to, Tony doesn't think that he'll self-publish a book again.

There are success stories in self-publishing, and Jarett Kobek's *I Hate the Internet* is one of them. Jarett suspected that his brutish diatribe about the Silicon Valley start-up scene was going to be a tough sell for commercial publishers, and after a bunch of failed submissions, he decided he was right. But he also knew the book had a potential that the editors weren't seeing. Along with two friends, Jarett founded the indie press We Heard You Like Books in part to publish his own debut, and also—as he describes in a profile at *Publishers Weekly*—"to make the world safer for its freaks."

An Instagram-friendly book title, a shiny blurb from Jonathan Lethem, and the fact that Jarett had the resources to work with an outside publicist helped get his novel into some important hands. Within three weeks of its publication, the book had taken off: Dwight Garner reviewed it in *The New York Times*, Bret Easton Ellis shared a photograph of him reading the book in bed, foreign rights started to sell, and Jarett was being interviewed by international publications like *The Guardian* and *The Irish Times*.

The way that you feel about your self-publishing experience will largely have to do with the reasons you self-published in the first place. If you are hoping to make money, you are going to be disappointed regardless of how you get your book out. (To put things in perspective, in December of 2018, BookScan showed that *I Hate the Internet* had sold 5,839 copies in its American print edition since its publication in 2016. I imagine that a great deal of this book's sales were made up of ebooks, a format that BookScan doesn't include, but still, this isn't a lot of copies for a book considered as a sleeper hit.) If your decision to self-publish is motivated by your desire to share your work with others, you might end up having a positive experience. Sure, there are people who are going to look down at you for self-publishing, but most readers—and especially people who aren't writers—don't care *how* you publish something; they're amazed you managed to sit down and write a book at all.

If you do think that your project has commercial value, however, you're better off revising it than publishing it yourself. Most publishers won't offer on manuscripts that have already been published in other forms.

III
....

Getting paid

I've heard stories of tough-love professors scaring the bejesus out of MFA students by insisting how few of them are going to "make it" on their first day of class, but few teachers move beyond this scare tactic to tell writers what it *means* if their art can't fund their art. It means that you need to get a day job and financially plan. Good writing necessitates that you think like a child: dreaming, playing, and creating worlds inside your head. But in order to make *money* off that writing, you need to gain financial knowledge and make decisions like a grown-up, or pay someone to do the adulting for you.

How to financially plan
....

"Although it has been many years since I've sat in a classroom, it seems to me that financial education is a hole in most curriculums," says certified financial planner William Dobbins, who works with clients across the country. "Even the most basic of financial concepts—income, expenses, and budgeting—don't seem to be addressed. Regardless of one's degree of education, we are all cast out into a world that revolves—in very large part—around finances, and we're expected to just figure it all out. Many—if not most—stumble."

William (who, it's worth mentioning, is married to a conceptual artist, so he's seen the ups and downs of the professional creative life firsthand) has come up with a four-step financial planning cheat sheet for writers looking to pursue a career in the creative arts.

1. Build a budget

"Know your expenses intimately," says William, "and work to get yourself to a place where your art income alone covers those expenses, and better yet, exceeds them." (For most people, satisfying our expenses with "art income" will mean Getting a Day Job. More about those soon!)

Living expenses usually include rent or mortgage, utilities, a car payment or transportation costs, cell phone and Internet bills, student-loan payments, and groceries, but, of course, they can extend indefinitely depending on an individual's situation: health insurance, gym memberships, therapist visits, medication, daycare . . . the list goes on. What one person considers a luxury might be a necessity to someone else.

2. Understand which of your expenses are deductible

"Learning which expenses are business-related and which are not is critical to your financial health," William continues, "because Uncle Sam lets you take deductions on your tax return for business expenses. Whether you research these deductions on your own or engage a good CPA, you might be surprised at what qualifies: Part of your rent might be deductible. Part of your electric, Internet, and phone bills might be deductible, as well. Getting a handle on which expenses are deductible will save you money in the long run. Don't give money unnecessarily to the IRS!"

3. Make saving an essential expense

Rule three is to invest early, even if you have next to nothing to invest. "If it's one hundred dollars a year when you're still living at home with your parents, early investment establishes a habit," William says. "As your sources of income increase, the amount that you can save and invest only gets greater. So if the time comes that you've got a windfall—say a big check from your publisher—you've already established a habit of saving and investing."

In terms of investments, William suggests both short- and long-term goals. "In the short term, ideally, one would have six months' worth of expenses saved away somewhere," he says. "That's an ideal cushion in a savings account, something you think of as untouchable unless your source of income is disrupted."

Over the long term, especially if you have taxable income, William advises establishing either a Roth IRA or a traditional IRA because they help build financial security for your future along with some tax benefits. Income restrictions, your age, marital status, and other considerations can impact whether a Roth IRA or traditional IRA makes better sense for you. The somewhat subjectively named RothIra.com has helpful information on the difference between these two financial plans.

4. Seek professional help

After a decade of my equally self-employed husband and I doing our own taxes to "save money," I now understand that a real-life human tax accountant is an imperative—nay, *priceless*—part of a long-term financial planning strategy. In addition to adding years to our marriage, our accountant pointed out significant deductions we were entitled to as self-employed people who worked from home, and he helped us understand how we could afford health insurance, as well. When we had a child, our accountant was back to bodyguarding our modest savings account, indicating the percentage of our child's daycare that we could write off as a business expense and other portal-to-another-world deductions that we otherwise wouldn't have known about.

In short, the years I went without a tax accountant actually *cost* me money, and I would recommend that all writers hire one (I am going to do this) as soon as it makes cents.

But when is that? "If you're no longer eligible to file a 1040-EZ tax form, that means you have income beyond a certain limit and that you're entitled to more sophisticated deductions," explains William. "At this point, it's time to engage a tax professional. It's also time for a discussion around what is the best entity form for you to take, a decision that will depend on your level of income."

In layman's terms, what this means is that if your income starts to roller-coaster (your book was turned into a TV show one year, or it sold like wildfire), you might want to protect yourself from the new tax codes put in place by the Trump administration by establishing one of three entities: an LLC (in which you and your business are united; the business's profits are your profits and vice versa), an S Corporation, which is *kind* of like an LLC except that the income is taxed differently and in a way (if you're up for the paperwork) that can bring you extra deductions, or a C Corporation, which is a separate living entity in and of itself that requires paychecks and a W2 and all kinds of other highfalutin stuff. Discerning which entity is right for you will depend on your level of income: LLCs are for the bronze-level earners, C Corps are for the golds. Unless you're trained in tax or business law, you should pay a professional to help you understand which form is right for you. "Seek tax counsel," William urges. "You don't want to realize that you have been overpaying your taxes for years because there is no getting that money back."

Whether you end up engaging a financial advisor or a certified financial planner, make sure that that person is a "fiduciary." What that means is that they have signed a fiduciary oath that they won't personally benefit from selling financial products to you. A fiduciary has your best interests at heart, rather than their own. They profit from your personal investments, so if they're not helping you make money, they're not going to get paid.

How will I get health insurance as a writer?

I have no idea, so let me know if you find out.

More seriously, the health insurance hurdle is one of the primary reasons that writers don't get to write as much as they deserve to. Very few writers can afford private insurance, which puts people in a situation where they either have to take a job that they don't want so that they can have health insurance, marry someone for health insurance, or risk illness and/or a serious accident by going without.

You might be able to find group health insurance (or information as to how to find it) through these organizations: the Authors Guild, Freelancers Union, the International Women's Writers Guild, your local chamber of commerce, or the National Writers Union. PEN America has a resource page on its website with a lot of lesser-known organizations to help writers (and other entertainment workers) find health insurance they can afford. There are also ways to get health insurance by using loopholes in the American government. Under current tax law, self-employed people can deduct health-insurance premiums for themselves, for spouses, and for any dependents they might have. But how do you prove self-employment to the IRS? Constant documentation will be your friend in this noble quest. Some freelancers have the bad habit of mixing their personal and business expenses, so one thing you'll need to do is to establish a separate business bank account (and debit or credit card) for business expenses alone. You'll also need proof of wages paid for services falling in your line of work, and past tax returns proving that you've been producing income in this profession for some time.

That previously mentioned change in tax codes sees many self-employed people finding it financially advantageous to turn themselves into small-business entities in order to prosper from a 20 percent deduction of business income on personal tax returns for pass-through entities. The *New York Times* columnist Neil Irwin has an informative article on this subject called "Under the Trump Tax Plan, We Might All Want to Become Corporations" that explains how the savvy can game the system by taking advantage of "the huge gap between the tax rate paid on individual income . . . and the low rate on business income the president proposes, of 15 percent."

Many of these same corporations can be used to acquire health insurance plans for their employees (and if you started your own corporation, you would be your own employee), but I wouldn't advise starting a company to obtain health insurance without consulting a business-law expert versed in the current tax codes first. The Business Formation section of the DIY legal-guidance website, Nolo, can help you find a business law attorney in your area, and they have helpful articles on health insurance in an English even a writer can understand.

Should I write for free?

IMHO, the short answer is yes, until you don't have to. I have a friend who has never published a story or essay she wasn't paid for, and I have about a hundred friends who have only recently started to get paid for their published work.

I started out publishing anywhere that would have me, online mostly, for nothing, and I was only too happy to do so. (It's worth mentioning that I had a corporate freelance gig at the time that made it easier for me to write for pleasure, regardless of what, or whether, I was being paid for a specific piece.)

Online writing was a positive experience when I was setting out: it helped me build relationships with editors and readers; it gave me clear feedback as to what was resonating; it established the kind of book-length projects that readers, agents, and editors might expect from me down the road. I found my current agent because of my online writing: she'd been following some of my humor columns and short stories, and wanted to know if I had something larger to share. It so happened that I did, and the rest is happy history. But do I write for free now?

The answer is rarely, and when I do it's an occupational necessity. When you begin to publish books, you're called upon to promote them, and this can take the form of blog posts, short essays, interviews, and other promotional items. There are exceptions, of course, but it's ethically dicey for writers to be paid for work that promotes something they have published, so a lot of these promotional pieces will be completed for free. Regarding other requests for uncompensated writing, these are the questions I personally run through as I make my way to yes or no:

Will the assignment be emotionally draining?

When I'm assessing how much time a given assignment will take me, I'm not just thinking about the time that it will take me to research, write, and revise the piece. That's physical time, real time, and finding it is a question of organizational management. But budgeting your *emotional* time is equally important. A negative collaboration can reverberate in your psyche long after the work is handed in. But how do you factor in emotional time when you might not know the editor you're working with, or the author you're interviewing? Pay attention to your initial correspondence. Does your interlocutor seem scatter-brained or passive-aggressive? The type to leave you for weeks without a returned email, or to request eleventh-hour edits? How many rounds of revisions will it take before you see eye-to-eye on the piece, and will you want to poke your eye out when that time comes?

If you're not getting paid for something, it should either better you in some way (make you happy, bring you knowledge, forge important new relationships), or it should be fun. Keep in mind that it's easier for people to share your writing online than it is in print, so you might take that into account if an online piece could bring you some positive exposure. (More about this mysterious "exposure" in a sec.)

What am I getting in return and how will I know when I have got it?

Sometimes publishing for free comes down to you owing someone a favor. Someone has written a blurb for you, and they ask you for a short guest post about writing habits on their craft blog; to me that's a no-brainer: yes. Scratch my back, and most times, unless I'm under a particularly crazy deadline or you believe the earth is flat, I am going to scratch yours.

But if an editor promises me "exposure," I need a way to know what "exposure" actually means. When you're publishing online, it's easy to track traffic and page views. Some platforms, like Medium, can even show you how far readers get into a particular piece. Publishing in print is trickier. If I'm asked to contribute to an anthology of essays for which my writing won't be compensated, I get a little bristly. What's the incentive? Will I get a cut of sales? Or is it payment enough to be published alongside a roster of other authors I admire? What's the project's audience? Is their audience mine? I'll often write for free when it involves giving advice to other writers, for example, or if the publication is for some higher cause or charity. Generally, though, if I feel resentful of the ask before I've even started writing it, I know I should say no.

Once you start earning money for your work, I think you should keep earning it. On social media, the author Alexander Chee has been forthright about the reasons he no longer writes for free. "My experience thus far is that if I give writing away, people don't respect it," he wrote in his TinyLetter. "I have been a writer online since the beginning of it and my experience now, for the last fifteen years, is that people with a new website and a need for content have often treated my writing, and me, badly. If they can't pay for my fee, they often can't pay for other things, like copyediting and editing, fact-checking, and design. They take it down off the Internet without warning, or they change things, or they might even make it look shitty. Or they forget to invite me to the big fancy party they throw after inviting people who haven't done anything for them once they're doing better after first getting the work I gave them for cheap."

Alex has come up with a fee that he will not write for less than, a sum he views as an "emotional boundary" that protects his ability to work well and to do so happily. "When I accept less than that," he continued in his TinyLetter, "I get angry, and I self-sabotage. I'm fifty years old. I work another job, as a professor, and I'm a busy literary citizen, as the expression goes, judging contests and showing up for my causes. I also have bills to pay. That all takes time I don't get back. And if I'm writing an essay based on my experiences, well, I don't get those experiences back either. I have started counting the working years I have left against the projects I want to write, and yes, that may not include your ask that you are hoping I won't ask for money for."

Alex sees asking for pay as part of literary activism. Even if the answer is no, writers should ask for pay so that the asker starts expecting to be asked.

Can I call myself a writer if I'm not making money from my writing yet?

Deciding when you "earn" the right to call yourself a writer is intrinsically linked, for many people, with their definition of success. If it's getting a book traditionally published, maybe you say you're a writer when your book has an ISBN. If you think successful writers get paid for their work, perhaps you call yourself a writer the first time you get a check for something you have written. If you equate success with establishing a readership, you're a writer when you publish something that is widely shared. The steely-nerved among us will consider themselves writers when they start taking risks. "I began calling myself a writer as soon as I had a book-length work in progress," says author Lara Lillibridge. "I didn't get paid for being a mother, so claiming an identity apart from money didn't seem weird. It was about the time spent and passion for it."

And there it is, the evil word that makes identifying as a writer even more fraught: money. When people ask you what you do for a living, they're also asking you how you *earn* a living, and most writers don't have any idea what they'll make from one month to the next. "Eight books in and I struggle to say it out loud 80 percent of the time," admits YA author Beth Ain. "I call myself a writer in the immediate wake of a deal and then not again until the next one." With two novels behind her, author Polly Dugan also struggles with fluctuating confidence. "I'm still trying to get comfortable calling myself a writer," Polly says. "Mostly because I've been stalled for so long on book three that the first two seem like they were written by a different person."

First things first: you have the right to remain silent in any conversation—real or digital—pertaining to your work. You don't need to make it easier for anyone to understand you, and you certainly don't need to play existential how-I-make-a-living Twister for a stranger. You don't even need to tell people what you're working on, if they ask. If you choose to engage, come up with a line to protect yourself from priers. Something along the lines of: "I'm working really hard on something, but it's too much in my head right now. I'll be excited to tell you more about it when it's done," might work.

The longer you go working on something that you're not being paid for, the more that people (even friends and family) will start to doubt this mysterious, time-consuming book. So if you're in the long-distance club, arm yourself with peers. There's no shortage of writers who took their sweet time getting their books right: Tayari Jones spent six years on her novel *An American Marriage*, an Oprah's Book Club pick. Donna Tartt works at the breakneck speed of one book a decade, and you don't hear her readers complaining (or the Pulitzer Prize committee, either). The childhood fans of J. R. R. Tolkien had to wait through an entire *world war* for him to perfect *The Lord of the Rings*, his follow-up to *The Hobbit*, and it took Gary Snyder forty years before his epic poem cycle, *Mountains and Rivers Without End*, was published in book form.

If you are going to be deep-diving for many years into a project, don't forget to tend to the seeds of your career. Although it's romantic to consider going off the grid for ten years only to reemerge with a game-changing tome, the writers who applied for fellowships and residencies, published essays, fostered writerly friendships, and/or deepened their presence on social media in a meaningful way during the decade(s) spent writing their debuts are competitively equipped to find a publisher when they finally type, "THE END."

Speaking of The End: you should try to reach it if you have it in you. "Not finishing the novel would have dealt my psyche a blow whose imagined pain was worse than the considerable frustrations of facing my limitations every day," wrote Matthew Thomas of the decade-long fight to finish his debut novel, *We Are Not Ourselves*. This quote (which appears in the book's author questionnaire) actually inspired Lisa Ko to finish the novel she'd clocked seven years on, the bestselling, prize-winning, took-her-around-the-world-on-book-tour book, *The Leavers*.

Whether your book takes you two years or twenty, whether you get a million bucks for it or it never finds an editor, you are the only person who gets to decide when—and why—you call yourself a writer. Once you do, don't stop.

Supplementing your income, a.k.a. the side hustle

Unlike full-time teaching or editorial positions, there is no annual salary for "writing." Most of the creative writers I know seesaw between perilous financial comfort and living hand-to-mouth, and this includes writers that the outside world judges as successful. With many independent presses offering advances in (and under) the $5,000 range, it's virtually impossible to live on such an advance unless you (or someone else) is supplementing your income. Given that they are divided up over a number of years, and that significant percentages have to go to a writer's agent, the IRS, and regular bill payments, even giant advances net a writer a yearly salary on par with that of an associate professor, but this "salary" comes without health insurance and it has a stop date:

you can't continue to earn such a wage unless you are writing, selling, and promoting new books every year. This is a grueling pace.

Accordingly, many writers (*most* writers) take on side hustles: short- or long-term gigs that supplement their incomes while keeping their minds engaged. For creative writers, the industries within which they can apply their skills are manifold indeed. Author Alex Marzano-Lesnevich found themself writing copy for a marinara-sauce jar label when the owners of an Italian restaurant reached out to them after reading a Modern Love column about snake ownership and sexual identity that they wrote in 2011. (Admittedly, it takes a few leaps to get from snakes to marinara, but the restaurant made those leaps.) Author Annie DeWitt wrote entries for *The Princeton Review*'s Best Law Schools while she was at Columbia ("It became the underground side hustle for a lot of MFAers," she admits). Rolf Yngve helps former inmates write their résumés through a veterans' program called Leave No One Behind, and author Nelly Reifler was a monthly columnist for *Electrical World Magazine*—a column, by the way, that she was in no way educated to write. ("The editor said it was easier to teach good writers how electricity works than to teach electrical engineers to write well," Nelly says.)

The host of the Rally Reading Series, Ryan D. Matthews, once wrote birthday party guides for Party City that focused on the plight of stressed moms with little time (Ryan remembers "Yoda Soda" as a particularly inspired article of his), and author H. W. Peterson taught writing to engineering students (they're coming for your job, Nelly!) until she found a gig writing dialogue for Amazon's virtual assistant, Alexa, through a contract company she still works for today.

Sex sells, but it sells better with good copy, and so it is that many of our writer friends have side hustles in erotica. The writer Kara

Leighann wrote DVD cover copy for gay soft-core films like *Hunkboat 1* (and *2* and *3*), *Joyland* publisher Emily Schultz wrote copy for a cable news show where the anchors stripped while reporting, and—while not exactly erotic, unless used in a certain manner—author Amy Bloom wrote descriptions for a line of body products scented like baked goods. (Shout out to edible products, y'all—I wrote about them for a year at Victoria's Secret, myself.)

As suggested by these examples, copywriting can be an energetic side gig for writers who know how to meet deadlines. Editing, proofreading, translating (if you speak more than one language fluently), ghostwriting, sensitivity reading, tutoring, and public relations work are equally great options, but how do you get these gigs?

First of all, you'll need a track record of your writing and/or other creative work. An author website is a good place to include links and excerpts, and it will spare you the hassle of sending potential clients your ten-gigabyte portfolio. The social-networking platform LinkedIn has a reputation as the weird uncle of social media, but employers do look for full- and part-time candidates on this site, so it behooves you to keep an up-to-date professional profile there. At the time of writing, Sophia Amoruso, the brain behind the Girlboss empire, announced that she was starting a LinkedIn-like platform exclusively for women, so keep your eyes out for that. Most of the writers cited above found their gigs through personal connections, friends, colleagues, or people they were already working with, but I've personally had success with job-recruitment agencies like 24 Seven Talent or Artisan Creative, myself. (Make sure to specify whether you are looking for full-time or part-time work and whether you're willing to commute or relocate when you sign up with one of these sites.)

Of course, many writers supplement any income they are earning from their writing with teaching positions, but it's important to note that you will need either an MFA or a published book (or both) to apply for most creative-writing positions in the academic market—a beast that we will tussle with in book two. If we can't actually help you find a side hustle, at least you know you're gonna need one. Blogger Elna Cain's informative article on finding freelance writing gigs on ElnaCain.com, as well as the online resource center for writers, The Write Life, are both great places to start.

To teach or not to teach

In *After the Book Deal*, we'll explore the finer points of going on the academic market, but at this juncture (especially if you're in an MFA program or contemplating attending one), it's worth asking yourself if teaching is the right career move for your future. Teaching is a popular—one might even say default—option for writers and graduates with humanities degrees, but with more articles and statistics coming out about the restricted job market for MFA and PhD grads, a young writer could be forgiven for asking *why*.

"I'm currently grading final papers and so I'm not sure that I should commit any of my feelings about teaching to print," wrote one college teacher who preferred to remain anonymous, "other than to suggest that writers explore ALL POSSIBLE ALTERNATIVES before deciding that teaching is the best career choice for a writer."

A few benefits up-front: teaching allows writers to stay engaged with the subject and discipline they're passionate about; it grants access to other great minds and minds that might be even greater with a little bit of encouragement; it provides exceptional networking opportunities along with a supportive community of like-minded people who understand the ups and downs of the writing life. And, of course, there is the lure of having your summers off to write. Except, hold on. Without even addressing a reality in which responsibilities/life/offspring exist, the truth is that most writers (especially adjuncts) have to use their summers to supplement their income, prepare the fall semester's courses if they have a teaching job, or try to find one if they don't.

For most writers who enter academia, landing a tenure-track teaching position is the Holy Grail. Job security! A craftsman bungalow! Sabbaticals! Tweed coats! It's worth slaving away as an adjunct for a couple years in order to make it to nirvana, right?

Unfortunately, young writers and students aren't indoctrinated to the reality of just how hard these tenured (and tenure-track) positions are to get. In an article for *Vox*, a former tenure-tracker named Oliver Lee put things into perspective. "I can't overstate how rare this opportunity is: Tenure-track jobs at large state universities are few and far between. Landing one without serving a postdoctoral appointment or working as a visiting assistant professor is about as likely as landing a spot on an NBA team with a walk-on tryout—minus the seven-figure salary, naturally."

A *Guernica* article by its coeditor Rachel Riederer showed that in 1969, 78 percent of professors were on a tenure track. By 2009, that percentage was down to 33.5. The rest of the teachers floating out there in the 66.5 percent of pie-chart land are doing so (with very few exceptions) without any job security. No health insurance, no guarantee that their classes will fill or won't be taken over by a full-time professor, no agency in deciding where they want to live (you go where the job is), and *very* little pay.

No, really. *Very* little pay. I interviewed an adjunct professor who preferred to go unnamed who was adjuncting at the time of our interview at three different colleges in three different states on the east coast for $2,500 per course. She was commuting, napping, eating, and writing in her car, teaching through a sleepless fog for $18,000 a year, without any health benefits. When I pointed out that quite a bit of that money must have gone to gas, she fell silent. She admitted that she had forgotten to set aside a gas budget.

Adjuncting is a great way to get your foot into the door of academia and carve some teaching notches in your belt, but you must be open-eyed about it. This is a generality, of course, but writers who have fulfilling adjuncting experiences often have one or all of the following: an outside stream of income, a supportive partner (through whom they have health insurance), and no dependents. If you have a mortgage to pay, a high rent in an expensive city, offspring, expensive medical bills, or any other number of life expenses that require regular investment, it's going to be hard to keep your head above water as an adjunct. Which is why it's doubly important that you love what you do.

"I notice that I enjoy teaching more every year, and understand its significance to my own work more every year," says author Marie-Helene Bertino, who has taught at the MA, MFA, and low-residency level nationally and internationally. "The more I teach, the more I realize that what I am actually doing is explaining to beginners and advanced writers how to get to know oneself as much as possible so as to know when one's self is trying to get away with something, so as to know when to push harder against our stubbornness, or when to go easy on oneself." Marie also draws inspiration from the activist position that teaching allows her to take on. "Specific to my work is a desire to teach the literature of the uncanny, to trace the improbable and impossible, as I am trying to correct what seems like an eon of privileged, white, affluent realist writers who never had to imagine their circumstances better or wilder or more magic, and so never did."

Author Ramona Ausubel, who recently started a tenure-track job at Colorado State University, finds that investing in other people's work helps her feel at peace with how much—or little—she herself is writing.

"I have however many books in me over the course of my life," she says. "The number is going to be finite. If literature as a larger project is going to be meaningful, it requires more voices."

Stories exist in every format, and the ones that need the most support are the stories that are untold. MFA holders can use their writing, editing, and interpersonal skills to help people outside of academia to hone these tales in deeply meaningful ways. Author and essayist Emily Rapp Black has worked with the LGBTQIA speaker's foundation, SpeakOUT Boston, to professionally train speakers to tell their coming-out stories in public forums (such as high schools and churches) in order to build awareness around queer issues in predominantly straight communities, while Alaina Leary uses her personal website to offer consultations and editorial services to marginalized voices across the publishing industry. The author Deb Olin Unferth was so influenced by the work she did at the Wesleyan University's Center for Prison Education that she developed her own program at a maximum-security Texan prison called Pen-City Writers that has grown into a full creative writing program with its own library, literary journal, and college credit for participants. "Nothing will convince you of the power of education to change lives more than teaching in a prison," Deb says. "Incarcerated people have unique voices, urgent motivations for wanting to learn how to write, essential stories for our time. And by teaching them you are offering what they so frequently lack behind bars: community, independence, self-determination, intellectual engagement, rigorous thinking, inspiration, and an outlet for creativity."

To teach a private workshop you will need impressive former teaching experience, along with stamina and resources if you're going to build something of your own. To pursue opportunities as a public-speaking mentor, collaborators will want proof that you're good at it yourself: including video and audio clips of past speaking engagements, along with testimonials, and a CV will help. If working as a manuscript consultant or editor-for-hire is the path that's right for you, in addition to the usual suspects (testimonials, bio, contact) on your author website, include a tiered range of services: for example, a consultation on a short story should not cost the same price as a novel.

Hey, Mister, where's my money?

If you go the freelance writing and/or speaking route, you will spend about 40 percent of your time writing, and 60 percent of your time chasing down the money that you're owed for whatever it was you wrote.

One way you can get out of this time-consuming spiral is by keeping track of who owes you what. Maintain records of what you wrote, for whom, and what is owed to you, and also note when you get paid. Another good practice is to specify a late fee on your invoices, and to hold your client(s) to them. If after numerous email reminders and/or phone calls, you're still not getting paid, the company And Co. will send a letter from a semi-official law firm on your behalf for as little as three dollars. You're basically paying for imposing letterhead, but it often works. Additionally, a professional membership in the Authors Guild gives writers access to legal advice, legal forms, contract reviews, and other resources that can help freelance writers get the money they are due.

Can I stay in my corporate job without losing my creative edge?

The French novelist Gustave Flaubert used to say that you should be bourgeois in your life so you can be bohemian in your work. With the financial security, health insurance benefits, and other comforts that corporate positions offer, this has proved true for a number of writers who were able to thrive in both the literary and the corporate worlds.

After nearly seven years of working full-time in an executive position at Amazon and writing on the weekends, an essay of Kristi Coulter's on Medium called "Enjoli" went unexpectedly viral. A self-describing pragmatist, rather than run blindly into the arms of her waiting book deal, Kristi took advantage of Amazon's sabbatical program to feel out what it would be like to write full-time. She was originally worried that it would make her stir-crazy not to go into work every day, but instead she found that a near decade of corporate experience had turned her into an expert time manager and an efficient taskmaster: two qualities needed to write a book.

Another author who directly credits her time in corporate America with her ability to multitask is Mira Jacob, who was working as an editor for various Fortune 500 companies during the completion of her debut novel, *The Sleepwalker's Guide to Dancing*. "If you're going to be an artist, you need to be a business person," Mira explains. "You need to learn to anticipate stuff: What will it take if I want to do this or this thing, or what do I need to do in order to do it. You know, you can't just 'write.' I think there's an essential kind of confidence about how competent you are that comes from working in the corporate world, and about how much you can get done. I'm a producer. I've learned to produce."

Many writers graduate from their MFA programs convinced that once they publish a book, they'll be able to get a teaching job to help pay the bills. This line of thinking initially seduced author Elliott Holt out of her career in advertising, after her debut, *You Are One of Them*, was a critical success. "I have an MFA and I have a book, a book that got decent reviews," Elliott remembers thinking during that time period, "now I won't have to work in advertising anymore. Now I'll write and teach!" Elliott laughs. "I didn't understand how hard it is to get teaching jobs," she admits. "There are fewer jobs now, the humanities departments have had to cut so many. It's a new model: professors retire and they replace them with adjuncts." Presently, Elliott is working as a visiting assistant professor in the Department of English at NYU, but it's a temporary appointment, and one that pays far less than she made in advertising. "I'm not naïve enough to think I won't have to work in advertising again."

If you're well organized, productive, great at multitasking, and have the kind of skills that would get you into corporate America in the first place, writing and jobbing are not mutually exclusive. But don't expect a lot of sleep. For the nearly ten years that Mira Jacob spent in white-collar America, she worked all day as an executive and mother, and then switched to writing her own novel from 10:00 p.m. to 1:00 a.m. each night. "I'd fall asleep writing," Mira admits, "you know, just drooling on the keyboard. While that was happening, it was hard to believe that I was getting anything done, that I wasn't just passing out at my computer. But I was, actually. I was writing a whole book."

If I have children, will I ever write again?

In my experience, when creative people are wondering whether or not they should try to have children, a lot of their fears stem from the idea of their creative time being usurped. When my husband was lobbying for a baby, that's the thing that most concerned me: my time, my time, my time. As a writer, time is my joy, my payment, time is how I make a living, I need time to write. When I was younger, I didn't know much about children except that they took a *lot* of time. But now that I have a daughter, what I realize is that while you can't say for sure how much time your child/children will necessitate, you can (should, must) create a budget to help protect your writing time.

It's a romantic idea to fall in love so hard with someone you want to make a child, but you're doing your future self a solid if you research what that kid is going to cost. For example: as we sit here chatting, a writer friend of mine is paying $2,650 a month in Brooklyn for daycare for his two-year old daughter. The daycare is open until 6:30 p.m., and it costs a dollar a minute in late fees every minute after that. Kind of like an overdue library book, except vastly more expensive. For part-time daycare (three days a week at most places in Brooklyn), the cheapest rate I was quoted by my interviewees was $1,350 a month.

Most of the New Yorkers and Brooklynites sampled pay $20 an hour for a babysitter, plus extra for the sitter's food and cab, which is pretty standard in the New York metropolitan area. One thing you'll have to get used to as a parenting writer is that the cultural activities you used to participate in for free might not be gratis anymore. A new-parent friend recently participated in a reading for the first time in a long while, and went out with friends after the series, a necessary reentry into literary life that cost him (and netted his sitter) a hundred bucks in cash.

Working parents outside of giant cities have it a little easier: a writer friend in Wooster, Ohio, pays $5,000 a year for full-time day-care; another in Corvalis, Oregon, found a "grandmalike" babysitter who charges a dollar an hour to sit; and a third friend in the Massachusetts Berkshires found a nanny saint who watches all three of her children for $20 an hour. But people working in suburbs complain of city prices: in Westchester, New York, for example, sitters charge up to $25 an hour, a half day of preschool costs $7,000 for nine months, and full time is $14,000, which might seem like an amount that is budgetable, until you hear that this school's concept of "full time" is five and a half hours a day.

This sample is in no way exhaustive, and some of these writers are sending their children to specialized Montessori programs, which can cost more than other daycares, but the point is that unless you have generous family members or a "grandmalike" hero in the area, the cost of childcare is significant and needs to be budgeted for if you are going to claim time to write.

Once you have the kiddo, though, and find a place to store the child during your writing time, the good news is that some writers saw their creative output *increase* in their baby's early months. "I think there's a way in which having a baby—for me, at least—allowed me to get my priorities in order," says the author Joanna Rakoff of her experience raising her first child. "All that mattered was my son and my book. (And keeping a roof over our heads.) Whereas before kids, I'd wasted time having lunch with 'friends' I didn't truly love, or browsing in shops, or organizing my medicine cabinet, after kids, I was able to cast off all unimportant obligations, to stop doing all the things I felt I should do, and only take care of the things that truly mattered."

Author Rumaan Alam also found that parenting brought him renewed focus. Despite working in the magazine and advertising industries, Rumaan never published a book until he was a father. "I learned how not to squander forty-five minutes at my desk," Rumaan writes in an article about writer-parents for *BuzzFeed*. "I learned how to read during the twenty minutes in which the kids' naps overlapped; I learned how to make dinner while the kids ate breakfast, thereby freeing up the last hour of my day; I learned that it was not the worst thing in the world if they watched *The Magic School Bus* so I could fold the laundry and know that, come bedtime, my own work (instead of the laundry) was waiting for me. The constraints on my time made me adept at finding and exploiting the few loopholes that existed."

But for most writing parents—women especially—finding writing time got trickier when their child started having existential needs. "Eventually, the fourth trimester ended," writes Catherine LaSota in an article called "Two Freelance Artists and a Baby," from a column she used to write for *Catapult* about creative motherhood, "and our baby became less a sleepy slug and more of an inquisitive, needy human. I couldn't be in the same space with him and have enough brain capacity to do anything else, and I didn't want my son always to be around a distracted adult; he deserved human interaction as he babbled at a stuffed giraffe or batted an elephant mobile."

"I have three kids now at very different developmental stages," Joanna Rakoff says of her own quest for the elusive thing called balance. "As my kids get older and engage with the world in a more mature manner, it becomes even more of a pleasure to spend time with them, and breaking away from them to work becomes even harder for me. But perhaps more importantly: they each need me in a very different but equally intense way, and I find it harder and harder to clear my head of their needs and challenges and voices, and enter the world of my new book."

If this section feels like I'm trying to position parenthood as a precarious alternative for a writer, that's not my intention, and it certainly isn't my point. I just think it's important to be clear that parenting is *tough*. It can be expensive, sometimes prohibitively so. It's also great and life-changing and mind-expanding, but I don't think it's necessary to write about that here. How many examples are there of wildly successful writers who are also parents? Michael Chabon and Ayelet Waldman are some of America's most prolific writers, and they have four children. Jim Shepard and Karen Shepard, another power duo, have three children between them. Jhumpa Lahiri has two children, Anthony Doerr and his wife had *twins* while he was in Rome on a prestigious fellowship, and his career turned out just fine. Lev Grossman, who wanted zero children, now has three, along with a bestselling book trilogy, The Magicians, that the experience of parenting inspired him to write.

IV
....

Getting it represented

For most writers, getting an agent will be one of the most important milestones in their careers. And while it's true that most writers do have agents, and that most editors acquire agented manuscripts, it's also true that the perceived importance of agent-having causes many a writer to sign with an agent before they need to, and/or to sign with the wrong one.

Whether you need an agent doesn't just come down to whether you have something marketable to sell. You also need to be in a place in your writing career where you know how to meet deadlines, cut extensive portions of your writing without having an emotional collapse, be moderately comfortable with public speaking, and have some sense of the kinds of projects you'd like to work on in the future if your current manuscript should sell.

If I want to get my book published, I absolutely, positively need to have an agent, right?
....

I don't think it would be an overstatement to say that most graduates leave their MFA programs convinced that they need an agent to start publishing—some even graduate with representation for works in progress. For writers who didn't attend an MFA program, the sanctity of the literary agent is less ingrained.

Author Chloe Caldwell credits her initial disinterest in "the agent thing" with the fact that she was working and writing without an MFA. "I wasn't in that world," she explains, "I didn't look into it. It wasn't what people around me were talking about or doing." The writers she admired—Elizabeth Ellen, Mary Miller, Chelsea Martin, and the Internet writer xTx—were putting out small, exciting books with micropresses and publishing inventive work online. Through her own contacts in indie publishing, Chloe got in touch with Future Tense Books, a micropress originally based in Washington that was excited about her collection of personal essays. For that book, *Legs Get Led Astray*, Chloe explains, "I didn't get a book advance. I didn't sign anything. It was under the radar and very micro." Chloe felt in control of the entire process and was even more confident in her DIY approach when *Legs* went on to do quite well, earning praise from the likes of Cheryl Strayed and Lidia Yuknavitch. In hindsight, given the positive attention the book received, it's surprising that Chloe wasn't contacted by agents upon her first book's release. But back then, she didn't know what to expect, and without expectations, she never felt let down. "I think that's the big difference between people who go to an MFA program and those that don't," she says. "I didn't think there was a right way to do things."

Buttressed by the reception of her first book, Chloe continued publishing provocative, accessible—and unagented—nonfiction. Her second book, *Women*, came out with Short Flight/Long Drive Books, where her friend Elizabeth Ellen was an editor. The book took off, especially when the celebrity Lena Dunham started publicly supporting it, proclaiming it "a perfect primer for an explosive lesbian affair."

Unsurprisingly, given the hype, literary agents started to come out of the woodwork. "It was like going on a date," says Chloe, "being asked things I'd never been asked before. But I didn't feel like I needed anything. I'd been fine on my own, because I knew people."

Flattered nonetheless by the attention, Chloe signed with an agent who urged her to put out another book of essays. This wasn't something Chloe wanted to do, and she felt unduly rushed. "I didn't love my first experience with an agent," she admits. "I felt a lot of pressure to follow up *Women* with this big thing and my heart wasn't in it. And that wasn't a feeling that I knew."

On her agent's advice, they shopped the new book to "Big Five" publishers. No dice. In talking with her author friend Emily Gould a while later, Chloe learned that Emily was starting her own imprint with Coffee House Press, an indie Chloe adored, and Emily wanted to consider Chloe's new book for publication. Against the wishes of her agent (who still felt like the book had commercial potential), Chloe signed with Emily Books, which left Chloe feeling like she hadn't needed an agent for a deal she basically negotiated herself.

Today, though, Chloe describes herself as being "almost out of the PTSD phase of agent-having," and has been working for a few years with Melissa Flashman of Janklow & Nesbit. For Chloe, a hands-off agent was what she needed: someone who wouldn't try to sculpt her work into what the market wanted, but would wait until Chloe handed in something that she was excited about. As her work has gained more attention, inviting trickier negotiations such as film and TV rights, Chloe says she is grateful to have an agent at her side, a sentiment echoed by Luke B. Goebel, who negotiated the publication of his debut, *Fourteen Stories, None of Them Are Yours,* without an agent's help. Though Luke was initially heartened by what he called an "art-first" approach, the unexpected critical success of his debut brought him opportunities that he wasn't able to successfully negotiate himself. In one disappointing example, a potential foreign-rights deal fell apart when the publisher Luke's imprint was attached to botched communications with a foreign publishing house. "At the time, I just wanted someone to be able to buy the book and to know that it was real," Luke says, "but looking back, I should have sent the book to agents and been attempting the more traditional big-business approach. I might have got real money for the book, it could have looked differently at the end."

I'm a poet. Should I be looking for an agent?

The agent landscape is different for poets, many of whom will spend their professional lives without formal literary representation other than the editors and prize juries who champion their work. "Although not all poets are unagented vagabonds," attests Futurepoem books editor and poet Ted Dodson, who is also a contributing editor for *Bomb* magazine, "I don't know a lot of poets that have agents specifically because they are poets."

One of the reasons for this is because poets—even successful ones—don't usually earn the kind of money that a decent-minded agent would want a swipe at. "In poetry, gigantic sales might be a couple thousand copies," says poet and National Book Award finalist Leslie Harrison. "My first press run with Houghton Mifflin was five hundred copies. We're never going to have the sales that an agent would be happy with."

Additionally, a poet's path to publication is much different from writers of fiction or memoir. For one thing, at most poetry presses, unagented collection submissions are the norm. "It's rare that we accept a manuscript from an agent," admits Ted. "If we were to receive one, it would be very weird."

Instead of the agent-to-editor route, many poetry collections reach publication via the contest structure. "Poets don't make money off their books," says Ted. "A contest that publishes a full-length collection might pay you a thousand dollars. Poets, though, have some income opportunity around private and government-subsidized prizes and grants. That's a possibility, though it's slim. As with the Ruth Lilly and Dorothy Sargent Poetry Fellowships, these prizes can be huge, like twenty-seven thousand dollars. They can propel someone's career or reward someone after a lifetime of work."

Propel their professional careers, yes, but not necessarily to a place where it makes sense for a poet to seek representation. After all, do you really want to part with 15 percent of the three hundred dollars you got for publishing a poem in *The Very Prestigious but Underfunded Such and Such Review*?

"You have an agent if you have market representation, period," continues Ted. "Poets need representation in the marketplace if they have something to sell—a novel or memoir, or a lifestyle cultural bent that can be capitalized on."

Sometimes a poet secures an agent to help them craft this marketable something: perhaps they're working on the structure of a novel together, or a proposal for a memoir. This was the case for poet Alex Dimitrov, who signed with an agent when he and fellow poet Dorothea Lasky started Astro Poets in 2016, a Twitter feed merging poetry, astrology, and humor. The feed quickly attracted a following significant enough to merit agents' interest. Marya Spence at Janklow & Nesbit was the best fit to help the team transform Astro Poets into a book, and she also agreed to represent a novel that Alex was working on. As for representing his poetry? "I don't know," laughs Alex. "I'll have to ask."

Poets who are agented only for their poetry have something that Ted calls "cultural pop crackle," and frustratingly for poets, it's made up of more than critical appeal. For poets with this elusive combination of raw talent and charisma, a speaking agent is a strategic—and potentially more useful—alternative to a literary agent. "For poets, in one way, it's the only representation and protection they're going to have in the marketplace," says Leslie Shipman, founder of the Shipman Agency, who represents poets such as Rickey Laurentiis, Aja Monet, and Timothy DuWhite. "Venues—universities—don't necessarily have the budgets they need to properly compensate writers for their labor, but it's just as often the case that they *are* negotiable, and like anyone else would, they start low. And I, of course, start high, and hopefully we can meet in a reasonable place that works for both the venue and the poet. There's this idea that poets should be happy for the exposure, so here's five hundred bucks. I think poets should be properly compensated."

I'm ready for an agent. Is my manuscript?

"If you are 100 percent happy with your manuscript, it's probably a sign that it's bad," says the novelist and Pulitzer Prize finalist Rebecca Makkai. "It takes forever to write a manuscript. So when you finally get through it, you think, 'It's finally done!' It's not done. I wouldn't send it out until you get the feeling that it's finally—finally—done for the third time."

Rebecca encourages both her students (and herself) to get as much distance as possible from a manuscript before sending it out. "Most people learn the hard way by getting it rejected," Rebecca says. She finds it far more useful to set the manuscript aside for a couple of months, to share it with some "beta readers," and then, once you have your wits about you, to revise it again with the readers' feedback and the thoughts that surfaced during the time away. Rebecca admits that it took her a while to learn to give a first draft time. "You think you know what done looks like," says Rebecca, "but with your first book, you don't know."

A mistake that Rebecca sees a lot of aspiring writers making during the query period is to assume that both agents and editors have time to edit something they like. "There are more writers than there used to be," she says. "There are so many brilliant manuscripts that you're up against. People have the impression that editors massively edit manuscripts, but the modern editor is busy acquiring, busy marketing. They don't have time to fix something that shows spark but isn't done."

I'm definitely guilty of sending a new manuscript to my agent along with a white flag: "This is as good as it's gonna get; I'm stuck; send help!" I'm not proud of this behavior, but I only hoist that flag up when I'm truly desperate. "You can get away with this when you've been working with the same agent and editor for a while," Rebecca assured me when I confessed my shameful habit. With established editorial relationships in place, you *can* get to a point where you can share something problematic, and expect—if not narrative assistance—at least some water and a snack. "But no one is going to fix an imperfect book for you your very first time."

So how will you know that your manuscript is ready? In the immortal words of Whitney Houston: Don't trust your feelings, love can be deceiving. It's not done when it's your first draft, and it isn't done when it's your second. And if you're proud of how long your book is, it's definitely not done. In most cases, a bloated manuscript is the sign of sloppiness, not genius. Of course, a book is going to be the length it needs to be and long books can be transcendent (I'm looking at you, *A Little Life*). But it's also true that an overly long manuscript is a sign to a potential agent that you don't know how to edit yet. Remember how we said that agents and editors don't have a lot of time? Your manuscript has to be effing *incredible* for them to get through 200,000 words.

How to find the right agent for your work

Writers usually find their agents in one of the following manners. I've listed the best-case scenarios first, followed by the more traditional (and time-consuming) paths.

Regardless of how you start your agent search: let go of the conviction that you NEED AN AGENT NOW. This is especially true if you're the one being courted. Many writers are so happy to be noticed, they throw themselves at the first agent opening their arms. That agent might wear a weird-smelling deodorant, or have a proclivity for exclamation points that is going to drive you batty when you start exchanging emails. It's important to find out!!!

Scenario 1: Agent finds you

Maybe the agent heard you read at a series and fell in (professional) love with your whole package: your work, your reading style, your jaunty little hat. Or the agent read something that you published online or in a magazine, and it resonated with them. They want to talk to you about your future projects, including whether you have anything "larger" (this is code for a novel) in the works . . .

Scenario 2: A friend finds you an agent

Perhaps your friend is a writer and recommends you to their agent, or your manuscript has already attracted attention from an editor, and the editor refers you to an agent so that you have someone to protect you during the negotiation process of the book.

Scenario 3: You meet the agent in person and you court them

You attend a writer's conference or festival where you're given the opportunity to sit down with an agent, and you meet one you really like. Or you meet an agent in a social situation, and—same thing—you click. You begin the potentially long process of combing through the work you have to see if you have ~~a novel~~ something the agent thinks that they can sell.

Scenario 4: Blind submission

You're either using a database such as QueryTracker, AgentQuery, or the Literary Agents Database on *Poets & Writers*, or you've identified books that are similar in style to your own and you have combed the author's acknowledgments page to find out who their agent is. You email them a query about your project, hold your breath, and hope. (You're going to have to exhale soon—it can take two months or longer for an agent to reply.)

Should an eventual offer come, consider this mind-bender: you do not have to sign with someone just because they want to work with you. Take time before signing with an agent. You should do your research, which includes paying attention to the way your potential agent talks about your work to *you*. "Finding an agent is such a strange blind-date/gut-feeling situation," says WME agent Claudia Ballard, "but I still believe that the way an agent reads and talks about your work, the edits they suggest, who they see the book being published alongside, what kind of career they envision for you . . . all these elements are a key part of the process."

In a perfect world, you and your agent will develop both a working relationship and an honest friendship. Regardless, though, there is an underlying dynamic at play: your agent works for you. You pay them. (You have to make money to give them money, but the endgame is that 15 percent of whatever you make is theirs.)

Accordingly, you are allowed to take action if you sign with somebody who ends up being a poor match. Because the publishing world is such a small one, writers rarely talk about failed author/agent relationships, which is how young writers get the idea that published authors have one agent for life.

Not so. I am on my third agent, and an informal poll on social media showed that authors Alexander Chee, Annie DeWitt, Marie Myung-Ok Lee, and Jess Row are on team number three as well. Jill Santopolo, Tanaïs, Scott Cheshire, Caitlin Horrocks, and Amanda Stern are on their second (Amanda admitted that she accidentally dated her first, whoops!); Kristopher Jansma and Matthew Specktor are on five; John Domini and Lucy Ferriss are each on number six, and Tobias Carroll and Robert Lopez are holding strong at zero. Over on team monogamy, Joanna Rakoff, Michelle Hoover, Dean Bakopoulos, and the cookbook author Bruce Weinstein have all been with their same agents for more than twenty years. Congratulations, guys!

Why do authors part ways with their agents? What in the world can go wrong? A lot of times, a mismatch in communication styles can be the dividing factor. In a blog post called "Is It Time, Dear Writer, to Ditch Your Literary Agent?" the writer and comic-book author Chuck Wendig posits lousy communication as the number-one reason that agents get the shaft. "Your agent is the champion of your book and ostensibly, your career," he writes. "They are its babysitter—and I don't mean that dismissively, I mean, you want your child to be in capable hands, and further, you want that babysitter to answer the phone if you would like to find out how your baby is doing. If you go weeks without hearing anything from an agent, or months, or forever, you have a problem. It probably means they forgot your baby at the mall."

Sometimes the author/agent relationship breaks down because the agent isn't selling any of the writer's stuff. Whether this is the fault of the writing, the author, the agent, or all three, the relationship starts to feel like a marriage in which there isn't any sex. I've also seen writers leave for greener pastures because their agents operate more as publicists for their publishers than bodyguards for their client. If your agent seems more interested in maintaining a good relationship with a potential publisher than you, this is never a good sign.

But we're getting ahead of ourselves! You can't fire your agent, you don't even have one yet! Here are some transpersonal ways to negotiate whether or not an agent's right for you.

Personality type (yours)

Whether you have a hands-on agent who is helping you revise a manuscript before they shop it, or a hands-off agent who only steps in when it's time to shepherd a book through publication, your agent is someone you are going to be speaking on the phone with and emailing a *lot*, so it's important that your working styles align. If you're a Type A person, like me, you'll need a taskmaster who's a communication ace; if you have a lot of complexes, you'll need a nurturer who's willing to reassure you when you're feeling vulnerable; if you want the big money, you'll need an agent who's not in the business to make friends.

Agent databases aren't going to tell you whether or not a literary agent is quick to answer emails or has a sense of humor, so if certain personality traits are important to you, you might as well be upfront about your needs. During your initial meeting you could say, for example, "I feel most supported by phone calls instead of emails for important topics—is that something you can do?" or "I keep track of my entire life on Google Docs, is that a format you're familiar with?" It will feel weird to ask such logistical questions of someone you're excited to work with, but if your emotional fulcrum is going to be knocked off balance because your agent doesn't text, you should know this before you hitch your dreams to their agency.

Some agents are open to working with their clients as developmental editors: they'll help you get a manuscript into salable shape before submitting it. If this extra service matters to you, make sure it's something that your potential agent provides. If you don't want to edit your manuscript until you have an editor for it, first of all, good luck with that kind of attitude, and secondly, make sure your agent is the hands-off type.

Personality type (theirs)

The mistake I made with my first two agents was that I was looking for a friend instead of a business partner. We liked the same kind of craft beer, were exasperated by the same trends, thought the same weird things were funny. It would never occur to me to seek out a like-minded personality in my accountant or my dentist, and yet, it mattered greatly to me that my first literary agent could also be my pal.

It took years of rejected manuscript submissions for me to realize that in addition to their being friendly, I also needed an agent to sell my freaking books. Obviously, you and your agent need to get along, and you should share the same sense of humor and intellectual interests, because your writing reflects your aesthetics, and your writing is what your agent is there to sell. But your agent also needs to make up for the social skills you lack.

If you're a timid person, it might feel contradictory to hire someone bold, but chutzpah is an essential agent quality. If you hate your book cover, your agent can suit up for this battle with your editor; if there isn't a marketing budget allotted to your project, she can argue to get one; if your publisher is asking you to travel for promotional purposes with no plans to cover your expenses, your agent can shame them into reimbursing you; if there's a prize you think your book is eligible for, your agent can convince the publisher to cover the submission costs. These are just a few examples of the awkward conversations you'll need your literary agent to start. So think hard before you hire an agent because they're just so "nice." Agents are knights in shining armor, and effective knights do not go into battle on a flan.

Do you and your agent agree on the right place for your book?

Wanting to be published isn't enough—the savvy will begin their agent search knowing *where* they want to publish. If you feel like your writing is a good fit for the Big Five, you'll want an agent who has connections and a publishing track record with commercial houses. If you're more of an independent-press type, it's important to make sure that your agent is open to working with small presses. The money in independent publishing is (usually) modest, so there are some agents that might not want to work with you if small presses are your goal. It's for this same reason that some indies and micropresses don't even work with agents, so if your agent says they're up for the indie-publishing route, you'll want to make sure that the agent is chummy with the indie crowd.

We'll get into the difference between publishing with the big guys and the indies in the "Preparing to submit to editors" section just around the bend, but suffice it to say here that they are different journeys: make sure your agent has the appropriate tires for the trip.

Does your agent have a vision for your future?

It's great to have an agent who knows how to support you through your first book's sale and marketing, but it's even better to have a partner who believes in (or even foresees) what you might do next. Forget about next, actually—while you're publishing your book, you're going to be encouraged by your editorial team to write your heart out on essays and op-eds, so you also need someone who can improve your short game, too. Take a look at the client list your agent represents: Are those authors publishing work in exciting places on the side? Are they on podcasts, paneling at festivals, are they part of the larger literary conversation in a way that you'd like to be as well?

Much like a primary-care physician treats your entire body and not just, say, your eyeball, you want an agent who can help you through all the various stages and professional iterations of your career.

Does your agent like your writing?

This question probably makes you laugh—why in the world would an agent sign with someone whose work they didn't like? The thing is, agents are part physical trainer and part trend forecaster: they might love the book you've potentially got in you more than the one that you have now.

When I started working with my current agent, we were initially discussing a novel I had written entirely from the fictionalized point of view of a mute John Mayer. Although the project intrigued her, my forever agent thought it was too weird and niche for my debut. Instead, she wanted to revisit an old manuscript of mine that I had given up on, a love story in reverse that she thought had broader appeal. That's the book we launched with, and she was right to put it first. (John Mayer, if you're reading this, I kinda sorta need your permission to publish the other one?)

Most agents have been in the business for a while and you are (in theory) new to it, so they really do have intel on what has the best chance of selling, when. (This doesn't mean that you can't write what you want to write or that you need to think about the salability of your projects, it's simply a reminder that your agent will.) But once in a while, agents might have their hopes set on a book you have no interest in writing, which is why you need to know—intrinsically—what you have the stamina to write.

Case in point: on the *Minorities in Publishing* podcast, the writer James Han Mattson shared a story about a meeting he had with his agent in which he planned to tell her that he needed more time than originally planned to finish his first novel because he was returning to Korea to meet with his birth family after thirty years of separation. Understandably, his agent got all googly-eyed and said, "Forget about your novel! Can you write a memoir about *that*?" James ended up trying to write that memoir while he was in Korea living the very experience he was writing about, inviting frustration on all sides.

Untested writers can benefit from the kind of agent who works with them (and their writing) developmentally, but ideally, you are looking for a coach, not a conductor. Make sure you find an agent who wants to represent what you want to write, and not what they want to sell.

The agent query process

The single most important part of the query process is to make sure you are submitting your best work. Your best work is not the first draft in your computer: it is the eleventh or the twelfth draft, it should come with a history of actual sweat, maybe some blood, tears on your keyboard. You should have already had your feelings hurt about it by people you admire. You should be physically and emotionally strong enough to have your feelings hurt again.

If thinking about your project makes you feel queasy because you know deep inside that you have done everything you can to make it shine, then you might be ready to send your manuscript to agents. It's time to find out!

Aim high

You might as well start your search at the very top. The aforementioned Rebecca Makkai has a great story in the craft book *Behind the Book: Eleven Authors on Their Path to Publication*, about how she kept the name "Nicole Aragi" on a piece of paper for three years, the agent she most wanted. She never dreamt that Nicole, a seasoned veteran who represents the likes of Colson Whitehead and Edwidge Danticat, would want to work with a debut author who hadn't yet debuted, but she still wanted to try. "I just felt like if I didn't try it, I'd regret it," Rebecca writes. "I also felt so sure she'd say no that once she did, I could move on to more realistic expectations. When I was twenty-one, I sent a story to *The New Yorker,* which is hilarious. There was 1 percent of me that was delusional, but 99 percent of me wanted it to be my first rejection. And I felt the same way about querying Nicole."

Except that Nicole Aragi said yes. She didn't say yes right away, but yes is what she said, and Nicole has been Rebecca's agent for all five of her books.

The neat thing about the querying period is that the possible outcomes are known entities: you will get a yes, you will get a maybe, you will get a no, or you won't get a reply. But you won't get any of these outcomes if you don't query, so start off by contacting the people you'd most like to work with.

Pull strings

Because agents receive hundreds of unsolicited manuscripts from strangers, it's worth doing whatever you can do to convince the queried agent that you are a lucid and reasonable person who will not upset their life. If you have a friend in common (or better yet, a friend already repped by this same agent), ask your friend to send along a note saying that you're a stand-up person, will she keep an eye out for your query? In the subject line of your query, mention that friend's name (i.e., Novel query via [Name of Friend]).

Don't falsify friendships to get your query through the slush pile. The only thing worse than having an agent mad at you is having their client angry, too. Ask someone if you want to use their name. Say thank you if they say yes.

Be succinct

If your email is overlong and frantic, the agent will assume that this is the way your manuscript reads, too. Just like everyone else in publishing, agents are overworked and low on time. Until you have sealed the deal and sold a bazillion copies of your prize-winning debut, a prospective agent has absolutely no reason to tolerate your crazy. You should be professional in your query. You should be succinct. You should give the impression that you are levelheaded, even if you're not.

Be confident but humble

Here's something you shouldn't do. You should not write an email to industry tycoon Binky Urban with the subject line "This book will change your life!" What kind of nincompoop sends a query like that? Well, me, as it turns out! I did this in 2003 with my first book and guess what? Binky's life didn't change.

The now (sadly) defunct Tumblr Slushpile Hell is filled to bursting with queries from writers suffering the delusion of extra-special greatness. In addition to assurances that their attached submissions would "save humankind," one writer admitted that their novel had been commissioned by Jesus, whom the writer had "met in person many times, while touring throughout creation together." It's okay to be proud of the accomplishment you are hoping the agent will ask to read, but it is generally frowned upon to suggest that your manuscript is divine. If the work really is that good, it will speak for itself.

How to stay sane while you're waiting for an agent's response

Agent querying is one of the worst periods of a writer's life, seconded only by querying for editors. The rare and precious thing that you have been tending to like an alien life source is out there in the ethers, and you have given up your power over its alien destiny. Your only job now is to wait. If you're lucky, well-connected, or you've submitted something especially timely, you might hear back right away. For the rest of us, a query could go unanswered for several months, or more.

Some agencies have instant replies that include their average response period. If they don't, I'd give the agency two months before confirming that they have received your manuscript. If anything has changed in the month(s) since your original submission (you have published something high profile, or other agents have expressed interest in your project), this is the time to mention that in order to put fire under their glutes. I have known writers to use the follow-up period to, let's say, *embellish* the level of interest their submission is getting from other agents. And by "embellish," I mean "lie." As a fiction writer, I cannot condone lying. But I can condone exaggeration. Sometimes exaggeration works.

If you haven't heard anything but silence and it's been three months since your submission, it's probably safe to assume that the answer is no. Follow up regardless, but do so with demoted hopes.

Even if you do get a positive response—the agent asks to read some chapters, or the entire manuscript—your inbox is going to become an instrument of torture. Agents have tons of material in their to-read pile, and they take Fridays off with a frequency rivaled only by the French. In the summers, their response rate further slows: it is hot, and they are time-sharing with their best friend the photography agent in a bungalow on Fire Island.

Waiting and waiting (and waiting) for a potentially life-changing judgment on something that you worked hard on is going to put hair where you have none and make you lose it where you do. Having been there multiple times, I beseech you to find something that you love as much (or more) than the manuscript in question while you're waiting for replies. If you're not in love already, find someone to lust for. Start another manuscript. Exercise a lot. Do not isolate yourself socially because you're convinced if you take just a step away from your computer, you're going to miss a life-changing email. The longer you stay by your computer waiting for it, the less likely it is to come. Go to the movies. If you can afford it, vacation. (Preferably somewhere without the Internet.) Volunteer or get a second part-time job. If this sounds insane, it's only because you have not yet experienced what free time is like when you are querying for agents. Do whatever you can to stay busy during this nightmare.

Holy crap! An actual human agent has replied!

If you have received a form rejection letter to your query, please know that you are not alone. Every single writer has been told that their work "has merit," but "isn't the right fit at this time." Every writer has been wished luck finding representation elsewhere.

Should your query result in an actual human being responding to you, this is fantastic news! If an agent is interested in your manuscript, they will ask either to see several chapters, or to read the entire thing. Regardless of their request, understand that while this is a promising development, their wanting to read more doesn't guarantee that they'll want to take you on. Few manuscripts can sustain the excitement of their premise, and agents might decide, while reading, that perfecting your submission would require too much work for them to undertake.

Another possibility is that an agent asks you for an exclusive read. This might occur when there is competition for the project (either the topic is hot or you are, or maybe, lucky duck, it's both), or when you have a relationship with the agent, or a shared connection—i.e., one of her clients is your friend. This isn't a common practice any longer, but asking for exclusive reads does occur. You don't want to agree to a period that is so long that it will kill your chances of getting anyone else to read it: one month should suffice. But don't grant an exclusive if you don't intend to honor it. The agent world is too small for you to get away with that.

Sometimes dreams come true, and the agent will love your submission and ask to work with you. This will be one of the most exciting moments of your life, but remember, you can take your time deciding. When multiple editors are interested in an agented submission, editorial calls are scheduled so that the writer gets the opportunity to feel the editor out. You can use this model during the agent search as well. You can have a phone call with the agent, you can have a lunch. You can also follow your gut feeling and shout, "Yes!"

Preparing to submit to editors

Query session number one is down (you have an agent! Well done!). Only one more circle of query hell to go! Submitting to editors is just as nerve-racking as the agent search, with the difference that you now have an official industry representative by your side. So when you start receiving passes (sorry, but you will), your confidence will have a parachute: "At least I have an agent!" your confidence will say as it plummets—slowly! safely!—to the ground.

Unless you've been in the industry a long time, have worked as an editor, or have a lot of well-connected friends, your agent will have a list of the editors they'd like to submit to on the first round. A "round" is the initial selection of editors that an agent will send a new manuscript to. The number varies by project, but generally, a targeted submission might include up to eight editors, whereas general submissions could include as many as thirty. The publishing world is a small one, so most agents will withdraw the manuscript from submission after a few rounds. When this happens, you might consider taking all of the feedback you have received from editors and incorporating it into a hefty revision, or your weary agent might suggest you write another book. When my first book hit its third round of rejections, my then-agent asked if I could write "a sexy memoir about my time in France." You will notice, maybe, that that book has not come out.

You can make suggestions to your agent about who you'd like the book sent out to. You need to trust your agent (this is a subtweet and what it means is that you shouldn't be on your agent's nuts all the damn time), but there is room for you to have ownership in the submission process.

Provide comp titles for your manuscript

"Comp" is short for "comparison," but nobody in the publishing industry has time for that whole word. It's worth putting thought into what existing or upcoming books resemble your own in content, length, and style, because in addition to providing you with a potential editor for your own project, you'll also start getting ideas for the way your book can be marketed. What kinds of audiences resonated with your comp titles, and do you think that you can reach them, too? How was the book described on the jacket copy? What does the cover look like? If this is your first book, don't only provide bestsellers as your comps. Put the work in to find under-the-radar titles that broke through and performed respectably. In addition to proving that you're not a narcissist, this will also imply that you have a notion of how publishing works.

Know your platform (and your boundaries)

Perhaps you were born at a time when the concept of a personal brand was already embedded in the cultural fabric, and you have tackled your digital life from day one with the goal of coherence, charisma, and accessibility. Or perhaps you are me, and you joined Tumblr without realizing that it wasn't WordPress, or you have an outdated iPhone and your Instagram photographs look like they were taken in a sea of Vaseline. Or perhaps you are old world in your persuasions, and when you are asked to promote your book on social media, you say you have a publicist for that.

A "platform" is the way you represent yourself online. It's a telegraph of your personality, a way to show friends and strangers what you're all about. It's also a tool to build an audience, reach new readers, and drive traffic toward your projects. Curating and maintaining a personal brand takes a tremendous amount of time. It might be something that is exciting to you. It might be your worst nightmare.

It's worth having a heart-to-heart about your platform with your agent before you search for editors, because your willingness to engage your current audience (if you have one) could positively impact an editorial board's feelings about your manuscript. If you have a substantial number of followers on any social media outlet, this should be reflected in your submission letter—make sure your agent does this. Likewise, if you have no desire to engage on social media, or an aversion to it, this is information your agent needs up front. Most publishing houses like game players: if they know from the outset that you are not going to participate in social media, that will allow them to switch up their strategy and think about your book's marketing in a different way. But if they offer on your book assuming that you are happy to use your social networks to post about your book, only to learn in prepublication mode that you've decided to delete all of your social media accounts, this is going to make for an awkward conversation with your team.

Will an editor turn your manuscript down just because you're not on social media? No: if the work is good enough, marketing will find a way around it, and in some cases (Ottessa Moshfegh, Zadie Smith, Elena Ferrante), the absence of a digital platform can make you more alluring. But it would be disingenuous to say that an author's social media aversion won't give an editor pause. An author's platform is free marketing for your publisher. Publishers have bottom lines like any other industry, so they like things that are free. But one thing you should absolutely not do is join social media if you don't want to. If you're really and truly against online engagement and you do it anyway, it will go full cannibal on you and eat your dignity and soul. Being on social media, for a certain kind of person, can make it impossible to produce new work. It becomes too easy to see what other people are doing (and publishing, and winning), it amplifies slights that are probably only perceived, it can make you feel alone even though you have hundreds of digital friends.

Do not join social media just to please your publisher and promote your book. If you look around at the writers who have enormously popular platforms, many of them have been there for a long time: connecting with people virtually and sharing what enrages and delights them is a pastime they enjoy. The people whose every tweet starts with: "Haven't posted for a while but wanted to pop in with news about my book!" are usually the last people picked for the proverbial team.

Weigh in on your pitch

It's good practice to understand how your agent is going to pitch your book *before* they actually do, so that you can course-correct for any discrepancies between your vision and theirs. You can even write a sample pitch letter yourself to emphasize how you imagine your book being presented to the world; just make sure you posit this as something you're doing in order to be helpful to your agent, instead of micromanage-y. Rather than, "I want to write my own pitch letter because I have a control problem," try, "Would it be helpful if I wrote a sample pitch letter so you can get a sense of the way I'm thinking about the project?"

Be aware of the existence of "the editorial board"

Many writers think that their book is going to one editor who has the all-powerful ability to say yes or no to it. But at most houses, if an editor likes a project, they have to convince an entire board—like, at an actual conference table, with iced water in a carafe—to offer on your book. I have been there: an editor at a big house loved my first novel but his colleagues didn't. This sucked. It felt like I'd been barred from sitting at the cool kids' table because of a hall monitor. But once it happened, and I realized that it was a thing that happened, I was better prepared for it to happen again.

"Writers should know that a rejection at this level doesn't have anything to do with you," explained executive editor of Henry Holt & Company Barbara Jones at a 2019 panel on publishing that I was also on. "Maybe I have something else on my list that is too similar, and I can't ask publicity to get behind two books that they'd be pitching in the same way. You want publicity to really be able to get behind your book—that comes into play, too."

Should I submit to indies or Big Fives?

In 2015, *The Guardian* interviewed the author Benjamin Myers about his decision to stay with his independent publisher Bluemoose even though bigger houses came a-courting after the success of his prize-winning debut, *Beastings*. "I feel like as a writer, I'm from the margins, or the underground . . ." Benjamin told *The Guardian*. "A lot of my heroes and influences are people who are on the edge . . . so I think, 'Why bother to chase [the big] publishers?'"

For most authors, it would be difficult—read financially impossible—to turn down a commercial offer in order to go with—or stay with—an independent publisher. But it's still worth giving thought to the kind of place that's right for your personality, values, and your future projects before you start submitting.

Hundreds of thousands of books are published in the English language every year, and a lot of them are great. With larger budgets and expanded resources, commercial publishers can give debut books a fighting chance at getting noticed. Authors at big houses might find themselves with an editor, a publicist (or publicists!), a marketing liaison, and social media support. Add to this a veritable fleet of sales agents whose job it is to sell your book in the regions that they cover, and you suddenly have a giant team of people out there championing your book.

This being said, commercial houses can allocate resources to untested authors because they are run as companies: for-profit enterprises that are hoping to make money off of the projects they take on. This doesn't mean that they are evil: it means they have a bottom line. There is simply less margin for risk with commercial publishing houses; and "risk" here pertains not just to the content these publishers are acquiring, but also the way in which the books are marketed.

It's uncomfortable to generalize, but I'm afraid that's what we're here for. Without the resources to mimic commercial houses' hardcover-to-paperback, social media coverage, a-tour-if-there-is-the-money-for-it formula, independent publishers have to be creative in order to connect their books with readers. Authors at independent presses might find themselves playing a more intimate role in both the brainstorming and execution of their marketing plans than they would at larger houses. Depending on your personality, this level of collaboration might be right up your creative alley.

With less overhead and fewer people weighing in on acquisitions, smaller presses can sometimes show more flexibility at the contract level, as well. An indie might be willing to adjust royalty rates to cushion a small advance, entertain a scenario in which your book only exists as an ebook or a paperback original, and/or leave room for experimentation in your next-project option clause. Again, a generalization, but an indie editor is less likely to balk than a Big Five editor if you decide to follow up your debut novel with a vegan cookbook slash poetry collection inspired by pagan gods.

Writing is hard. Publishing is very hard. You can make it slightly easier on yourself by realizing that sometimes a book is right for the indies, and sometimes it's right for the Big Fives: it isn't either/or. Many writers—myself included—toggle between commercial and independent houses based on the nature of the book that's up to bat. Granted, you have to establish a name for yourself to do this and accept the complications of having multiple publishers, but take comfort in the fact that writers like Roxane Gay, Joy Williams, Lacy M. Johnson, and Jim Shepard have.

Can we sell my first book on a proposal?

In order to sell your first book—regardless of its genre—on a proposal alone, you need to have proven expertise and credentials in its category or you need to be a star. For example: Does Gwyneth Paltrow need to write an entire book about vaginal health in order to get a vagina-book deal? No, friends, she does not.

If your first book is fiction, it will be next to impossible to submit anything to editors but the finished manuscript. There are exceptions, of course: if you have astonishing publication credits or you have a short story that went viral, you might be able to sell a project because of your reputation alone. (But we all know how many times a short story has gone viral in the history of publishing. Once.)

The landscape is different for authors of nonfiction. Essayists and op-ed contributors are more likely to have viral articles and essays in their publication wake. Editors want proof that your message can reach readers: if you've already penned popular articles, you've got a good track record for yourself.

You can also sell a book on proposal (or try to) if you are an expert in your field or you've lived a unique story. Perhaps you are the Backpack Kid who started the viral dance move, the Floss. No one is better positioned to tell your special tale.

Anthologies and collections can be sold on proposal, especially if a community already exists around your topic. The popularity of Michele Filgate's *Longreads* essay about an abusive stepfather, "What My Mother and I Don't Talk About," allowed her to sell an anthology by the same name to Simon & Schuster, in which high-profile writers explore what topics are off-limits with their own moms. The cofounders of the website *Modern Loss*, Rebecca Soffer and Gabrielle Birkner, proposed a witty essay collection about grief (not a typo: witty) that sold easily thanks to the way their signature tone resonated with readers online and at community events.

Cookbooks are an entirely different animal, an exotic, lovely beast, and it would be exceedingly rare to sell one on anything but spec. On one hand, cookbooks are expensive to develop: it's a big risk to write recipes, buy the ingredients, pay for a great photographer, *and* write the cookbook if you don't know if it will sell. "Cookbooks are a rapidly aging industry," says Alana Chernila, author of three cookbooks to date. "Each publishing house will have a certain number of cookbooks they can publish each year, and a publisher might already have their own list of titles coming out. Your project will morph so it can fit into their landscape. Having early editor and publishing feedback could make it shift into another book entirely." Alana cited an example from the proposal for her first cookbook, *The Homemade Pantry*, which went on to be a bestseller. A line in her proposal that suggested her book's recipes be organized around aisles in the grocery stores—her publisher adored this concept and ended up molding the entire book around it. "That one angle stayed the same," Alana says. "Everything else changed."

It bears repeating: proposals function best when your project has commercial value and a proven audience. If you have a niche project, which is to say that its value is artistic (not commercial), or its target audience is highly specific, you're better off submitting the entire manuscript. Successful proposals will emphasize *why* the reader is going to care about your book more than what the book is actually about. Accordingly, most proposals will include the following information (not necessarily in this order):

- Project summary
- Analysis of comp titles

- Definition of audience
- Your bio
- Marketing plan
- Table of contents or chapter summaries
- Sample chapters
- Praise

Book proposals aren't like article pitches: they take a very long time to write. So much time, in fact, that some writers would be better served by writing the entire book before trying to turn it into a proposal. If the topics tackled in your chapters aren't evident from the chapter title alone, or if you're submitting fiction, your chapter summaries will have to include a synopsis of the ideas put forth in every section, about two hundred words per chapter. That's a lot of words about a book you've yet to write!

If we consider patootie-in-the-chair time, book proposals make sense for writers who would be unable to proceed with their particular project without financial support. Maybe your project involves art photography, and you need the resources to pay a professional photographer. Perhaps your nonfiction book is going to require years of research and travel. If you need money up front, and your agent thinks your proposal has a good chance of selling, it's worth putting the time in on a proposal. Proposals are also appropriate for anyone curating an anthology: writers are more likely to contribute to a contracted project than a pipe dream.

Finally, keep in mind that the proposal system is better suited to writers who have a certain level of confidence and resilience. If your book doesn't sell on proposal, it might stifle your desire to write it. Maybe this will be an acceptable outcome for you. Maybe it will kill you. Only time can tell.

We've got nibbles! (a.k.a. setting up editorial phone calls)

Once an editor expresses interest in your manuscript, your agent will let the other editors on your submission list know to make them nervous. Then your agent will set up phone calls between you and the interested editors so that you can feel each other out.

Most calls will start with the editor telling the author what they love about the book. The editor might share their editorial vision, as well as initial marketing and publicity ideas. If they don't bring up these topics, ask them for their thoughts. Books, unfortunately, do not sell themselves. It takes a lot of forward-thinking and elbow grease to get a book into a reader's hands, so you should go with an editor who knows how to improve your book, and support it through the sales cycle as well.

These calls are generally positive and exciting: most editors won't want to scare off an author that they're interested in, so you can expect mostly flattery with a modest serving of whatever reservations the editor might have. The real criticism will come once you accept their offer: that's what the editorial letter is for!

It's worth noting—or heeding, rather—sometimes editors set up calls with authors before they're sure they want to offer on a manuscript . . . and then they never do. "This is something that can happen when an editor is unsure about whether they have a concrete editorial vision for the project," explains a literary agent who preferred to remain anonymous, "but wants to use the conversation to get a sense of whether they can find their footing in real time. Sometimes those conversations can be great and warm, but not really help clarify anything for the editor. So the editor ends up saying some version of, 'I feel like I can't really wrap my head around how to get this book to the place where I'd want it to be,' or, 'With some distance from the conversation, and having talked it over with colleagues, I feel like the amount of work I'd want done that needs to happen before acquisition—I'd need the assurance that s/he/they can get it there, before being able to offer.'"

These are highly unpleasant emails to receive. You are allowed to cry.

How do I know which editor to choose?

If a potential editor says your book is perfect and it doesn't require any changes, run. It's a nice thing to hear, but it can't possibly be true. Editors exist to edit: if they don't find any flaws with your manuscript, the editor's the problem.

Though this is far easier said than done (and might not be a discernment you're in a financial position to make), don't automatically leap for the editor who offers the most cash. As we will learn in the subsequent section on advances, a big advance for a book that underperforms can be a bone-rattling experience with negative consequences for your career. It's also important to remember that a big advance isn't always commensurate with an editor's enthusiasm. I have a friend who received a $140,000 advance for her first book. This was a momentous amount of money for this writer—money that was going to impact her life positively for many years to come. Accordingly, she proceeded with the conviction that she had received a huge advance. She assumed her book was a big deal for her publisher—after all, they'd paid so much to have it. The problem was—or rather, the misunderstanding that developed—is that for her commercial publisher, this was not a big advance. It was a good advance, a very respectable one for a first book, but this number was more of a rote commercial transaction for them than an all-hands-on-deck pledge.

The writer's publicity support ended up being lackluster; her marketing support, too. She had to hire her own publicist to launch her book during a summer when her regular publicist was busy with bigger, buzzier titles. This isn't to say that big advances come with nonchalance or disingenuousness, absolutely not. But if you get a sizable advance, you should verify that your editor and her colleagues have actionable ideas and the energy to support your debut so it's not just a flash in their pan. (And for the record: a modest advance does *not* mean that your book won't generate that all important "buzz." Quieter titles can get picked up by the media, celebrity endorsements, shiny early reads on Goodreads; they can trend on Instagram because of a hot cover: dreams really do come true.)

Your gut will probably tell you the editor your book needs. Your editor should be passionate about the project, passionate enough to convince their colleagues, assistant, sales agents, celebrity book bloggers, Instagram influencers, booksellers, and readers to buy and read your book. This takes energy and faith. And faith from you, as well! As the Grail Knight says to Indiana Jones as he contemplates the spread of holy receptacles before him, "You must choose. But choose wisely, for as the true Grail will bring you life, the false Grail will take it from you." This is as true for publishing as it is for Christian relics.

What if the offer sucks?

Advances are such a taboo topic in the industry, many writers don't even tell their author buds how much they received. This discretion, although understandable, can do a disservice to the writers whose egos it's meant to protect. "The only offers we read about are the astronomical advances in *Publishers Weekly*," says award-winning author Mitchell S. Jackson.

"It skews us toward thinking that for a debut, the norm is a big advance. For my own first book, it got me thinking: if I don't get six figures, I've failed. Not only did I not get six figures, I didn't get any offers period."

When Mitchell eventually did get an offer, it came to him by way of an editor who had originally turned down his debut, *The Residue Years*, but was unable to stop thinking about it. "I was in the eye doctor when the offer came through," Mitchell remembers. "I read that number three times. I mean, I had an eye patch on. I called my agent and was like, 'Did I read that number right?'"

Despite the editor's change of heart about the project, the number was hugely disappointing to Mitchell, who had spent twelve years working on his book. His then-agent defended the low offer, saying it was what the market could bear. "I didn't want what the market could bear," says Mitchell. "I wanted what I wanted."

Mitchell said he needed time to think about it, but his agent encouraged him to decide quickly. (Side note: if your agent is rushing you toward a decision you're not comfortable with, this is probably proof that you and your agent are ill-matched.)

Mitchell took the deal, published with Bloomsbury, and when his editor moved to Scribner, he was given the option to go with her. At that point Mitchell had a second book ready to sell, and thanks to the critical success of his first book, he felt he was in a favorable position to net a significantly higher advance.

Unfortunately, his new publisher had access to the numbers from his first negotiation. "Scribner knew I took this crappy deal from Bloomsbury," says Mitchell. "It was the worst thing." This time around, however, Mitchell had a powerful tool in his arsenal: he was working with a new agent, the revered Jin Auh at the equally respected Wylie agency. So when Mitchell rejected Scribner's first offer, and their second, and their third, he had the support of not just his agent, but the agency's big boss. "I get this call that Andrew Wylie wants to meet with me," remembers Mitchell. "I go in—he has my whole manuscript—sticky notes throughout it—and the first thing he says is, why did you call this *Head Down, Palm Up*, it's not that, it should be named after the essay, 'Survival Math.' He told me, 'I'm going to get you what you want, but you might have to leave Scribner.'"

Mitchell and his agency agreed to send a revised version of his manuscript to a larger group of editors on a Friday, and to demand offers by that Monday. But before this plan could be put into action, Scribner came back to Mitchell with the number that he wanted. "Something that I learned through this," Mitchell concludes, "is that really good agents demand respect for their clients."

Should I take a two-book deal?

There are different reasons why a two-book deal might be proposed to a new author. "The two-book offer usually happens when you have an author selling a short-story collection who has a partial of a novel," explains literary agent Sarah Bowlin, who was also a longtime editor at Henry Holt. "It also occurs in a competitive situation in which offering more money for a second book can give a bidder the advantage. When a writer is proven," Sarah continues, "when you know what you're getting, what the author is like and the pace at which they work, this can also influence the likelihood of a two-book deal."

The incentives of a two-book package are financial, first. Writers will receive more money up front because they are selling two books instead of one. Likewise, the two-book offer is a vote of confidence in the author by their publisher, and many writers will feel validated knowing that their next move is already scored. "For me, the two-book deal was even more important than the advance money," says an author we're going to call Amelia. "I thought it would ensure that I wasn't a one-hit wonder, that I could fund my next project, and that I could live the life of a 'real writer' that I so dearly wanted."

But there are risks that come with a two-book deal, both for the writer and the book. "The second book can be overvalued, or undervalued, by combining it in a two-book deal," says agent Sarah. "There's a stability question, also: Will the house exist by the time the second book comes out? Will the editor still be there?"

There's the possibility of professional dissatisfaction, as well. Your working style might have proven incompatible with your editor's during the first book's inception, or you might be unimpressed with the way the publisher handled your book's marketing and distribution. "Sometimes the reality is that the first book tanks and then the house unenthusiastically publishes the second," Sarah explains. "Whereas if you could move the second book, another publisher might put a different kind of energy into it."

The risks of a multibook deal are less tangible for the writer, but equally important to consider. There is a big difference between signing a two-book contract when the second book is underway, and doing so when you have no idea what you're going to write next. For author Akil Kumarasamy, who signed a two-book deal with FSG for her debut, working on her second book has been a positive and straightforward process. Her agent sold her first collection of linked stories as an exclusive to an editor, and Akil had already written a good chunk of her next book. For Amelia, who had no idea what her second novel would be about and agreed to a contract that only gave her a year to conceptualize and write it, things got . . . kind of weird.

Amelia was aware of the pressures around the sophomore book thing, but she thought she'd rise above them. "When I signed the deal,

I thought, I *got* this!" she remembers. "I quit my job, I went on tour with my first book, while trying to write my second simultaneously. Then began the nervous breakdown."

With a critically acclaimed debut behind her, Amelia found that her writing process had been adulterated by fear and anxiety: she couldn't sit down to write without wondering how her second novel would be received. "The second book is the real test," she says. "Will this person stand up as a novelist? Was that first book a fluke and now people are going to want to take you down because you got lucky the first time? My work gathered this energy; the psychology of my situation has come through in my writing as a kind of nervousness. In the story itself, I find myself grappling with the idea of early success or nonsuccess."

Performance anxiety is an occupational hazard for any first-time author who intends to write a second book, but the condition worsens when you're working against the clock. When I sold my second book (not in a two-book deal, but as my first book was coming out), against my agent's sage advice I, too, gave myself a year to write a second book from scratch. I've always been a quick writer, with the qualifier that I'm quick when I know what I want to write. A year did not give me the time I needed to screw up, to experiment, to doubt, to feel unworthy; it did not give me time to sob. A year left no room for failure, there could only be success. I cracked under this pressure, and I missed my book deadline. Amelia missed hers, too.

From Sarah's vantage point as both an editor and an agent, the outcome of the two-book deal depends on what kind of writer the author is. "Just as signing up with an agent can fuck with a writer's head because the business is encroaching, too much advice about how to plot or how to sell can ruin the writing for some authors. It can get into your head. The stress of not knowing whether this thing will come into the world is bad for some people and motivating to others."

In short: two-book packages are excellent if you are short on cash, work well under pressure, and are far along in a new project. They're less excellent if you have reason to worry about your publisher's (or editor's) job stability, break down when you're on deadline, or have started doubting your commitment to the book you're meant to write. It bears mentioning that if you accept a two-book deal, you must deliver a book that adheres to the style and genre you signed on for. If you're contracted for a novel about rabid woodsmen in 1800 Colonial America, for example, you can't hand in a memoir about The Important Thing That Happened That One Time at Summer Camp. "If a publisher is buying it," concludes agent Sarah, "it's hard to get vague contract language—like, they're not going to purchase your 'undetermined next work.' It's a valuation problem, it's hard to determine what a writer's ideas are worth until you see the writing."

What if everyone says no?

Although it won't feel that way in the moment, the fact that your manuscript is receiving rejections doesn't mean that it will never be published. *Harry Potter and the Sorcerer's Stone*, the first book in the Harry Potter series, was rejected by twelve editors who probably don't feel so hot about their decisions now. Herman Melville was encouraged by the editors reading *Moby Dick* to reimagine his antagonist as something other than a whale. Joseph Heller famously named his classic novel *Catch-22* for the number of times it was rejected, and a French editor rejected Marcel Proust's Herculean *In Search of Lost Time* with this Gallic zinger: "I rack my brains why a chap should need thirty pages to describe how he turns over in bed before going to sleep."

In more recent examples, Alexander Chee's *Edinburgh* was rejected twenty-four times before it found a publisher, and this despite the fact that it had been recognized with an award from the prestigious Iowa Writers' Workshop while it was still in manuscript form. (It would go on to win another award, the $50,000 Whiting Award.) On the eve of her first novel's publication, author Tara Isabella Burton admitted to her Facebook followers that *Social Creature* was not her first manuscript: it was her ninth, and that three of her earlier books had already been universally rejected by numerous publishers. My own first novel, *I Am Having So Much Fun Here Without You,* was rejected by eighteen editors over three targeted rounds. I put that novel in a box and didn't do anything with it for ten years until my third agent asked me to revisit it. I wrote it over from scratch, then wrote it again, and one more time for good measure, and we had Big Five editors interested on its first trip out.

So what gives? Are editors foolish, fearful, blind? Is it a question of timing? Is it a question of revision? Perseverance? Should we do as former librarian and author Kristen Arnett suggests and "type a bunch of words into a document, close the computer, throw it in the trash, change your identity, start a new life"? What is a writer to *do* with all their nos?

Unfortunately, there isn't a clear-cut answer. Publishing a debut author is a risk, and even the bravest editors have to answer to publishers who are risk-averse. It is very, very hard to get a book published. Nonetheless, new books come out every Tuesday (see the #happybookbirthday hashtag for proof), so while it's difficult to publish a first book, it clearly isn't impossible. The hardest part of the publishing experience is believing in yourself—year after year—when editors do not. Of her trek through acres of rejection to her first book deal, Tara reminisced, "I'm as proud of having kept going, despite the rejections, and the general devastation, as I am of the work itself."

If you feel that your book's rejections are proof that it simply hasn't met the right editor yet, by all means, press on. But press on while you are doing something else. After a certain amount of rejection (let's say three rounds), it's essential for you the writer, the editors who are reading the submission, and your bewildered agent to take a lengthy break. The book is written, and unless someone steals your computer and you haven't backed your files up, it isn't going to disappear. You will have an occasion to revisit it in the future, and perhaps with the benefit of time and distance, you'll find a new—and exciting—way back into the work.

On the flip side, if trying to sell your novel has ruined the affection you had for it, made it impossible to even *consider* undertaking any revisions because you're so damn tired of the project, put it in a box. (I'm partial to the black Tjena Ikea storage box model for mine.) Bury the manuscript underground, put it under lock and key, do what you need to clean up the energy between you and your failed masterpiece, and then move on to something else. Everyone's experience is different, but the best way I've found to heal after a forsaken project is to get lost in the pleasure of building something new.

V
....

Everything you've ever wanted
to know about advances,
but were too afraid to ask

If you're human, and fallible, when you find out what your advance is, you're either going to be happy about it, or think it's not enough. Your feelings will go through another transmutation when you find out what other writers got. This learning-about-other-peoples'-business business is an argument for never leaving the house, but you have to leave the house, writer! You have a book coming out!

How do I know whether or not I got a good advance?

Because it's taboo to talk about advances, a lot of first-time authors don't know if they received a "good" advance or not. In fact, many writers have gone for so long without receiving any kind of payment for their work, anything upward of two thousand dollars seems like money they can actually save.

There are several ways to do reconnaissance regarding the size of your advance. You could ask your agent. But your agent gets a 15 percent cut of all your life's happiness, so that conversation could be awkward. You could ask another author friend, but if their advance was bigger than yours, you're gonna be so pissed. One fun and neutral way to compare your advance to other people's is to understand the codes of the Publishers Marketplace weekly book-deal announcements, which you can access with the tool best suited for online stalking: the World Wide Web.

Decoding Publishers Marketplace announcements

"in a nice deal": *1 to 49K*. Author better not quit her day job.

"in a very nice deal": *50 to 99K*. Author might be able to afford health insurance in a couple years.

"in a good deal": *100 to 250K*. Author is wondering if her second book will get a million dollars. Author is showing the first signs of debut-author delusion. If not already teamed with a licensed practitioner, author should enter talk therapy right away.

"in a significant deal": *251 to 499K*. Author has opened up a Zillow account and is wondering just how much "fixing" goes into a fixer-upper.

"in a major deal": *500K and up*. This author's flying bizness class!

Not part of the Publishers Marketplace deal lingo, but very much the stuff of dreams, there also exist "preempt" and "best-bid" scenarios that you might see mentioned in a sale announcement. In a defensive preempt, a publisher eliminates the competition by ponying up an amount of money so attractive that there is no reason for the book to go to auction. The value of the preempt to an author is pretty evident: they're spared the drawn-out nail-biting of an auction, and will most likely net a large advance. For the publishing house, the thinking behind a preempt is a little trickier: by throwing a large sum of money out before the book is tested at auction, it's possible that they'll overpay. But in most preempt scenarios, the publisher doesn't care. Perhaps the publisher has a clear idea of the audience the book will resonate with and how they're going to market it: they've got a surefire hit on the table, and they want it in their hands. Sometimes, it's a courting tactic: the preempt is a dramatic gesture that shows the author that they are valued, and will be treated as a VIP if they join the fam. Other times, a preempt can be orchestrated by the agent or even the author. Perhaps it feels like there is only one editor for this book, someone the author is motivated to work with. In such a case, an agent might contact that editor and say, "You're the perfect editor for this. Make us a great offer and we won't show it to anyone else."

Designed to give publishing professionals the temporary feeling that they work on Wall Street, the practice of best-bidding started to catch fire in the early aughts. In this round-robin scenario, interested publishers are given the opportunity to bid on a project without knowing what the competition is offering. As opposed to auctions, which can move slowly, with editorial phone calls and modest increases in the advance money over a period of weeks, best bids move quickly, closing in a day. These round-robins usually result in a sack full of money for the author, but this practice has its cons. Most editors in a round-robin scenario won't have had time to sit with the project, or think through how they're going to market it. They'll probably only have had time to read a chapter or two, and in some cases, they haven't even seen the manuscript. What you're getting here is effectively an arranged marriage with no guarantee that you'll get along well with your assigned mate, or that the mate in question "gets" you. But they might!

What is everyone else getting?

Not only is it bad manners among publishing professionals to discuss who's getting what, if you dig a little, you'll realize that there's no hard reason why one person gets a lot of money and someone else very little, which makes the topic of advance-giving not only contentious, but unfair.

I have a friend who received a million dollars for her debut novel and another friend who got six thousand dollars for his. I have a friend who was paid four thousand dollars for a two-book deal. Another friend received a million dollars for a second book proposal.

Some big-pocket publishers turn down manuscripts that go on to be critically acclaimed and win major awards. These same publishers sometimes overpay for untested debuts that grossly underperform, while smaller presses underpay for books that go on to be cult classics.

Above, we explored the Publishers Marketplace industry guide to advances. Here, we'll look at numbers supplied by agents, editors, and writers attached to a wide variety of houses, specifically referencing the kind of money they see being paid out for first books. These numbers are generalized and don't take into account the nuances of a debut author's platform or credentials, which can significantly alter an advance. It's simply a big picture of advance ranges for first books:

> **Micropress:** 0 to 1K
>
> **Nonprofit indie press:** 1 to 8K
>
> **For-profit indie press:** 5 to 20K
>
> **Midlist title at a Big Five publisher:** 30 to 100K
>
> **Lead title at a Big Five publisher:** 150 to 500K

You can be enraged, befuddled, or mystified by the fact that there are untested authors out there earning millions for their first books while more critically acclaimed, "literary" authors are earning a few months' rent for theirs. This is easier said than done, but do not spend your precious time comparing yourself with other people—you will, quite literally, make yourself sick trying to analyze a lawless game.

In terms of advances, your first course of action should be to save what you can and come up with a game plan to cover the rest of your financial needs so that you can live and write in relative stability for the next year or two. Your second course of action should be to write something new that makes you feel like ~~a million bucks~~ sixty thousand dollars.

Merits of small advances

A friend of mine who received an advance well under a hundred thousand dollars recently admitted that "she'd been carrying around some weirdness" about friends who got significantly larger advances, two to three times what she received herself. "It really bothered me. I wondered if it wasn't good enough, why am I not at that level, does it mean there's something wrong with my book?" But her debut did unexpectedly well, and she earned out—earned her advance back—much earlier than her publisher expected her to. Now she feels elated: "Relieved and grateful . . . all of the things I should have felt in the first place."

Although editor Masie Cochran* believes that authors should receive a fair wage for their work, she has seen the merit in small

---

* The reader should be advised that at the time that Masie was interviewed, she was an editor that the author of this book greatly admired. Now she is the editor of a book by this same author. Isn't life surprising? The author did not want to take Masie's quote out of the manuscript because it is a good one, but the author does want to disclose her changed relationship to the person polled.

advances during her time editing for the independent publisher Tin House. "It used to be that people had 'establishing books,'" Masie explains. "It's weird now, the expectation for the first book to be a hit and sell thirty thousand copies. That's become the expectation instead of the surprise."

Many of Masie's authors have earned out during their first year of publication, a confidence-booster for emerging authors. "Regarding advances for a first-time author, there is breathing room in small advances; you don't have to feel like the first book has to be the best book you're ever going to write," she says. "If it does well, you can make more than your advance in royalties. You're on top of that advance, instead of under it, which can be encouraging."

The pros and cons of big ones

Aside from the obvious (money!), big-league advances (we're talking $350,000 and up) can significantly increase your sales potential. "A large advance can have a snowball effect," explains a Big Five editor who preferred to remain anonymous. "It can make foreign publishers more likely to offer on a book, or purchasers of film/TV rights. In most circumstances, it probably does mean that the publisher will expend a greater-than-average effort in trying to make the book work, though for many reasons a large advance is not a guarantee of a book's eventual success."

Large advances are often given to debut authors when there is a lot of competition for a project. But "competition" means that there were numerous editors bidding to acquire the book at auction, it doesn't guarantee that readers are going to *buy* the book when it comes out.

An author friend of mine (we'll call him Billy) had a buzzy

short-story collection that garnered him offers from ten different publishing houses. On his agent's advice, he went with the highest bid, a
hefty advance that happened to come from the most commercial house.
Billy's book came out to critical acclaim, but disappointing sales. He
had a frustrating experience with his publishing house, who, Billy says,
"walked away from the project when it was clear that it wasn't going to
be a megahit."

Important opportunities began to fall through the cracks. Billy's
publisher rarely shared his glowing reviews and interviews on their social media, and they neglected to include his reviews in his paperback.
One time, at a signing after a university reading series, Billy opened
his book to find it already autographed. He wondered how this was
possible, since the paperback had just come out. While the student who
wanted to buy the book patiently looked on, Billy realized what had
happened: in order to save money, the publisher had cut out the pages
from his unsold hardcovers (many of which he had presigned) and
pasted them into the new package for the paperback. This practice isn't
unheard of, and a publisher who has overpaid for a project has every
right to try to recoup their costs, but for Billy, it added insult to an in-
jury he already felt. "It was a deeply personal book," Billy explained. "I
became horribly depressed. I couldn't stop wondering if it would have
been different if I had gone with another publisher, accepted a smaller
advance."

Even authors who enjoy a positive relationship with their publisher
can feel an untenable amount of pressure to succeed when they get a
big advance. For one thing, it's hard for such authors to keep their advances secret, especially when a project goes for a high amount at auction. "That automatically puts the author in an awkward place where
most writers don't find themselves," our anonymous Big Five editor
explains, "which is financially exposed in a way that might color the

response to the book." Indeed, if a reader knows that an author received a million-dollar advance for the book they're currently perusing, a cloying cocktail of envy and confirmation bias could see the descriptor "buzzy" swapped out for "overrated." Haters gonna hate.

Sales numbers are also public: anyone in the industry with access to BookScan can check how a given book is performing in the market. Though useful, BookScan is a flawed resource in that it only reflects around 85 percent of your true sales. Your publisher is the proprietor of the real-deal numbers, but BookScan is what industry professionals are going to look at when your second project goes out on submission. [Insert a collective sigh from a million authors here.]

A large book advance represents an expectation, and if the author doesn't meet that expectation, her future projects could be impacted by that discrepancy. "In the event that the book isn't profitable," says our Big Five editor, "the process of negotiating for subsequent books becomes more fraught than it would be for an author who has received a lower advance. I think that it's very hard for a debut author to be prepared for these scenarios."

Do you have to earn out to be successful?

Legend has it veteran agent Andrew Wylie once said that he's not doing his job if his client's book earns out. A provocative statement, it nevertheless supports the numbers. In 2009, a *New York Times* article entitled "About That Book Advance . . ." stated that "seven out of ten titles do not earn back their advance," and publishing expert Jane Friedman says this percentage still holds true. "It's not that books are failing," Jane explains. "It's that some publishers are knowingly paying a higher royalty rate. They do care, on some level, about paying authors an amount that is respectful."

An advance is a financial risk that a publisher is taking on an author. Normally—not always—the advance reflects the amount of books they think that the author can sell. But as Jane's statement suggests, this risk isn't always conservative: sometimes editors overpay for a timely project, or for the cachet of working with a certain author or celebrity. That is to say, if it feels like a publisher has overpaid for a project, they probably know why they did.

Publishers don't have to earn back every penny of an author's advance to be profitable, but at the same time, the advance isn't the only money that they're spending on the project. There are marketing and publicity costs, printing and shipping costs, contest submissions, fees for graphic design . . . the bill isn't necessarily settled once (if!) an advance is earned back.

Publishers aren't going around boasting that most of their authors aren't earning back their advances. If not an elephant, it's at least the baby rhino in the room. "There are a number of reasons to publish a book, and it's almost never to make back the exact amount that you invested," says another Big Five editor who also preferred to remain anonymous. "All advances are an investment in an author's long-term career."

If the 70 percent figure gets thrown around a lot, that's because most agents and publishers would, indeed, consider a title successful if it earned back this percentage of its advance. "Behind the scenes there will be people who know they have paid more for a book than it can earn out," explains Jane, "but they're not going to hold it against the author."

Our second anonymous Big Five editor concurs. "The best thing an author can do regarding earning out is to not think about it. There are so many different ways that you can define success. Given the amount of books that don't earn out, publishers are realistic about expectations. It's basically not for the author to worry about."

Even if you never earn out, your publisher is generating cash flow from your book sales. Most publishers get a whopping 50 percent of the retail cover price for every copy sold, and 70 percent for ebooks. (Jane believes that a chunk of a book's advance is, in fact, the publisher acknowledging that the ebook royalty rate is too low.)

There are intangible benefits from your publication, too. If your book was critically acclaimed, the award nominations and positive press are building (and/or improving) a publisher's reputation. Even if your book didn't perform well commercially, the good press alone will make your publisher happy. Your book might convince other authors to work with such and such an editor, positively affecting the caliber of authors their imprint can attract. Advances are like a combination of Monopoly and the Greek myth of Orpheus: take your money when you pass go, and don't ever look back.

Budgeting your advance

Many advances are paid out in four installments: 25 percent upon signature of the publishing contract, 25 percent upon the completed manuscript's reception, 25 percent at publication, 25 percent at the publication of the paperback, even if there doesn't end up being a paperback. If your book was a paperback original, these installment terms will be adjusted to reflect that. If your hardcover isn't going to have a paperback edition because of disappointing sales, try not to hate yourself. Find something productive to hate instead, like climate-change deniers, or people who think cilantro tastes like soap.

Regardless of whether your advance came in one payment or four, the important thing is not to spend it all at once, because there really isn't any way of knowing how your book will perform, and also because you are going to need that extra money for therapy once your book comes out.

If your advance was modest, get an accountant. If your advance was significant, get a money manager and some life insurance. Whatever you do, don't do like my friend [name redacted] and spend all of your advance on a speedboat. Set some money aside for thank-you tokens for your editorial team and agents at pub time. (A heartfelt, hand-written card is thoughtful, but some authors also send on gifts, flowers, alcohol [when appropriate], or something handmade.)

If you're publishing in America, remember that we have something called "taxes" that happen every year. If you can afford to, pour some of your advance back into the industry that you want to support you. Giving money to PEN America, Girls Write Now, We Need Diverse Books, and other writing advocacy groups is much more meaningful than giving it to the IRS. And don't forget to use some of your new cash flow at your favorite independent bookstore on books and thank-you notes.

Book Two

....

☐ Before and
☑ **After**
☑ **the**
☑ **Book**
☑ **Deal**

Anybody can sympathize with the sufferings of a friend, but it requires a very fine nature to sympathize with a friend's success.

—OSCAR WILDE

I

....

Prepublication

You have realized a long-held dream and acquired a book deal for something you've worked hard on. As if this isn't enough of a thrill and achievement, it also means that your book—yours!—is going to exist in the real world. Not tomorrow, not next month, either (actually, it's kind of weird how far away your pub date is?), but very, very soon! If you thought you would get to spend the next few months basking in the achievement of your book's forthcoming publication and the glory of its content, I'm here to burst your bubble. It's time to get to work, my friend.

Reining in your ego

One thing most writers share in common is a wildly unstable ego. In the space of twenty minutes, we can go from thinking we are the only writer who matters, to believing that we should never write again.

The experience of having a book published will only intensify these existential ups and downs. Anthony Doerr, author of the international bestseller *All the Light We Cannot See*, experienced his first major reality check during an event for his debut, *The Shell Collector*, at a Barnes & Noble in New York. Tony's event was on the fifth floor of the Union Square location, and when he stepped onto the elevator, he was feeling pretty great. "I'd gotten a twenty-two-thousand-dollar advance for a short-story collection," Tony remembers. "I was thinking, I'm with the publisher who published Hemingway! My life is totally figured out!" But as the escalator brought him past bigger, standout books, his confidence began to plummet. "I'm going up, and I'm realizing, there are *so* many books here. There are just so many books."

Realizing that there are going to be other books available in the world aside from your own is a major milestone. It's essential to your emotional and psychosomatic success that you not only accord that people have the right to read books you haven't written, but that you continue reading such books yourself. Reading powerful literature—especially by your contemporaries—will go a long way toward keeping your ego in check while your book is coming out.

Just as you're entitled to your fits of desperation (an author friend of mine said prepub made her feel like she was removing wallpaper with nail scissors), you are also entitled to your bouts of mania and self-aggrandizement and pure, unfettered joy. When you're in one extreme or the other, don't post anything online.

The social media announcement about your big book deal

Remember a couple of moments ago when we decoded the way book deals are announced in Publishers Marketplace? When your publishing contract is finally sorted, you'll get one of these announcements, too. It's become fashionable for writers to wait to announce their publishing deals on social media until they have the link or screenshot of the official deal announcement. This is the first time you will be publicly sharing good news about your book, so it's an opportunity to set the tone for the way you will announce good book news in the future. Authors have several options regarding the way they communicate this tiding.

Baby as prop

Some people like to write the gist of their good news (i.e., "Mama got a book deal!") on a sturdy piece of paper and prop it up against a baby. Sometimes the baby is theirs, and that's why they wrote, "Mama." Sometimes they use somebody else's kid. Sometimes they use a cat. There are all different kinds of people in the world.

Tears

Other writers take a selfie of themselves crying, or at least welling up, while holding up some section of their book contract. Most authors usually know about their book deals about two months before they publicly announce them. But authors are very good at holding on to tears!

Stone-cold announcement

This is when the writer just uploads a link to the announcement or writes something like "News." This person has seen the future, and they're going to be a Very Big Deal, so there's no sense acting like this news is anything out of the ordinary. This shit is gonna be happening all the time.

Oscar speech

The good thing about the Oscar speech is that the author can use the same copy for their book's acknowledgments. The Oscar-speech announcement sees the writer thanking everyone and everything who has ever helped them on their long and winding path toward publication. These posts sometimes include hashtags like #grateful or #blessed or #dreamjob and just generally involve a lot of text.

What? Who? Me?

Some time after my first book came out, my first publisher released a memoir by a celebrity called *Scrappy Little Nobody*. I really liked my publisher, and the celebrity seems like she's probably a fun girl to share nachos deluxe with. But the thing about the celebrity author was that she was famous and talented and super attractive, and she sure as heck wasn't a nobody when the book came out. This kind of titling is an example of the What? Who? Me? posturing that sees the author who has been to MacDowell three times, would have been a Bread Loaf fellow if they hadn't already been teaching experimental nonfiction in Portugal that August, made the National Book Foundation's 5 Under 35 list before they even finished their MFA, and has generally been working their ass off acting as if their book deal has hit them like an unexpected blessing from motherfucking outer space. Friends. These types of writers have known their book deal was coming since the third grade when the poem about a dead apple tree they wrote for National Poetry Month got hung up on the classroom wall with some sticker stars. It was just a matter of time, bitches. And now that time is here.

The publishing contract

The publishing contract is a long document that will take about two months to get to you because your publisher's lawyers and your literary agency's lawyers need to email it back and forth to each other for a

while, or else it doesn't count. Your publishing contract is the first official document you will encounter as a professional author that outlines
just how challenging this new role is going to be. Like, for example,
your publisher might decide to charge you sometimes for FedEx shipping envelopes, but other times, not. Don't think about the potential
FedEx shipping charges. You just let them go. Also, your hardcover
might not make it to paperback if it doesn't sell well, but don't think
about that either. Just initial everything and sign the last page with
your full signature, and have something with bubbles! Remember to
be optimistic about the publishing process. If you can't do this without
assistance, ask your literary agent to help.

Speaking of every writer's favorite intellectual bodyguard, your
agent is the person to help you translate what your contract actually
means. Pay special attention to your option clause because it can impact
what you can and can't do with this particular house for your second
project. If you don't have a two-book deal contract, the option clause
will tell you how long you have to present a new idea to the publisher
and how long they have to accept it or reject it. Audiobook rights are
also deserving of your attention. A lot of the big publishers will retain
these because they have an in-house recording studio, whereas smaller
publishers might sell the rights to audio publishers, sometimes for a tidy
sum. Make sure you're clear as to whether the money from that sale is
going to your publisher (and against your advance), or directly to you.
Publishers will usually offer one sum for North American rights and a
different sum for world rights. If you have retained your world rights (or
they didn't sell), make sure your literary agency is equipped to handle
foreign sales. And finally, the serial-rights clause becomes important
during the prepublication period when you're trying to build buzz for
your book. Publishing excerpts in a respected outlet is a popular way to
build anticipation and (hopefully) cinch some preorders, so it's worth

giving up first serial rights if you have a publisher committed to helping you place excerpts.

Surviving the editorial letter

The dichotomy between the editorial feedback you are hoping for ("You're perfect, it's perfect, let's go make you rich") and the feedback you probably will get ("You are flawed, it is flawed, but I believe that you can fix it") is a disunion that will be experienced by most writers in the editorial letter they receive once their book deal is signed.

"For most authors, you are coming off the happiness of having sold the book after having already been through however many drafts with early readers and your agent," says Veronica Goldstein, a literary agent at Fletcher & Company, which is the same agency that provides me with ample opportunity for manuscript revision. "And then to get your first set of notes from your editor and hear that there's still more work to do . . . This is someone's editorial opinion and experience that you really, really value, who is going to be responsible for the fate of the book. You'll generally know what level of edits are coming based on your initial conversations, but still, it can be a point of anxiety. If they are giving you notes that point to a major flaw, things that need to be totally rethought or rewritten, endings that need to be changed, the author might have a hard time gearing back up for that kind of revision. It can be hard, because of course an author is sensitive to the realization that maybe, even though you've had this triumphant moment of the sale, that the book isn't as ready for the world as they thought."

You are allowed to respectfully disagree with some of the feedback in your editorial letter. If you disagree with *all* of it, however, you'll find yourself in an unpleasant standoff with your editorial team. In most cases, your editor wants what is best for you and your book, and the requested edits are there to help your book connect with readers. Think of the editorial letter as a schedule from a personal trainer: a list of exercises that will deliver a healthier and stronger body at the workout's end. It can be difficult to start a workout, but you always feel better afterward, right?

How to set—and meet—your book deadline

As you and your agent begin negotiating your book contract, one of the main questions is going to be when you can get the book finished versus when the publisher would like it to come out.

The length of time between the signing of a book contract and the publishing of the book in question is shocking to people outside of the industry. It is exceedingly rare for a book to take anything less than a year and a half to publish after the book deal is inked; two years or longer is the norm. Why does it take so long? First of all, there might be more writing to do, and there will certainly be revisions. There will be rounds (and rounds) of copy edits, a creation of a marketing plan, pleas for blurbs, back-and-forth about the cover and the title, discussion of your platform, outreach to press and book clubs, a push for you to pitch and generate personal essays to support your book's publication . . . it takes a lot of time and legwork to get readers excited about your book.

Depending on your professional background, you might be approaching your first book deal with a history of successfully met deadlines behind you. Perhaps you've worked in journalism or as a copywriter, and you're no stranger to the effort it takes to turn clean copy in. Or maybe this is the first time you are encountering a deadline, and you don't have a track record of working under pressure.

Regardless of whether you are a taskmaster or a procrastinator, give yourself more time to get your book in, rather than less. A year is never a year, after all. Even if you arrange your schedule to devote your free time to your book, outside events can throw you from your path: a Twitter feed is elected president; a person you love is hit by illness; a person you love dies. Happy things can also happen: maybe you'll fall into a new relationship that chews up all your time, or you adopt a pet who chews up your computer cord.

Missing your book deadline might feel like a necessary indulgence if you haven't gotten the book right yet. But when you set back your own project, you're inadvertently taking money out of whatever marketing budget your publisher has set aside for it. Delays cost time and time costs cash. Readying a book for publication is tough business, so gift yourself with more time than you think you'll need.

Developmental edits

The late writer Terry Pratchett has a quote about the revision process that always comforts me: "The first draft is just you telling yourself the story." A key to success during the revision process is thinking about developmental edits as writing support instead of criticism. Your editor is your partner, not your enemy. This bears repeating: your editor/partner is working to turn your manuscript into something readable by a wider public, instead of something that can only be appreciated by you.

Developmental edits are both an expansion to the notes that you already received in your editorial letter and a reminder that your manuscript is far from finished yet. Either on a hard copy or via Track Changes, your editor will point out where the manuscript lacks focus, where the plot could be tightened, where there isn't any plot at all. Together, you'll consider ways to strengthen and develop character, while watch-guarding for narrative continuity: you'll have to fix the places where a character admires a sunset that should be a sunrise or has two lunches in one day. (Conceivable, if the main character is a writer and they are on deadline. I get very hungry when I write.) Another thing that you'll do during developmental edits is press DELETE a lot.

Meeting your book's team

At some point after the book contract is finalized, if you live close enough to your publishing house to make this happy event possible, you will meet the people who are going to publish your first book.

It's a good idea to bring along your agent to this meeting, during which you will meet your editor and their assistant, if they have one. If you are going to get a publicist, it's too early at this point to know who that will be, but you might meet a publicity director whose job is going to be to discern whether or not you'll be difficult to work with. Don't bother trying to act one way or another. These people have read your book, so they've got your neuroses figured out. There's nowhere to hide!

Someone from sales might pop in, flanked by someone in marketing, and if your head is swimming in names and job titles by this point, the good news is that your agent will remember who was there. Ask them for a cheat sheet afterward so you can go forth in your adventure knowing who does what.

Within twenty-four hours, send a group email to everyone you met expressing how great it was to meet them, how lucky you are to be working with them, and why [enter name of publisher] is simply the best house for your book. Then send a handwritten note to your editor, reiterating the same. The goal here is not just to show gratitude, but to prove to the team that you are conscientious, detail-oriented, and polite, characteristics that will leave some people in publicity thinking that you might just be the kind of writer that they can send on tour.

Did anything go wrong during your meeting? Did someone come up with a really bad idea for a new title, or like, weirdly compliment your hair? Now is not the time to take to social media to publicly make fun or vent about anything that happened with your publisher. From here on out, no more bitching about publishing is allowed on social media. Don't complain about your editor, agent, your alarming cover concept, nothing. Pick one trustworthy person in your life who will be your bitch bucket, and share all your complaints with them, preferably through a messaging service with end-to-end encryption.

You drive me crazy: the things authors do that drive publishing professionals nuts

Writers tend to have inflated egos, and those egos go into overdrive when our books are coming out. Whether it's forgetting that our agents and editors have other clients, or that people have the right to read (and enjoy) books we haven't written, we sometimes need to be reminded not just about our place in the world, but of our manners, too.

Here, an anonymous group of publishing professionals share the author habits and character traits that put their nerves in overdrive.

Agent 1: "The biggest thing that makes an author difficult to work with is being a poor communicator and only looping your agent in when you have a problem. I like to be a true partner and consultant all the way through the process, and the more info I have, the better I can protect my clients. In other words: tell your agent where the bodies are buried, yes, but also involve her in brainstorming and planning."

Agent 2: "When they send a draft of something and a week later say, 'Don't read that draft, here's a new one!' And you've already read half. Ggggrrh!"

Editor 1: "Your editor has other authors. If they work with more famous people, don't assume you're being treated like a peon and that the Pulitzer winner is sucking up all the oxygen. In an ideal world, you are getting responses. If you're not, use the power of your agent. Use your agent to have the awkward conversations."

Publicist 1: "I could really love a book, but if I'm treated badly, there's always going to be a subliminal barrier about how hard I'm going to work for you. If just thinking about you gives me a bad feeling ... well. Take a deep breath before you take it out on the publicist! Understand that publicists can't control things at a certain level; we're not paying other people to review your book, so we can't guarantee that it's going to happen or that it's going to happen in the time or way that we would like."

Publicist 2: "One of my authors spent all his time complaining about his hotel to me. Time I could have been using to pitch him!"

Editor 2: "When an author doesn't track their manuscript changes, and just says, 'Oh yeah, I changed some things,' and I have to go on an Easter-egg hunt to find what was changed, where."

Agent 3: "The only character trait I can't cope with is humorlessness. I'd say I've encountered the full gamut of behaviors and I can cope with them all just fine, but if someone can't laugh when things are difficult, and there are always difficult moments in publishing, I lose patience."

Agent's assistant: "When authors mail forms and contracts back without a little note. Even a 'Hello!' on a Post-it Note goes such a long way toward making you feel appreciated."

Editor 3: "A writer once sent me a screenshot of a particular font she liked and wanted used in her book. The screenshot wasn't even of words. It was a hashtag. She liked the font used for the hashtag. None of us had any idea what it was, but I'm pleased she thought my powers of font recognition were that strong."

Veteran author: "Nudging potential blurbers who have only had your book a few weeks! That's a no-no! You have to give your readers time."

Agent 4: "Sending projects to editors before your agent gets a chance to pitch!"

Agent 5: "When writers only post about themselves on social media. Good literary citizens celebrate other writers, too. Or when they complain about something professional, a bad review they got, and put it on their Facebook."

Publicist 3: "Expecting me to get their books reviewed in *The New York Times* and their stories published in *The New Yorker.* I'm sympathetic to these ambitions, but I'm not a magician. Instead of asking for the second, third, or hundredth time why your book hasn't been reviewed in particular literary Holy Grail outlets yet, perhaps offer an idea or initiate a conversation about how you might be able to collaborate to make something unique and meaningful happen in the way of promoting your book."

Agent 6: "When authors compare themselves to their friends."

Publicist 4: "When authors point out all the things that haven't happened for their books yet. Trust me, we *know*."

Agent 7: "Expecting the agent to be all things; therapist, loan officer, tax accountant, computer specialist."

Editor 4: "You have to understand that there are people on the other end of everything. Cover design, interior design, publicity. They're human beings. When you say, 'This campaign sucks,' these are people I work with every day. Don't put your editor in a position where they have to choose between the author and their coworkers. These are our teams, too."

Editor 5: "Email tone can be hard to read. All of us would do better to save our reply as a draft before we send it."

Publicist 5: "Authors sometimes treat me as a personal valet or therapist—I knew my job was to ease their nerves so they could do a good job in their interviews, but sometimes I felt like my time wasn't respected."

When your title's not your title

Early in the editing process, you might hear that the title that you've chosen isn't the one that the publisher wants printed on your book.

Won't this be surprising! Case in point, my first book was called *I Am Having So Much Fun Here Without You*. To my editor's credit, I didn't have to convince her why it was a great title, but we certainly had to do some hand-holding with marketing and publicity, who had valid concerns about the social media friendliness of a forty-character title.

I'm of the mindset that your title is worth fighting for if you really like it. On the other hand, if you're apathetic about your current title and your editor's lacking inspiration, just pick a plural noun that ties into your book's subject and put a definite article in front of it. Not convinced that this approach makes for a good title? Think about all the recent blockbuster bestsellers that combined *The* plus *Somethings*. See?

Manuscript acceptance

The final delivery of the finished manuscript is an important part of your transition from writer to author; it marks the transformation of your secret project into a public product. Yes, a product: an object that consumers can purchase, can enjoy or not enjoy. Relinquishing control now, when your book is still months away from being published, will buttress you over the long term when strangers dismiss the "thing" you spent years working on with a one-star review because they didn't like your epigraph.

Your book is for the reader now. From this point forward, your efforts, and your team's efforts, are going to be about connecting this book with the right readers. Congratulate yourself heartily on reaching this major milestone. And then keep walking forward.

Setting a launch date

Your launch date is a key component of your publishing success because it is the deadline by which you absolutely need to have a competent therapist. Once you know your pub date, schedule something enticing to look forward to six weeks after that date. That is the duration of time that people will be excited about your book. After six weeks, most people (your friends included!) will have moved on, which is why you need that therapist—or at the very least, a vacation—to cushion that weird blow.

The blurb discussion starts

Like or hate the practice, blurbs are here to stay. Just as a Yelp review assures a potential diner that they can eat in such and such a restaurant without getting dysentery, a blurb lets readers know that someone intelligent has enjoyed this book before.

It used to be that blurbs appeared exclusively on the hardcover. These days, they're on galleys, they're on pregalleys, they're on agented manuscripts. To both readers and industry insiders, endorsements matter. A great blurb builds buzz, and can earn your book extra attention at your publisher's internal presentations, at book conferences, among booksellers, and in trade reviews.

Asking for blurbs is an uncomfortable experience for all authors, but it's especially unpleasant for debut authors who are less connected than their seasoned colleagues. While writers who attend MFA programs have a leg up on the process (they can ask the program's professors and alums), not every writer goes for an MFA. I didn't, and when the blurb discussion started for my first novel, my high-school English teacher was what I was working with by way of professional contacts. To beef up my Rolodex, we relied on the respect that other writers had for my book's editor. I asked some of her former authors, I asked some of her author friends. The takeaway is that there are human beings out there who are truly generous. The other takeaway is that you will spend a lot of the blurbing process writing to people you don't know.

Here are the top four questions that you are probably wondering about this blurbing thing:

How many people should I ask?

There's no tried-and-true arithmetic for this, and your editor will steer you toward the number that's appropriate for your project, but if you have paltry contacts and even less in terms of platform, I'd write a dozen people and expect that you'll probably get three or four blurbs out of that. If you're somewhat established or you have writer friends who will definitely go to bat for you, I'd contact three more blurbers than you actually need. Inevitably, some people aren't going to have time to read your galley, and others just won't like it, so you'll want a safety margin.

Having said this, it's imperative not to write more people than you need to. If one of your blurbers finds their endorsement moved to the interior pages because there wasn't any more room on the back cover, this makes you feel like a hotshot, but the blurber will feel slighted. If their blurb gets cut because you simply got too much praise for your new book, you've lost a colleague and gained a saboteur.

How should I ask?

With my first novel, I was advised to send handwritten notes to all our potential blurbers, even the long shots we were pretty sure wouldn't ever respond. Although thoughtful, in hindsight, I think this was over-kill. For the initial ask, a well-written email can suffice. If an author says yes, though, *that's* a great time to pop a handwritten note in the mail for your editor to include when they send out the galley.

Authors have different opinions as to whom the request should come from. Some authors would prefer that the ask come from an agent or an editor, so the request is easier to decline, while others think it should come from the author for this very reason. Having been both the asker and the askee, I think it's nice for the writer to personally contact other writers when the blurb is for their debut. I see it as a rite-of-passage moment; it's an opportunity for you to let some of your favorite writers know how they've inspired you. Postdebut, you can pick and choose the people that you write personally for blurbs. I do think the reaches should always be contacted personally by the author. Presumably, you don't have a personal relationship with these long shots, so you'll have to work harder to woo them. A personal note helps.

How should I thank someone who blurbs me?

A traditional gift to blurbers is a finished copy of the book that they endorsed for you. This is a nice memento, but it won't arrive for many months and . . . they've kinda read your book already, you know what I'm saying? Blurbing takes so much time out of an author's already busy schedule, if someone agrees to blurb you, you should thank them right away.

A thank-you email from your editor is de rigueur, and a handwrit-ten note from the author will mean a lot as well. Some authors go a step further and send an actual gift: flowers, baked goods, the promise of their firstborn child (you should not send this, or any humans, through the mail). If you're thinking of sending alcohol, you'll first want to ver-ify that your recipient drinks, and also that the reception of such a gift won't be an inconvenience (most states require the signature of someone twenty-one years or older to accept booze). Again: a thank-you note is appropriate and historically sufficient. You do not have to blow all of your advance money on presents for your blurbers.

And how do I get rid of the resentment for the writers who did not?

If someone didn't respond to your request or flat-out turned you down, don't take this as a signifier that they dislike you personally, or think your writing sucks. Until they start receiving galleys themselves, newbie authors can't fathom the volume of advance copies that veteran authors receive. In fact, there's a troubling new trend in which agents are asking established authors to blurb manuscripts that don't even have a book deal yet. In October of 2017, the author Lauren Groff tweeted that she received at least two of these a week, and these kinds of requests are in addition to the advance reader copies that are delivered day after day to an author's mailbox. In November of 2018, writer Yahdon Israel Instagrammed that he received between fifteen and twenty ARCs a week; when writer and *AM to DM* host Saeed Jones was executive culture editor at *BuzzFeed*, he received thirty galleys a week. Thirty books a week is almost 1,560 books a year. That's a literal flood of galleys. A murmuration of new books.

Big-name authors receive more books than they could possibly provide blurbs for, so sometimes they have to cheat the system for the books they want to support. I myself have blurbed books I've never read (not yours, obviously), and I've ghostwritten blurbs for other authors to use for someone else. Blurbing can feel like a racket sometimes, but once in a while, you'll get a blurb from someone you admire who has closely read your book, understood what you were going for, and said something that is deeply, deeply generous about it. These people are good literary citizens, and they're out there in spades.

A couple of dos and don'ts regarding blurbs:

- Do review the way you've thought and spoken about an author publicly before asking them for a blurb. If you've ignored our advice about not posting bad reviews and you posted some bad ones, do not ask the authors that you've two-starred for a blurb.
- If you go the handwritten-note route for the initial ask, don't send anything else along with the note. The author probably doesn't need a chest X-ray of your grateful heart or a friendship bracelet. They have enough of those!
- Don't brag to other writers about the super-duper big-name author you got to blurb your manuscript unless you are willing to share the personal email address of the big-name author with them yourself. It's hard for most writers to hear good news unless they understand how to turn it into good news for themselves. This will be true forever until the end of time. It's not just true for blurbs.
- Do be specific about why you're sending this particular manuscript to this particular person. "Because your book was a bestseller" is not a reason, even though it is. The reason you provide should prove (or at least suggest) that you have read this author's writing, and that you like it a whole lot. Restrain yourself from using your blurb request as an opportunity to point out any reservations you have about the author's latest book.
- For the handwritten-note route takers: Do write legibly and don't spill anything weird on your nice note. If you do spill, don't be like, oh, I'll just send it anyway, Bigtime Author is probably a rooibos-tea drinker, too, and she'll think we're simpatico. Stains are weird. She won't.
- Give people time to read your book. Time as in *months*. You're

not going to get a blurb from someone if you give them three weeks to read your book.

- If you're sending a handwritten note for your publisher to include with your galley, don't address and stamp the envelope for the author. Your publisher will enclose that note inside your galley, so if the outer envelope is addressed, it will look like you have poor communication with your editor and/or you just don't understand how the postal service works.

- Do understand that if someone blurbs you, you kinda sorta have to blurb them back.

Gulp! Your cover concept is revealed

My first novel was a dark comedy about a married couple in Paris trying to work through the aftereffects of the male partner's infidelity. Accordingly, I lived in fear that my book cover would feature a shiny red heel and a discarded cravat strewn lasciviously underneath the Eiffel Tower. Instead, I was presented with a cover that nailed my book's themes and relegated the admittedly salable icon of the Eiffel Tower to a postage stamp. The first cover I saw was the cover that we went with. This minor miracle repeated itself with my second novel. I saw the PDF, and I enthusiastically signed off on it.

I am here to tell you that this is not the norm. Especially for women writers, who will have to fight harder than their male counterparts for covers that honor the intelligence and complexity of their book's prose. A friend of mine eventually had to ask a graphic-designer friend to create a book cover for her when her publisher presented her with only one concept for her debut: a stock image of a man in a crosswalk. "A man in a crosswalk is a man who follows the rules," my friend argued, a misleading image, as her darkly comic novel was about a wayward man. When she asked her publishing team why the man was crossing the street, the art department responded by adding a tote bag to his shoulder. "Is he going to a farmer's market?" the author asked.

Another friend's highly awaited debut, a sardonic and fiercely intelligent comedy of manners, was reduced to a stock image of a white woman in a scoop-back bathing suit on a generic beach, her face turned toward the sea. This friend raised hell about this cover, which, to her, would mislead people about her book's accessibility. The stock lady lost her place in the sun.

I hate my cover, what now?

When author Rumaan Alam received the proposed cover for his first novel, *Rich and Pretty*, he remembers being completely taken aback. "The adrenaline was pumping—this was my book! It was going to be real!—and it was hard to tell if I was having an honest response or not." After some reflection, he felt that it just wasn't spot on and was pleasantly surprised to find his team agreed.

"There was no argument, just a round of brainstorming," Rumaan remembers. "I surely went overboard. I emailed pictures of paintings I love, and then my agent kindly told me to relax. She reminded me what I had forgotten: the cover isn't my job."

For his second book, this process repeated itself—Rumaan didn't feel like the first concept was exactly right. But he was able to be more objective this time around. "It's not just a matter of throwing together a beautiful painting and the author's name," he says. "The art director and publisher and editor are talking about whether the cover looks like another book, whether the color palette feels right for the season, whether the type will be legible when your jacket appears in a grid of book covers on some Internet list."

Most publishers will indulge authors in a month of back-and-forth before the editorial team starts to feel they've got a problem cover on their hands. A Big Five editor who preferred to remain nameless said that the clearer an author can be with their feedback, the more likely they are to see additional concepts. "The typography doesn't feel fresh"; "the color palette isn't what I envisioned." These, the editor says, are helpful comments that the art team can actually work with. "The absolute worst thing an author can say, that I don't want to hear, ever, is that a cover feels 'uninspired.' That's offensive to my colleagues in the art department, and it isn't useful."

Remember that the art department is made up of actual humans, not robots. Your editor can only ask for so many rounds of changes from the art department before losing their goodwill. When your cover is finally signed off on, send those thank-you notes.

Everyone likes my cover except the people selling it

The more buzz your book has, the less control you have over the cover. This shouldn't be the way the world works, but there are a lot of problems with the world. Another debut-novelist friend of mine had a story-driving book jacket showing a roughed-up snow angel for her first book (snow being a plot point in her novel) and a vertical typographical treatment over it, and this was the cover she thought her book would have until she learned that one of the country's biggest booksellers didn't like it. If her team didn't change it, the bookseller threatened not to carry it.

Can you put your dukes up to fight for the cover that you want? Yes! Your agent will be your advocate in these arbitrations, and sometimes you'll get to do the "I told you so" dance when the book comes out. (You know who had to fight to defend her debut's cover? Stephanie Danler. And I heard that *Sweetbitter* did pretty well . . .)

You get assigned a publicist. Or you don't.

Once you have a cover and a title finalized, you might be assigned a publicist to help you promote your book. Other times, because of budget or resource restrictions, you won't. Sometimes you'll be assigned a publicist, and you'll want to hire one externally anyway. These are all interesting scenarios. Let's discuss.

How do you know if you've been assigned a good publicist? Look at the books they've previously supported. What kind of press did they get? A book's acknowledgments page is usually a good place to discern an author's feelings for the people on their editorial team, but don't run for the hills if the author doesn't thank her publicist. Lots of books are put to bed before an author is assigned a publicist, so they might not have had the chance.

If your publisher is generous enough to provide you with a publicist, I'd caution you against doing much more than Recon 101. If you know a writer that they've worked with, for example, it's fine to ask them for some pointers, but I wouldn't go cold-calling every author on the planet about your publicist's credentials. You want to start your debut publishing experience off on the right note, and the right note is not having your publicist find out that you think they're incompetent before your collaboration has even started.

There are, of course, situations in which you might want to hire an outside publicist even if you already have one. Perhaps your publicist is going on maternity or paternity leave, or doesn't have a lot of experience representing your book's genre. A debut-novelist friend of mine (let's call her Linda) shared the same publicist as another first-time novelist whose book unexpectedly hit *The New York Times* bestseller list and was being featured on every talk show in the country. Linda's book was about to come out, and it was pretty clear that her Big Five publicist had her hands full with her breakout star. So Linda hired an outside PR company called BookSparks to help her with her launch.

Hiring an outside publicity team can be costly: esteemed companies like BookSparks charge from $10,000 to $15,000 for digital PR campaigns, and $15,000 to $25,000-plus for national (digital and traditional) PR campaigns on average. Freelance publicists can be more affordable, but they're still gonna cost you: depending on the amount of outreach you're expecting, you can find someone capable for upwards of $3,000 a month. Most independent publicists will require a three-month retainer, and many will push for six months of collaboration to get the best results.

There are a lot of hidden costs involved in hiring an independent publicist: talking through logistics with your agent and publisher will help you unearth what they could be. Will your publisher provide the outside publicist with a minimum of twenty-five complimentary copies of your book? And who is paying for shipping each time your publicist sends one of those books out? (Hint: probably you.) Some publicists will also request a cut of any speaking engagements, development deals, product collaborations, and other lucrative opportunities that come your way thanks to their efforts. Share your publicity contract with your agent before you sign it to protect all parties from misunderstandings down the road, and make sure that there is some kind of termination provision so you can exit the building in an emergency.

Looking back at her experience, Linda feels the investment was absolutely worth it. "Your outside publicist will often work harder than your publisher's because they're being paid to," Linda came to feel. "They know after they cash the check they have to show what that's getting you."

Without exception, the in-house publicists I've worked with have been responsive, thoughtful, and tireless taskmasters. But that doesn't mean there aren't publicists who are unable—for whatever reason—to do a stand-up job. If you're hearing that a publicist never contacted an outlet that he promised to, or didn't send a galley to someone you'd requested, or they sent a galley without any accompanying material (especially if you'd written a note to send along), these are warning signs that you might have a substandard publicist.

The good news is that your assigned publicist might be grateful, rather than offended, about you working with an outside PR firm if you position this decision as a way to provide extra support to your publisher, instead of proof that they're doing a bad job. Freelance publicist and founder of Nectar Literary, Alyson Sinclair, says that she rarely encounters territorialism with in-house publicists. "They're really happy to have the extra help," she says. "Especially if you're communicating well. The independent publicist has to share their information, though. If you're sending emails to someone whom the in-house publicist also goes and contacts, you're not helping the author. You're just confusing things."

If you're going to hire an outside publicist, the earlier, the better. Long-lead titles—print media—have their editorial calendars booked at least six months in advance. You're not going to make *O, The Oprah Magazine*'s Summer Reading List if your publicist contacts them in May.

A publicist can work with a shortened lead time, but they'd prefer not to. "Even online outlets like *Electric Literature* or *The Millions* are getting galleys now, rather than finished copies," says Alyson. "I don't often take on last-minute projects unless they're very targeted: for example, the author is going to this particular city and needs this particular thing to happen." Alyson explains, "If I have less than four months' lead time, I am really honest about the return on the client's investment. I can be helpful with dailies or radio, and with the tour, but sometimes I suggest that if they're that close to publication, they spend the money on marketing because there is more they can control. Some publicity is always better than none, however, so it's worth throwing that Hail Mary."

If you can't afford to hire an outside publicist and your publisher dropped the publicity ball (or there was never any ball to start with), there are still ways to right the situation before your book comes out. Start by taking heart: just because you're not hearing from your publicist doesn't mean that they're not working for you. Some publicists keep their clients in the dark because they don't want them to be distracted with disappointments. If it's important for you to keep track of where the publicist's pitches are landing (and not landing), ask to see their spreadsheets. Your publicist is not a mind reader. Let them know what amount of information sharing makes you feel the most secure.

If there are real concerns that need addressing, your literary agent is the one to initiate these conversations. Your agent will most likely start by talking things through with your editor, who will then address the situation with the publicist. Are things going to get uncomfortable with your publicist? Ergh . . . probably? The situation is delicate, but I do think it's better to have a respectful heart-to-heart when there is still time to address frustrations, and course-correct before launch.

There is another scenario we must address, and in this alternative the publicity problem is you. If you're experiencing a certain crispness from the members of your editorial team, it might be time to assess whether you are doing something to antagonize your colleagues. As a debut author, it's crucial to understand—and accept—that your book isn't going to get everything you want. ("How common to meet one who thinks what they're writing entitles them not just to public consumption, but to fame," writes Sigrid Nunez in her novel *The Friend*.) Publicists control how much effort they put into promotion, but they have no control—whatsoever—about what a magazine includes (or doesn't) in their book roundups, whether a review is good or bad, whether a celebrity book club will choose their client's book. Books don't always get media hits because of their quality alone. Sometimes great books get dropped from best-of roundups because an art director didn't like the title's font, or the cover of book *X* looked too similar to the cover of book *Y*, and book *Y* is by a person that the magazine editor's sister-in-law owes a favor to. Publicity can be political. Or not political. There aren't any hard-and-fast rules in book publicity. That's the only rule.

Little orphan writer

Just like in other industries, people in publishing change jobs, they lose jobs, they go on maternity leave, they disappear and show up two years later in Andalusia where they've purchased a marine shrimp farm and married a stone carver. Nine times out of ten, the editor you sign your book contract with *is* the person who will accompany you across the finish line, but should you encounter an editor switcheroo en route to publication, rest assured that this has happened to scores of other writers before you, and their books made it through just fine.

If an editor changes jobs, he or she might invite you to follow them to the new publishing house. This is something of a rarity because it involves a lot of begging and prickly financial transactions: the new publisher will have to buy out your book contract, usually with interest, and your current publisher also has to agree to let you go. More often than not, you will be assigned another editor at your current house. There are horror stories out there, of course: bestselling cookbook authors Mark Scarbrough and Bruce Weinstein lost their editor to turnover eight times. Memoirist Jessica Lamb-Shapiro went through three editors during the launch of *Promise Land* along with a fleet of editorial assistants and publicists. But all of these writers are still standing on their feet. Roxane Gay's memoir *Hunger* was orphaned twice during the lead-up to its publication, but that didn't stop it from becoming an instantaneous bestseller the week that it came out.

Even if you stay with your editor through your book's life cycle, it's essential to forge relationships with people beyond your editor. Get to know the members of your publishing house's publicity and marketing team, if they have such a division. Get to know the copy editors, the art team, the social media interns, the COO. The more champions you have at your publisher, the more likely you are to find yourself with allies eager to support and help you should your editor move on.

Internal presentations and book conferences

Your book has a cover, a title, a publicist, maybe a blurb or two. That means it's time to present it to industry movers and shakers. This will take place at both internal presentations and launch meetings (when your editor pitches the book to the wider sales and marketing teams) and—if you're really lucky—at book conferences around the country. The most noteworthy of these are BookExpo (formerly known as Book-Expo America) and the American Booksellers Association's Winter Institute. If you've sold world rights to your book, your publisher might present it at conferences overseas, such as the Frankfurt or London Book Fairs. If you are a nice writer, maybe they will bring you back foreign-rights offers along with some good tea!

First-, second-, and third-pass edits
(a.k.a. the last time you can change something)

The first-pass edits let you see how the manuscript will flow into the designed pages of your finished book. Galleys are often produced from first-pass pages, and accordingly, they sometimes head out the door with minor spelling or grammatical mistakes, or sections that will be cut later, which is why early readers are implored not to quote from advance copies in their reviews.

Second- and third-pass edits are when the fun begins. This stage requires attention and steeled confidence from the author. Even the most minute queries won't *feel* that way when you realize that this is your last chance to decide, once and for all, if your main character says, "Scram!" or "Beat it!" in your book's final line.

In addition to word selection, these final edits are when narrative continuity takes center stage. Be kind to your copy editors: they're saving you from publishing a book where the main character celebrates Christmas on November 23, drives on the wrong side of the road in England, or fights in a war for Switzerland.

Some detail-oriented authors make it to fourth-pass edits, but most lose the ability to read their manuscript without wanting to tear small hairs out by the third. Traditionally, the third pass is the last time you'll have the opportunity to make changes to your manuscript. This includes the acknowledgments page, which is challenging, because this early in the process, you might not be aware of the people you need to thank yet.

On acknowledgments

The acknowledgments page didn't used to be the ubiquitous literary finale that it is today. In olden times, a book's dedication was the place for the big thank-you. Today, however, acknowledgments are a standard expectation for an author and a legitimate point of stress: you have to pen these thank-yous half a year before your book comes out.

As an author, I'm of two minds on the acknowledgments thing.

On one hand, I resent the spell-breaking that they perpetuate at the end of a great book. For me, it ruins the book's final note to hear that the author was unmoored during the writing of their book, except for the "transcendental" month they spent at Yaddo. (A terrific anti-acknowledgments rant in *The New Yorker* by *The Wall Street Journal* columnist Sam Sacks suggests that authors hide acknowledgments on the book's copyright page, or on their author website. You could also make them extra-special invisible by not writing them at all.)

On the other hand: books become books with an awful lot of help. Agents, editors, copy editors, graphic designers, interns, publicists, publicist's assistants: the list of literary helpers is long, and it's important, and their work is hard. There is a certain coarseness to *not* saying thank you to your accomplices, especially in a culture where everyone else does.

Here is a list of the people and entities who are usually thanked in acknowledgments in the order that they commonly appear:

- Editor and agent (or agent *then* editor, depends on who you prefer)
- Other key members of the author's publishing team
- Early readers
- A nonliving entity, like the coffee shop the author always wrote in or their favorite yoga class
- Institutions that the author wouldn't be authorial without: MFA programs they attended (with a shout-out to their instructors, who doubled as their blurbers), residencies they attended, fellowships they won—this section is basically for the places that the author has either spent money on or been given money by
- Favorite friends
- Favorite family members

- Favorite pets or offspring
- A final, heartfelt declaration to the person they are having sex with

The concern that you might forget to thank someone important is real. Ask your agent and editor for a list of the people that contributed to the book behind the scenes. Many authors never thank their copy-editors, or the designer of their book jacket. Editorial assistants are often left out, too.

Personally, I admire the authors who get their acknowledgments onto one page—I have never achieved this, but there's always room for hope. Remember, you don't have to thank everyone and anyone who makes your life worth living. Just thank the people who helped, directly, with the book.

The author photo

Similarly to acknowledgments, I have issues with the author photo as a working concept. I think it's absurd to expect one photo to communicate your emotional and intellectual essence. And you can't even use your entire body; you can only use your head. And a little of your neck, and maybe, like, your shirt collar. But nothing more than that! It would be truer to life if the author's headshot was a slideshow (the author as an infant, the author's first writing desk, the night the author self-medicated with too much Tempranillo after not getting into Bread Loaf yet again), but most books don't have the capacity for multiple photographs.

Traditionally, authors have to pay for their author photographs out of pocket. Standard pricing for author photographs is around $500, unless you have a photographer friend and can get a discounted rate.

Remember to include the cost of your author photograph in your end-of-the-year taxes along with the receipts for every single latté you drank while thinking about books.

For my first author photograph, I didn't put a lot of thought into it, and the photographer put me on a silver children's slide in a playground because, I don't know, good light. This resulted in a photograph that made me look friendly and maternal, which is not how I self-describe.

So I tried to remedy this with my second author photograph, an artistic effort that resulted in something moody that no outlets chose to use. This seems kind of reactionary to me, but it turns out that magazines and newspapers are more likely to run headshots of authors who aren't sitting in the dark.

You certainly can use the same headshot for different books, especially if you're prolific and/or genetically blessed, and still look like the author of your first book when you're on your fifth. Or you can take a new photograph for each book. Some standard tips:

- If you're uncomfortable in front of a camera, maybe have an alcoholic beverage before your shoot. If you don't drink alcohol, you probably have really good skin, so don't worry, you'll be fine.
- If you wear a bra, tuck in your bra straps. Just basically tuck everything in. If you have hair, it might be worth bringing a friend along to discipline your flyaways, especially if you plan to shoot outside.
- Unless you have won a Pulitzer or were born before 1973, avoid the use of props in your author photograph. This includes cigarettes and pipes, which shouldn't have to be stated, but there you go. The jury's out on pets. Some people look out of touch when photographed with their domestic pets, but the author Jim Shepard posed with his three beagles, and really made it work. Kind of depends on your pet.

- Don't give your publisher full access to all the photos from your photo shoot. If you have a favorite one, show them only that. If you welcome their help deciding, narrow the selection down to three. You can select one photo for the hardcover and one for the paperback if you desire, but you should use just one author photo for promotional photos, so people get used to seeing your official author face.

- If you took your own author photo, ask a friend if you can substitute their name in the credit line. Unless you're cool with having a selfie as your official author photograph.

- The standard author photo format is five by seven at three hundred dpi (TIF or JPEG). Most publishers will want both hi-res and low-res versions of your photo, and they will cut up your book contract if you send them a thumbnail.

- Are you the author Joy Williams? No? Then you cannot wear sunglasses in your author photograph.

- Send a finished copy of your book to your photographer. Make sure they receive photographer credit any time the image is used. Include the photographer's name in the image file so that this is more likely to happen.

- If you've sold foreign rights and the publisher intends to use your author photograph, make sure with the photographer that it's cleared for international use before the translation goes to print.

Writing your author bio

The author bio on your book jacket is going to be the one that literary-festival moderators and reading-series hosts read to the audience by default, so it shouldn't make you cringe when you hear it read out loud.

Your bio should contain the titles of any other published books or collections you have, along with the publications and prizes you're most proud of. If you list every place that has ever published you, you will sound unhinged. You have a book. Calm down. Some writers like to include a quirky detail in their bios. I used to drive a Corona®mobile, and I get a lot of mileage out of that. I have an author friend who used to be a dominatrix. Worth mentioning, I think! You don't have to reference *all* the jobs you had before becoming a writer. I'd cut it off at three.

Readers like to know where authors live, their marital status, and whether they have children. Volunteer this information at your discretion. If nothing else, it's useful to indicate the general region you live in so that you can be more easily considered by local literary festivals and conferences, but you don't need to be giving away your social security number in your author bio, for goodness' sake.

Author bios should run around one hundred words and look more or less like the following:

> [Author full name] is the author of [enter book title/s], [include anything major that these books were nominated for, major lists they were included in, or prizes that they won]. Originally from [name of the place that you were born in], [author first name] now lives in [location] where [insert preferred gender pronoun] currently [list the occupation that helps you pay your rent]. A graduate of [insert name of your graduate program; if you didn't attend an MFA program, just insert some self-effacing copy about a weird job you used to have], [insert preferred gender pronoun] is currently working on [what the hell are you doing next? What are you doing with your life? Where are you to *turn*?!]. A recipient of [insert any prizes or fellowships you have won or residencies

you have attended], [insert preferred gender pronoun]'s writing can be found in [list up to three outlets where you have published. If you haven't published anywhere, insert a self-effacing joke about how many times you have been rejected from [insert name of publication who has hurt your feelings the most]. [Insert author website and/or the social media handle of the feed where you are the funniest].

Creating an author website

Although it involves a little energy in the beginning, having a website will save you time in the long run. You'll receive less email (and direct messages) asking for your bio, your publicist's contact, whether or not you're coming to such and such a town on tour, because all of these answers will live in one neat place. Even if it's just a landing page, an author website is an efficient and low-cost way to keep your audience informed about who you are and what you're up to, without actually having to be in touch with them.

Plus, with all the drag-and-drop website builders currently available, even the most technologically challenged writer can make a website cheaply, with relatively few headaches. For writers who need guidance through the process, the Authors Guild offers website-building, hosting, and marketing services at most of their membership levels: even for members who haven't published a book yet.

You can keep your author website barebones if you'd like to, but at the very least, your author website should include:

- An "about" section with your author photo (with photographer credit), an updated bio, and high-quality images of your book(s)

- Tour information and your upcoming events
- Top press and/or blurbs
- A contact page with your publicist's information (if you don't have a publicist, ask your agent how he or she feels about being listed before you include their contact information). And sleep on it before you put your own personal email address on a public website. You can use a contact form if you prefer.
- Social media buttons and a way to sign up for your newsletter, if you have one
- Links to selected publications

If you're going to include a buy link, check with your publisher as to which accounts you should link to. Linking only to Amazon will not go over well with the other bookstores that are carrying your book. To avoid this stickiness, some authors link their book to their publisher's website. No conflicts, no mess.

Keep in mind that a lot of people browse the Internet with their cell phones, so your website should be suitable for viewing on a mobile device. And for the love of all that's holy, do not use white typography on a black background, unless your author website lives on the dark web.

The marketing brainstorm

Six months or so before your launch, you'll probably have a brainstorm with marketing and publicity about how to bring readers to your book. Budget will play a huge part in how much (or how little) your publisher does to get the word out, but even houses with modest budgets do many of the following:

- They'll pitch your book to radio, print, and online outlets, and to targeted podcasts.
- They'll encourage you to pitch and place articles, essays, and op-eds that support your book's main themes. (Please see the "Getting your voice out there" section for more on these travails.)
- Lead titles will be promoted at trade shows and book fairs.
- Organization of advance reader copies (ARCs) giveaways on Goodreads and other early-reader programs
- Social media support from the publisher's corporate accounts

Publishers with expansive budgets might pay for advertising through social media banners, place ads in print and online magazines, or run bundle giveaways with partner companies or brands. Some authors might have merchandise made to accompany their ARCs, such as totes or T-shirts. Almost every author will be asked to promote their book on social media, but if a publisher has the resources for it, they'll also help brainstorm a social media campaign to build up the book's buzz.

Social media campaigns are easy (and exciting) to discuss, but very hard to execute. When used improperly, social media can make a lot of people uncomfortable, and artificially generating early enthusiasm for your book is difficult to pull off. That's why your best bet (if you're given the opportunity to run an online campaign) is to do something that feels authentic to the project and to your own values and interests. By way of an example, when the author Edan Lepucki came out with her second novel, *Woman No. 17*, which explores the creative process and less-than-stellar mothering, she started an Instagram account called Mothers Before that features photographs of people's mothers before they were mothers, with accompanying text from the submitters. The photos were bawdy, beautiful, sometimes kind of sad. As a writer and a thinker, Edan has always been interested in femininity and motherhood, so the Instagram account was a complement to issues she was already tackling in her work. The account might have been created to support her second book's launch, but because it reflected her true interests, it took on a life of its own, including the publication of a book based on her Mothers Before account.

A social media campaign like Edan's takes dedication, hard work, passion, and not a little luck. But at the end of the day, even if you have free time to sink into the project and a willing publisher, you can't control for what your readers think is cool. If your publisher is supporting a social media campaign for you, here's hoping that it works. If they aren't, there are a lot of things that you can do on social media to positively support your book that won't make you upchuck. A selection:

- Create a banner that shows your book cover and release date and scale it for use on Facebook and Twitter. You don't need to be a graphic designer to do this: a lot can be accomplished with the Pictures tool in Microsoft Word and a little screenshot. (Proof positive: all of my daughter's birthday invitations to date.)

- Update your email signature with a link to your website, if you have one, or to your publisher's webpage if you don't. Include the title of your book. Don't use wacky font. Don't use animation. Just calm down about it.

- Update all of your social media accounts (including LinkedIn. Really!) to reflect that you have a book out. If you want to include the places where the book is available, check with your publisher before doing so. Many publishers have a bookseller hierarchy that they'll want you to use.

- Start sharing the books you are reading and enjoying on social-cataloging sites like Goodreads, and begin following authors you like on various platforms in a respectful way. (If you don't have anything good to say on Goodreads, do not use that site.)

- Create Facebook Event pages for your different book events, but only share invitations with people who live within a short drive's distance of the event. Your friend Rachel loves you, but she isn't going to fly from Los Angeles to your Brooklyn book launch, for Pete's sake.

- Apps and websites such as Social Print Studio and Vistaprint allow you to make good-looking, double-sided business cards with your book cover on one side and your bizness on the back for cheap. These cards come in handy when you meet someone who genuinely sounds interested in your book, but will probably forget this once your conversation ends because reduced memory recall. These cards help them remember their intrigue! Include your author website, email address, and a blurb or pull quote so the recipient knows what your book's about.

- Start a newsletter or TinyLetter that gives subscribers a view of your larger interests. Although you can certainly communicate the key things happening with your book (where you'll be on tour, for example, or when it will come out in paperback), newsletters should share the limelight with other people you admire. Include a list of what you are reading, or looking forward to reading. What songs are you listening to? What podcasts are easing your commute? Subscribe to other author newsletters to get a sense of who's doing it right.

- Remember that you had a life before this book. Keep living that life.

Understanding foreign rights

If you sold world rights to your publisher, your publisher will handle foreign sales. If you didn't, the rights holder might be your agent. If you self-published, the lucky foreign-rights holder is you.

If your first book is a buzzy one, you might start selling translation rights before your book even publishes—for other people, rights might sell if the book starts picking up momentum once it's out. Regardless, the process starts with book scouts, who are skilled at determining (or rather, forecasting) what upcoming projects could hold commercial or literary appeal for the imprints that they scout for. When scouts are interested in a project, they'll try to get it into editors' hands before the competition so that the publisher can make an offer on the foreign rights. The film-scouting process is different, because these readers will be judging whether or not the material can be adapted for the silver screen, but the end game is the same: identify projects that have potential and move to acquire them quickly, before the competition does.

Foreign-rights sales are brokered by foreign-rights agents who try to play matchmaker between a book and a foreign publisher. There are exceptions, of course, but deals are commonly brokered with the U.K., France, Germany, the Netherlands, Italy, Portugal, Scandinavia, and the Baltic countries. Because of the time it takes to translate them— except for the U.K. when the original work is in English—simultaneous publications are rare. Most translations come out within a year or two of your book's publication, and in addition to the money you received for the sale, you will usually get a few copies of the translated book.

Foreign-rights sales vary wildly, from a few thousand dollars to forty thousand or more, based either on how well the foreign publisher thinks the book will do, or how much competition there is to acquire the rights. Rights are often acquired during big foreign fairs that lots of American publishers and agencies attend, such as Frankfurt or London.

"Often there is a big book of the fair," says book scout Cathrin Wirtz. "You have certain territories picking it up very quickly—the Netherlands, Germany, Italy, Scandinavia, France." Although the race to acquire rights to "It books" is exciting, there can be a price tag for the frenzy. Not only will foreign publishers frequently end up overpaying for a buzzy book, the noise around such acquisitions distracts buyers from acquiring other books that might actually perform better in their markets. "It's an iceberg situation," continues Cathrin. "We hear about the books that sold to a number of territories overnight or within a matter of days. But there are all these people writing beautiful books—we need to take the time to pay attention to overlooked books, the ones you fall in love with regardless of how 'hot' they are. There is only so much time during a book fair."

If your book's rights don't sell abroad, don't take this as a reflection of how your book will perform in the United States. There are books that do enormously well in the U.S. that don't sell in England, and vice versa: the fact that the book doesn't even have to be translated isn't a factor. These are different markets with different readers who have disparate literary tastes.

Sometimes there is a reason a book doesn't sell abroad (a book can be too voicey, or its sense of humor too culturally specific), and sometimes it's just a question of timing. But the good thing about the book-as-object is that it can be revisited. "It's so nice to return to the backlist," Cathrin says. "To find the sleepers. To be surprised. To say to someone, 'This book is still available, and I think it would be perfect for your list.'"

Many foreign publishers are not required to use the same cover as your original, and the title might change, too. Even your author name is malleable. To the utter delight of my friend Sebastian, who finds this totally hysterical, I'm "Kopni Mom" in Greece.

Audiobook land

Some good news for writers and the people who publish them: audiobooks are a hot commodity. A giddy *Vulture* article in September of 2018 proclaimed that "audiobook sales are the fastest-growing sector of publishing by far." Audio divisions are experimenting with audio-only content, original staged pieces, and other exclusive content to ensure that the consumer's love affair with audio keeps on going strong.

Publishers were a little slow to jump on the audio train, but they're riding high and happy now. Small and midsize publishers alike are reaping the benefits: books that would have previously sat unrecorded are selling at auction for up to three times what the author was paid as an advance. In the *Vulture* article, Grove Atlantic publisher Morgan Entrekin admits he isn't sure how sustainable the feeding frenzy is. "You wonder if the prices they're paying for audiobook-only are really justified," he says. "But they're all thinking market share. We're getting involved with acquisitions that we probably wouldn't go for because of the price that Audible and others are paying."

Audio rights are a bundled-rights package like film, foreign rights, or first serial. Literary agents can hold on to your audio rights and sell them to audio publishers like Audible, Recorded Books, or Brilliance Audio, they can sell them to the author's publisher and copublish them with the in-house imprint, *or* they can sublicense them elsewhere.

The extent of an author's involvement in their audiobook recording can vary widely. With my first book, the audiobook showed up one day at my doorstep narrated by a British actor who does an awesome job. With my second book, I was asked to choose the actress who would perform the protagonist and I had input on the artwork, which motivated me to promote the book in audio form.

Most audiobooks are narrated by professional actors, but if you have a lot of stamina, a particularly melodious voice, and/or a vested interest in narrating the book (i.e., your book's a memoir), you can certainly pitch yourself as your book's narrator. But do you want to?

"It's exhausting," says audiobook narrator and actor Nancy Wu. "It's a skill you learn to build up. Ten years ago, I'd get recording sessions that were spaced out. You'd record for three or four hours every few days, but now they crank them out. Sometimes I'm in the studio for seven-hour sessions, six days in a row."

Nancy absolutely loves what she does, but she acknowledges that it's not for the faint of throat. She suggests that authors who are interested in narrating their own books try reading out loud in a confined, windowless space for two hours a day for a few days to see if it's something they could manage for longer stretches of time.

Author John Freeman Gill wanted to throw his hat in the ring as a potential narrator for the audiobook version of his debut novel, and he appreciated the professionalism with which his publisher, Penguin Random House, treated his request. "I liked that they didn't say, 'Oh, sure!' They said I had to audition. They had the book's best interest in mind."

Motivated by the challenge of a new experience and his conviction that "it would be a really meaningful artifact for the grandkids after I'm gone," John prepared his audition. The publisher had suggested he read the first five pages of his book, but the prologue contained only one line of dialogue, and it was important to John to show the producer range, so he submitted two selections instead.

John did get the job, but the time he spent recording his audition didn't prepare him for the physical trials to come. "There is a huge difference between reading into your iPhone for twelve minutes and recording for eight hours for four days," John says. "It's incredibly taxing on your voice. You become attuned to the environment of the world of moisture inside your own mouth." For John, who has written about his debut recording experience for *Literary Hub*, mastering the tricks of the trade helped him refine his performance. He quickly learned when a lozenge went from being "soothing" to "sticky" for the throat, how much water makes a voice sound "wet," and that a pillow held over the stomach can cloak the sound of a narrator who needs lunch.

For author Mira Jacob, narrating her debut novel was one of the most meaningful creative experiences in her life. Mira lost her father before her book was finished, and she was thus unable to share the story she had been working on for the past ten years with him. At first, she had a hard time managing her energy during the recording—her attention would wane, her voice drifted, the production team (Mira also recorded in-house with Penguin Random House) had to constantly remind her to keep the energy up in the second part of each sentence. But a few hours into the recording, Mira decided that she was reading the story to and for her father, and it shifted things completely. "I was really *reading* it, all of a sudden," she remembers. "It became so energetic. Imagining that I was reading this to my dad gave me so much purpose, I really felt like I had a telephone and that he could hear me. It was one of the most gratifying creative experiences I have ever had." Mira acknowledged that the physicality of the recording is "Olympic level"—she spent eight days in the studio, recording six hours a day, repeating some sentences as many as twenty times. "If you're going to keep your energy up and you're not a professional," Mira advises, "you have to imagine you are telling the story to a real person."

The actual salary will vary on the length of the project and the narrator's experience and cachet, but nonprofessionals (i.e., authors who don't have union backing) can expect to earn between one hundred and two hundred dollars per hour if they're chosen to narrate their own audiobook, and most book projects will take up to a week of an author's time.

If you'd like to take charge of your own audiobook production, Audible.com has a division called ACX (the Audiobook Creation Exchange) where authors and rights holders can cast their own actors and hire producers to self-publish an audiobook—for a price. Because ACX is an Amazon company, your audiobook is eligible for sale on Amazon, Audible, and iTunes when it's finished. The actual cost of self-publishing an audiobook varies widely depending on the length of the book and the talent that you hire. Unlike other SAG-AFTRA contracts, there isn't a single national minimum rate for audiobook actors: minimum rates are negotiated with individual publishers and producers and a number of factors affect the outcome of those negotiations. This being said, the professional narrators I spoke to said that Screen Actors Guild members tend to receive a fee per finished hour rate around $225, so if you want to produce your audiobook in a professional manner with equally professional talent, you should budget between $3,000 and $6,000 to do so.

Or you can double-down on the DIY experience and—truly—do the entire thing yourself. For his own debut novel, author Dave Essinger produced an audiobook using his own voice and equipment, and although he says he has no regrets, he can't exactly endorse the undertaking either. "If you are technically inclined and want absolute creative control and enjoy staring at waveforms and doing meticulous tiny edits for hours a day, then go for it. If you would be frustrated by losing those weeks or months of creative time for new writing, then maybe not so much."

Dave had no experience recording or editing, so a great deal of time was spent troubleshooting. All told, he thinks he spent about eighty hours on an eight-hour finished product. It cost a lot in time, but not a lot in cash money: he estimates that he spent under two hundred dollars on out-of-pocket expenses for his audiobook.

If your book contains ideograms like emojis, illustrations, electronic messages, or other copy that is text specific, you will have to put some thought into how you can convey these sections via audio. "In the case of Mary Adkins's debut novel, *When You Read This*," explains HarperCollins editor Emily Griffin, "the audio version required some reimagining. One thread in Mary's epistolary novel is the found blog posts of a young woman, which tell a story through designs in squiggles, dots, waves, and other shapes. Adkins wrote a script for the audiobook narrative in which she wrote out descriptions of most designs. So instead of a panel that said, 'I used to think lungs looked like this,' and included an illustration, she directed the narrator to read, 'I used to think lungs were the shape of upside-down teeth: wider on top and narrower on the bottom.' The result was an audio version that stayed true to the book's tone and themes but was also accessible to a listener."

OMG someone wrote the same book as me!!!

As with ready-to-wear clothes and heirloom vegetables, book publishing also follows market trends. Writers, after all, are natural-born observers, our cultural referees. It makes sense that the issues that fascinate and concern one writer would also concern someone else.

Accordingly, there are publishing seasons in which it feels like everyone is obsessed with the same topic. In 2005, vampire-themed novels were hot, and the success of *Twilight* ushered in a welcome era of dystopian books with angsty female heroes. Then things got post-apocalyptic: Emily St. John Mandel's *Station Eleven* catapulted onto the scene alongside Edan Lepucki's *California*, and Ben H. Winters's *The*

Underground Airlines came out one month before Colson Whitehead's *The Underground Railroad*. The challenges of the Trump era have added fuel to the postapocalyptic fire, with so many books devoted to the collapse of civil society that *The New York Times* has referred to this publishing trend as "a collective panic attack."

Nonfiction is also subject to market trends: Rebecca Weller's addiction memoir *A Happier Hour* was followed by Leslie Jamison's *The Recovering*, a few months before Kristi Coulter's *Nothing Good Can Come from This* met the wider world. Feminist accounts of motherhood hit the spring of 2018 like a tsunami: Meaghan O'Connell's *And Now We Have Everything* was followed by Sheila Heti's *Motherhood* and Rumaan Alam's *That Kind of Mother*, then Angela Garbes's *Like a Mother* came out, chased by Emma Brockes's *An Excellent Choice* and Kim Brooks's *Small Animals: Parenthood in the Age of Fear*. (And this is just a sampling of that season's titles!)

With the popularity of social-cataloging websites like Goodreads that offer hyperspecific reading categories ("motherhood and ambition" is one example; "school novels" is another), it's easier than ever to take the pulse of what is trending. With publishers taking fewer chances on niche books, it's highly possible that your book is going to come out with another book (or several) that explore a similar theme.

But is this bad news? No. When multiple books come out at the same time on the same subject, individual titles can receive more press than they might have by being grouped into roundups and think pieces. The authors of thematically linked books might find themselves with invites to conferences and festivals they might not have received if their book hadn't hit a nerve.

This was certainly the case for some of the aforementioned motherhood-related titles. In April of 2018, *The Guardian* asked "Is Motherhood the Unfinished Work of Feminism?" That same month,

The New York Times followed up with "Motherhood from (Almost) Every Angle," and that July, *The Paris Review* wondered, "Why All the Books About Motherhood?"

Memoirs and novels aren't the only literary genres that go to the ball in the same dress: essay collections, children's books, self-help titles . . . everything publishable is subject to a trend. When cookbook author Alana Chernila published her first book, *The Homemade Pantry: 101 Foods You Can Stop Buying and Start Making,* it followed the publication of Jennifer Reese's *Make the Bread, Buy the Butter: What You Should and Shouldn't Cook from Scratch.* "They were constantly put up next to each other for comparison," Alana remembers, "and I really love Jennifer's writing so I couldn't even be snarky about it!"

We don't want to think of other authors as enemies, and you're better off in the long term if you believe competing titles can *help* your book rather than hurt it. So read the books that yours is in conversation with. Reach out to their authors and compliment them on their work. Work together as a united force instead of one divided: pitch together for festival panels on your given theme, pitch group interviews about your shared (and unshared) influences. Believe in the common good.

Trade reviews start to come in

Trade reviews are different from traditional media reviews in that they aren't consumer-facing. A potential reader can easily pick up *The New York Times* and skim through their book-review section, but the same reader would need a subscription—or at the very least, a password—to access some of the trade publications.

If you're going to get any, the first trade reviews to trickle in are usually from *Kirkus Reviews* and *Publishers Weekly,* followed by *Booklist* and *Library Journal*. Just like with the announcement of book deals in Publishers Marketplace, there's a hierarchy of review shorthand to decode. You can get a review, a starred review, or you can get a starred review that is also boxed. This system is straightforward: if you get a star, you're a big star! A box is like having your own red velvet rope. It means that the trade reviews think people should pay attention to you. You don't need to thank the reviewers personally because the reviews are usually anonymous, but if you get a review that pleases you, it never hurts to positively mention the publication on your social media.

You should know that in some circles, *Kirkus Reviews* is referred to as "Cranky Kirkus." Where *Publishers Weekly* is usually evenhanded in their reviews, *Kirkus* has no problem taking books *down*. Their curmudgeonliness is so legendary, there's even a (now defunct) Tumblr devoted to it, Sick Burns: The Best of *Kirkus Reviews* Worst.

Some samplers:

> "If you finish this monumental collection and find yourself with an appetite for more, consider seeking professional help."

> "The characters reach their happy ending, but you might not care."

> "If you've ever wondered what it's like to feel simultaneously bored and nauseous, this is the book for you."

Trade reviews are far more likely to publish a negative review than glossy, female-centric magazines like *O, The Oprah Magazine* or *Glamour*, where reviewers focus on the positives of the books they share. The good news about getting a bad trade review is that they're easy to bury, because they're hard to find. Equally good news: your book can go on to have a long and happy life whether or not a trade review likes it. I have a friend whose book *Kirkus* found "appalling," and it went on to be voted one of the most-anticipated books of 2017 by numerous publications. Another friend's debut was labeled "yawn-provoking," and it was optioned by a major film director and was a *New York Times* bestseller. If you get a bad *Kirkus* review, take it with a grain of fancy salt.

Not every book gets a trade review, and your book can thrive without one, but it's true that trade reviews lend your book a certain clout. If it doesn't look like you'll have trade reviews and you can afford it, it's worth hiring an outside publicist to compensate for this missing coverage with other media hits.

When the private becomes public

For most people, writing is an intensely private activity. Poetry collections, novels, memoirs, short-story collections, all of these projects can take years to complete, and it's not unusual for some authors to spend a decade getting something right. For emerging authors who work outside of academia or publishing, it's not only that their colleagues don't think of them as writers, they might not even know they write.

"People get very weird about fiction writing in D.C.," says author Amber Sparks, who, in addition to writing, works as a digital strategist for a nonprofit in the nation's capital. "It's almost . . . suspect. I've tried to explain that it's no different than gardening or marathoning, but people seem to have this idea both that it's profoundly unserious, but at the same time that you're going to be so wildly successful that you'll up and leave your day job any minute."

Debut author Michael A. Ferro hadn't shared the fact that he was writing a novel, let alone trying to publish it, with anyone but his immediate family right up until the point where he had radio interviews lined up for his book's release. The fact that he will soon be speaking about (and promoting) this thing that has been a secret for so long is frying his nerves. "I can't imagine what I'll think when everyone has the opportunity to read it," he admits. "I think I'll just change my name to Mario and shave my beard off and say I moved into Michael's old house after he moved away to Alaska. If anyone doesn't believe me or still asks me questions about the novel, I'll pretend I don't speak English and will wander off."

People *will* end up reading your book, and your private thoughts (and sense of humor) won't be so private anymore. Author Dave Housley remembers that when his mother read the first line of his book ("I shaved my balls a week after Claire left"), she turned to him and said, "Well, I hope you know your grandmother is never going to know you wrote a book."

Writing comes with numerous risks (including never having dental care) and writing a memoir makes these risks run even hotter. Authors Melissa Febos and Alex Marzano-Lesnevich both had high-profile memoirs come out in recent years that tackled difficult subjects: Melissa's *Abandon Me* examines her relationships with the birth father who abandoned her and the sea captain who raised her, while Alex's memoir and true-crime hybrid, *The Fact of a Body*, recounts their experience working as a lawyer on a death-penalty case for a child murderer while simultaneously grappling with their own sexual abuse as a young child.

Alex worked for ten years on the research and writing of their true-crime memoir, so when publication approached, they thought they were prepared. "I'd published essays on the topic, and I'd done readings from the book, so I thought that I was ready, but it was so intensely, emotionally jarring to have the book in print. It was the most moving and profoundly emotionally impactful thing, to hold the finished book. To make a place for the past to live."

Both Alex and Melissa had loved ones in their lives who might be hurt or offended by material in their memoirs, so they shared advance copies with these readers before the book went into print. "I worked on the book for ten years," recalls Alex, "so my family had a lot of advance notice. But because my book is about people trying to control the narrative, I didn't want to give them the chance to do that. I gave it to them when it was done."

Melissa also shares her books with a select group beforehand without giving recipients the power to make edits. "I make a short list of the people in the book who will be affected by it with whom I want to maintain a relationship," she says. "I send the book to those folks, without any promise but to hear their thoughts. By going through that process before the book is published, I've minimized the stress after publication."

While both authors nurtured hopes that their stories would connect with readers, neither of them could have anticipated the extent to which readers would ask—or even expect—them to carry their own tales. "I got a therapist three or four days after the book came out," Alex recalls. "I had been prepared for people reaching out about their own trauma because I'd been reading from the book for a long time, but I wasn't prepared for the volume. I'm profoundly thankful for it, it's mind-blowing, but it's a lot, people self-disclosing about abuse in their family, and I needed someone to talk to about it."

Both authors had to learn to temper their appreciation for their readers with their own need for time and privacy. "I'm endlessly grateful to those who have read my work and identified with it, but that appreciation doesn't come with strings," says Melissa. "I wrote the book.

I'm not a life coach or a therapist or a guest on a never-ending talk show. In order to preserve my sanity, I have to conserve my energy. People can project a lot onto memoirists, and it's not our job to negotiate that, to correct anyone's misinterpretation, or do emotional labor for strangers. It was really liberating when I realized that."

Melissa manages her energy by taking breaks from social media and spending time with people who truly know her. As for Alex, they gave themself permission to enjoy the heck out of the summer after their book came out, without putting any pressure on themself to start writing something new. "If a book is going to be as risky as it needs to be, take as many rests as you can," they advise. "I wanted to feel what it was like to let go of something that I'd been working on for ten years." Alex went hiking, they went swimming, they said yes to whatever opportunity they had to get outdoors.

Poet and performance artist Joanna Hoffman also found exercise to be healing when her poetry collection, *Running for Trap Doors*, came out. Long-distance running helped her cope with the stress of publishing a book that was going to change the way that certain family members thought of her, and of her relationships to them. "My family is incredibly private," Joanna says of that experience. "Having a book out is an outing in a way. It outs certain parts of yourself that people might not have been anticipating. Some people learned very quickly that I'm a lesbian and have issues with depression."

In addition to using exercise as a form of therapy, Joanna also had sit-downs with certain family members before the book came out, guiding them through the material that might be challenging to them. Although these heart-to-hearts ultimately helped, Joanna still struggles with the balance of making the private public. "At events, I sometimes request that people not film me doing new material because I don't know where the footage will end up," she admits. "I've had other poems that I wish I could put in a book, but it just wasn't worth it. Certain people would never talk to me again."

It can be terrifying to have a book out in the world, and if you're doing the work right, it's never going to be easy. "It's intimacy," concludes Joanna. "It's forced intimacy. It's an uncomfortable reckoning of personal truths."

How to share good book news on the Internet

Much like the initial social media announcement about your first book deal, it behooves you to come up with a system for sharing news as your book nears its publication. Most writers who are active online tend to share everything: every blurb received, each positive review, every foreign sale . . . they are like toddlers whose every piece of artwork must be magnetized to the refrigerator, until there are so many things there, you can't find the refrigerator anymore.

I'm of two minds about this. Sharing good book news can help perpetuate either the truth (or the illusion) that your book is a success, thus keeping your book in the cultural conversation and momentum underfoot. If people are thinking about your book and discussing it, you're more likely to get invited to festivals and conferences, and an on-the-fence potential reader might transition into a buyer of your book.

But good things come in doses, and this is particularly true for happy news. If it's clear that your book is on track toward bestsellerdom, maybe chill out with the posts. Writers are doubting people with fickle, fearful hearts: if you post too much good news, they'll go from rooting for you to envying you, and envy can be toxic. Even if your book is the hot read of the season, seasons turn, turn, turn. At some point, the good news train is going to stop, and it's going to be so awkward when you have to go back to posting funny pictures of your cat after we haven't seen that cat of yours for months.

A good rule of thumb (although a pretty transparent one) is to post one book-related piece of news for every three regular-life ones. True champions of social media will continue to post nice things about books (and films and artwork) by people other than themselves throughout their careers—both before, during, and after their own books have come out.

And don't forget—just like you are allowed to post non-book-related news during your publication, you're also allowed to publish disappointments, fumbles, bumbles, politely worded regrets. Propagating the good-news cycle actually does us writers a disservice: it disseminates the idea that once you get a book deal, all lights are green ahead. This couldn't be further from the truth, as we are learning. Writing is hard, and although it gets easier to publish once you've published, it does not make the act of writing easier, or the doubts disappear. So if you're down about something, you might be surprised how comforted it will make other people feel to share that human doubt—if it's worded right.

A few words on envy

Whether you're hate-liking an Instagram post about a writer who just sold the TV rights to a book you couldn't finish, or sharing a signing table with someone who's selling five books for your zero, envy is going to happen to you, and it ain't gonna be pretty.

Unless you experience a personal loss or serious health issues during your book's promotion, envy is the number-one thing that could jeopardize your happiness as your first book heads into the world. If you allow that envy happens, you'll be better prepared to cope with it when it rears its ugly head.

Stay active—and offline

Envy thrives on inertia. The more you cyberstalk the writers that you're jealous of, the more the spores will grow.

Combat the envy monster by switching up your habits. Leave your computer at a friend's house and write longhand for a week. Read writers you can't easily compare yourself with: start with writers who are dead. Engage in literary citizenship at the local level: help a high-schooler prepare their college essay; review a book for a newspaper; volunteer to read to a senior citizen. Nourish your better self with healthy activities and keep your lesser self offline.

Compare down, not up

Instead of comparing yourself with the people who have "more" than you, consider the writers who are working to achieve the kinds of milestones and successes that you've already had. Remember when you didn't have an agent? Remember when you had to *query* for an agent? But look where you are now!

Workshop your enemy

If you're jealous of a particular book, read it with the generosity you would show someone in workshop. Does the author excel at food descriptions? Is their dialogue inventive? Are they good at plot? (Come on. Their book was more successful than yours—you *know* they're better at plot.)

Consider envy as a life coach

Sometimes your envy is telling you something negative (but improvable) about yourself that no one else has the guts to. If, for example, you come away from a literary festival feeling like you were outshined by another writer, interrogate your envy until you figure out *why* this person appeared to get more praise. If their reading went better than yours: Was it because they picked a shorter/better/funnier excerpt to share? Or are they just a better reader? And if they *are* a better reader, would it be the worst thing if you took a public-speaking class? Take your envy out for a beer once in a while. In its own perverted way, it wants to be your friend.

Don't give in to the envy. Or fuck it. Do.

I know writers who have tried to fight the good fight to be a better, envy-free person, but they did not win. They just freaking gave in to it. Identified one person as their nemesis, one book against which they will always compare their own. In time, they developed a twisted tenderness for the person that they decided to envy more than any other. They do not let this person know that they are "their" person. They learn to cherish this unrequited form of love.

Getting your voice out there (also known as essay time!)

Up to six months before your book comes out, your team will urge you to "get your voice out there" by placing off-the-book pieces in newspapers, magazines, and online outlets. Sometimes these publications will solicit something from you. More often, you will need to pitch them. These articles and essays aren't supposed to promote your book overtly, but rather fondle your book's themes. Such assignments are tricky because they can leave you feeling like you're doing things out of order. Why are you writing this piece dancing around your book's subject when you've already written the book?

When executed properly, though, these prepub personal essays can garner you not just new readers, but fans who are actually looking forward to your book's publication and who might get other people excited about it as well. In the months preceding the launch of her acclaimed story collection, *Sour Heart*, author Jenny Zhang published an essay called "Your Best American Girl" in *The New York Times Magazine* Music Issue that used Japanese American Mitski Miyawaki's music as a vehicle to discuss the immigrant experience in America. Author Alissa Nutting preceded her second novel's publication (*Made for Love*) with a balls-to-the-wall food diary published in Grub Street that was so sardonic and full of DGAF joy, it prepped readers for the similar register of Alissa's books. Over a year before her second book, *Good Talk: A Memoir in Conversations*, came out, author Mira Jacob began sharing excerpts with *BuzzFeed* from her graphic memoir exploring questions of race and identity in a Trump America. These posts all went viral and helped position Mira as a popular speaker, performer, and de facto sociologist for our troubled times.

You'll notice that these examples are all of female writers. I've found there's a lot more pressure on women than there is on men to churn out personality- or issue-driven personal essays in the period leading up to their book launch. A lot of these prepub essays appear in magazines or outlets with mostly female readers: *Elle*, *Cosmopolitan*, *O, The Oprah Magazine*. When men do publish something in these glossies, it's often filtered through the lens of the female experience. The author Rumaan Alam, for example, published an essay in *Elle* before the publication of his debut *Rich and Pretty* (which tells the story of two close female friends) that ran with the headline "Can a Male Novelist Really Write, and Get, Women?"

Happily for Rumaan, he found himself enjoying the personal-essay tour of duty. "It is kind of crazy that we now expect writers to mark the occasion of having published a book by . . . writing more," he jokes. "But I do see the value in doing this, especially for a writer who is making their debut. It's wise to develop some kind of profile, to get your name out, to establish expectations for readers about who you are, what you care about, and what your sentences sound like."

He credits his agent and editor, who were extremely helpful in "making introductions to smart editors at great publications." Rumaan's experience was so positive, he has continued freelance writing in between the writing and editing of his next book, and his short-form writing helped him land a job as a special-projects editor at *The New York Times*.

"If your editor or agent want you to do something, you should at least hear them out," Rumaan suggests. "They're experts, and if they think writing an essay about how you missed your junior prom because you had chicken pox will be good for your book, then why not write the essay?"

When you're in the heat of publication, jonesing with the desire to refresh your Amazon sales ranking (don't), your mind is going to be scattered and unwell: this is not the time to think up personal-essay topics unless you can do a bunch of iterations on the question *When will I feel like myself again?* If you want to try your hand at off-the-book pieces, start brainstorming ideas and pitches during the year leading up to your publication, when you still have your wits about you. Make sure that these ideas are ones you're actually willing to turn into a full essay in case one of the editors you pitch says yes.

And on this note: you can turn down the personal-essay tour of duty. Your editorial team will probably tell you that such pieces can help contribute to a swell of buzz, but in order for that to be true, there needs to be a swell, and the pieces need to be timed right. If you resent the articles you're being asked to write before you try to write them:

abort mission. The resentment you're feeling could seep through the copy and rub readers not just the wrong way, but away from your new book.

Planning your book launch

Most book launches take place in bookstores because bookstores sell books. To the extent that this is possible, try to hold your launch in a store you actually frequent. You're bound to have a pleasant event (and boosted sales) if the booksellers already know you as a supporter of their store.

Try to keep the event simple. For my first book launch, I decided to serve individual red-and-white checkered baskets of French fries because my book had to do with France (it was a reach, I know), and it wasn't until launch day that I realized French fries get kind of limp and gross-looking when they're not served fresh out of the fryer, which wasn't possible, because I'd ordered them from this anarchist throwback hole-in-the-wall fry shop in New York's East Village that I wanted to support, and the event was in Brooklyn, so my editor, my publicist, and I had to spend the hour leading up to my book event trying to "refresh" the French fries in the apartment of someone who lived across the street from the bookstore and also was kind of famous, famous enough that I really felt like I was imposing with my French fries. Long story short, there were just too many resources diverted to those fries.

Launch with a fellow author or a moderator if you can, preferably someone who actually likes you and has a healthy social media following they will use to talk up your book and launch. This kind of strategic thinking isn't "using" people, this is real life in the literary world, where people scratch each other's backs, nicely and softly, with hand sanitizer and stuff.

If you don't have a publicist to do this for you, ask a friend to hand out Post-it Notes to the people lined up to have their books signed, and have that friend insist that everyone write their names down, even if one of those people is your mom. You will be surprised by the brain freeze that hits you when you are faced with a signing line, especially when you're feeling jittery or tired.

Send a nice note to the bookstore that hosted you thanking them for everything they're doing for your book. And continue to buy things from their store.

The prepublication e-blast

If you're an absolute nightmare when it comes to email management, the prepublication email blast might be a point of stress. I'm the kind of person who never updates any of my contacts, so when I have to send out large group emails, it's par for the course that I'm going to get hundreds of Delivery Status Notification (Failure) messages back.

But what is this email blast I speak of? It's become common practice for authors to send out a massive, digital mailing before their pub date that tells everyone whose email they could get ahold of the following information:

- That they have a book coming out
- What the name of that book is and who decided to publish it
- That they are really excited about this! Can you believe they wrote a book?
- No, but really! Did you think they had it in them? Insert name of the high-school teacher who did *not* think they had it in them. Did they show that guy or what?

- Happily though, the book exists, and they would like you to pre-order it, because preorders can really give their book needed attention in the marketplace.
- That they will be in this city and that one, and that same city again, to promote this amazing book, and that even though you don't live in any of those places, they would love to see you there
- That they are super grateful for your attention
- That you should feel free to share the above information with everyone you know!

These emails will come hyperlinked and adorned with early praise for the book in question. It's true about preorders, by the way. Hearty preorders suggest buzz or at least elevated interest in a title, which perks the ears of industry insiders right up. Strong preorders can earn a new title better placement in a bookstore, or even cause a publisher to increase a book's initial print run. But preorders can also prove that someone just has a superdedicated group of family and friends, and thus don't always indicate that a book will reach a wider net of readers, so don't conclude that your book is going to be a runaway hit based off of its preorder sales alone.

What if I die before my book comes out?

When you've worked for years on something and your dream of publishing is about to come true, the worry that your own untimely death could screw everything up might seem overblown to some people, but it won't feel that way to you.

A little-known fact: Stieg Larsson, the Swedish journalist and author of the Millennium trilogy of crime novels, received a sixty-four-thousand euro advance for his three-book pitch from his Swedish publisher. He completed his three books, and then, climbing up a set of stairs one day, he had a heart attack and died. That trilogy, which was published posthumously and consisted of *The Girl with the Dragon Tattoo, The Girl Who Played with Fire,* and *The Girl Who Kicked the Hornet's Nest,* has gone on to sell more than 90 million copies, has been adapted into a successful film and franchise empire, and has also royally messed up the lives of Larsson's loved ones because the good man was too busy writing runaway bestsellers to also pen a will.

You are probably not going to die before your book comes out. But, you know, you could. If precaution comforts you, you can take these following steps to protect your (burgeoning) literary estate:

- **Draw up a (real) will.** Use an attorney or a reputable online software program so that your last testament is legitimate and notarized. Otherwise, you've basically got a diary entry that won't hold up in court. Specify your desires for your literary inheritance. Does your agent have the right to broker deals without you? Can a ghostwriter be hired to complete one of your manuscripts? Who should receive your letters and project notes in the case of your death?
- **Keep your files organized.** Both your digital and physical workspace should be organized, labeled, and easy for other people to navigate if you plan on croaking soon. Projects under contract and manuscripts in progress should be clearly labeled, unlike my system, which involves misfiling all of my documents and giving them weird names. Save your files frequently and clearly label versions of your different drafts. I don't do any of these things right now, but I'm going to try to take my own advice. Soon.
- **Choose an understudy.** The fantasy juggernaut *Wheel of Time*

was originally planned as a twelve-book series by its author, Robert Jordan. Except Robert left us after the eleventh book. Before his death, however, he had prepared an extensive outline for his final book, and personally briefed another fantasy author, Brandon Sanderson, on how he should conclude the series in the event of his death. If there is a writer whose style and intelligence you admire, whom you would trust to finish a book for you if you weren't around to do so, let your agent know. And let that writer know, as well.

- **Revisit your book contract.** Your contract should include a clause that deals with the author-death scenario. This clause will include language about the publisher's rights to hire someone to write the book under your name, or to revise it for you in future additions, so make sure you agree with the language there, preferably *before* the contract is signed.

- **Live a little.** If you are plagued by the idea of your own death in the months leading up to your first book's publication, you're probably experiencing anxiety. And not just *anxiety* anxiety, the term that's become so fashionable for a certain kind of stress, but the real thing. Anxiety is a psychiatric disorder that can lead, among other things, to depression and panic attacks. Remember when we told you in book one to get a therapist? Did you?

II
....

PUBLICATION! (-!@#$%^&*¡:o)

Elation, doubt, despair, pervasive unease, and bolts of white-hot pride: the only thing you're *not* going to feel during your first book's publication is centered. While you were in control for much of the process up to now (you wrote the book, revised the hell out of it, and have been working hard with your agent and editor to do what's expected of you and meet all of your deadlines), on pub day, control is yanked out of your needy hands and sent away to a dicey time-share situation in the Florida Keys. It's not likely to come back.

For better or for worse, a lot of writers spend the first months of their publication trying to gauge whether their book is a success. Success means different things to different people, but many writers have been socialized to equate success with making lots of money, which most books will not do. If you can focus on the fact that you finally got the opportunity to share your art with the world (and that you might get that chance again!), and ignore how your book is doing commercially, you'll have a swell debut. But you know who's capable of doing this? NO ONE. And if you think you *are* capable, this is only because your book hasn't been published yet.

Managing expectations on (and around) pub day

True story: the first time I drove to a bookstore in a town I didn't live in for a book event, I allowed myself visions of grandeur: a throbbing parking lot. A signing line outside the door. I knew the place wouldn't be *that* packed, of course, but I honestly did think there might be some excitement. I mean, my book had gotten great reviews in important magazines. Magazines a *lot* of people read! This was going to be it, my first time as a big deal. Imagine, total strangers coming out to hear me read. From my own book!

Then I arrived at the bookshop. There was plenty of parking. Parking on the main road, parking in the lot behind the store. Like, a *lot* of spaces. And that's when it hit me. Something fairly obvious. My book had come out two days earlier. No one, even my friends, had had a chance to read it yet. Plus, I was a nobody, in that I wasn't known. Sure, I'd had stuff published in literary magazines and so forth, but never anything *big*. So who the hell was going to come out to meet a person they didn't know for an event honoring a book they hadn't read yet? Not a lot of people, as it turns out.

In the guide book *What to Do Before Your Book Launch*, authors M. J. Rose and Randy Susan Meyers suggest that only a dozen debut books break out every year, with "breaking out" defined as selling thirty thousand hardcovers or fifty thousand ebooks. The esteemed editor of *this* book says the number of literary debuts that move that many copies annually is more like five, and this book's publisher argues that it's three, but regardless of who's holding the right number, it takes a lot of sales to make a book break out.

Publishing guru Jane Friedman is of the same mind as this book's publisher. "When I'm asked by writers at conferences about how many books they should hope to sell, I tell them to expect to sell between three and five thousand copies." This is realistic and empowering advice, but these aren't numbers that you'll often hear out loud. Whether the benchmark was put into their heads by a publisher who thinks a particular book has a chance at a bestseller list, or the author put the pressure on themselves, most debut authors equate success with a sales number that only a handful will actually reach. The truth is that most debuts—regardless of genre—will perform conservatively, and *all* debuts will be disappointments if you grow attached to a sales number that is physically alpine.

When your debut isn't your debut

I was at a lecture recently that the author Simon Winchester was giving at my local library. The event organizer treated him to a heartfelt introduction, and concluded by saying how excited she was for Simon to share the unique success story behind his first book, *The Professor and the Madman*, with us.

Graciously, Simon took the stage with a slight correction. "It wasn't my first book." He smiled. "The previous nine disappeared so rapidly!"

When an author encounters breakout success with a particular book, people start to think of it as their debut, especially if they weren't familiar with the author's work before. Many readers who declare themselves diehard fans of Anthony Doerr are shocked to learn that Tony wrote *four* books before *All the Light We Cannot See*. In an interview with *Politico*, author Jami Attenberg admitted she'd had "the debut thing" happen three times. "I had a story collection . . . so then they were like, 'Okay, now it's your first novel'—and people keep saying that *this* is my debut because no one's ever heard of me before. Which was entertaining!"

Author Chloe Benjamin has adopted a special smile to use when people refer to the bestselling *The Immortalists* as her debut. "I don't want to embarrass them!" she says. "But I also feel like I've earned my stripes and want people to know I've worked hard enough to have two books out. The ingénue label can be obnoxious, you know?"

You are the ambassador for all your published projects. Make sure your previous book titles appear on your book jacket, in your author bio, and in the also-by page in the front of your new book. During book events, ask booksellers to keep a modest number of your other books on hand. Don't be snippy when people act surprised that you've published titles other than the one they're thinking of buying. Get them excited to read you. Hand-sell your own books!

Typical print runs

A print run is the initial amount of books your publisher is going to market with. The higher the number, the more confident your publisher is that the book is going to sell.

In the bygone days of publishing, print runs communicated power and prestige. Publishers would take out advertisements boasting that a new book was already in its second printing, because the standard print run for a buzzy book three decades ago was twenty thousand copies.

With technological advances, quick printing is a bottom line's best friend. It hasn't become any easier (or less awkward) if a publisher prints too many copies of a debut, but it *is* easier for publishers to get fresh copies out to a demanding market if they underestimated a book's commercial appeal.

An editor at a Big Five publisher who preferred to remain anonymous explains the delicate art of determining when to print more books: "If a book looks like it's getting traction," says this editor, "if stores are reordering frequently and regularly, the publicist books a big

PUBLICATION! (-!@#$%^&*;:o)

media hit, a celebrity posts a photo on Instagram and the book shoots up on Amazon—the publisher is able to make an educated guess about how soon the rate of sale of a book will eat through the current stock in the warehouse and can decide to order another printing(s) to make sure the book doesn't go out of stock right when momentum is hitting (our worst nightmare). And again, based on an educated guess and historical data, that next printing can be one thousand copies or it can be ten thousand. And depending on the size, it affects how soon those books can be printed, those jackets can be printed (these two units are printed at different printers), how soon these two components can hit the bindery, how soon the bindery can put them together, then ship the jacketed books to the warehouse to either wait for reorders, or to go out immediately to fill backorders from stores and wholesalers."

Improved technology (which includes not only printing techniques but the way that publisher's sales reps keep track of sales estimates from the different accounts they pitch to) mean that publishers are better positioned to get their print runs right. But warehouse pileups still happen, and it's costly when they do. Although debut authors don't usually receive big opening orders (or any orders) from big chains like Target and Costco, these accounts sometimes do decide to back a new title by a relative unknown, only to watch the title flop. Big chains have rapid turnover: if a book doesn't perform well in its first few weeks on their shelves, it might be replaced by a competing title. (It's a cruel world, writer friend. We never said it wasn't.) A literary ousting such as this could suddenly see thousands of books headed back to mama publisher. If these copies don't find new homes, and/or the author doesn't have the room, budget, or desire to live alongside six thousand remainder copies of their own project, the books are going to be pulped.

As with all the statistics in this charmingly subjective guidebook, the numbers below are offered as an example, not law. You'll find variations from house to house, but here's an idea of standard print-run margins in the industry right now:

- **Independent publisher print run for a debut with decent buzz:** From two thousand on the low end to ten thousand on the high end would be considered standard, but there are exceptions of course. One of the independent publishers we spoke with had a twenty-five thousand print run for a debut author whose memoir garnered unusual attention in the months leading up to launch. An independent press's print run will be influenced by any number of factors: What kind of audience is there for the genre? What kind of platform does the debut author have? Is the author based in America and willing and/or able to tour to support their book?

- **Midhouse publisher for a debut with decent buzz:** "Initial print runs aren't a huge indicator of success because things can change very quickly, depending on what ends up aligning for a book," says an editor at a midhouse independent who preferred to remain anonymous. "Does it get a Barnes & Noble Discover pick? Does it make the Indie Next or the ABA Indies Introduce list? Is it chosen by a big book club that will want its own kind of stock? Is it picked for a first-edition club? These things can happen six months out, three months, even two months before publication. The range is so big, I don't feel comfortable putting a number on it, but it can go from five thousand well up to twenty-five thousand, and beyond."

- **Big Five print run for a debut with a lot of buzz:** Most of the publishing professionals surveyed agreed that it was impossible to affix a true range to initial print runs because there are so many factors that can change the number as launch date approaches, but Big Five editors did say that twelve to twenty-five thousand copies was a common range.

As long as your publisher is nimble enough to print new copies quickly, a small print run can be your friend. I know a writer who published a first book with an independent publisher who scheduled an initial print run of two thousand books. A surprise selection as *People* magazine's Book of the Week drove demand out the wazoo, and her publisher was able to print a bunch more copies quickly. Her book's surprise success also meant that she earned back her advance way faster than expected. Win-win for everyone!

How many books does my publisher want me to sell?

So much emotional attention is devoted to advances, writers often overlook (read: forget to stress about) a more actionable question: How many books does your publisher hope you'll sell?

Most publishers don't expect you to earn back the entirety of your advance. In fact, many houses would be pleased if you earned back 70 percent of what was given you, as we mentioned in the Before the Book Deal section on advances. But *all* houses hope you'll sell through your initial print run. If a publisher overpaid for an author's debut, that often results in a happy author who feels like someone has invested in her career and in her talent. But if a publisher overshoots a print run, they'll have thousands of unsold books taking up warehouse space.

Using the same delineations as above, here's what select editors consider successful sales numbers for a debut novel:

- **Independent publisher sales for a debut with decent buzz:** A veteran indie publisher who preferred to remain anonymous said they considered five thousand copies a successful sales number for a debut. "Anything under two thousand I would consider a disappointment. Anything over eight thousand I would consider a hit." Another independent publisher who also preferred to remain anonymous echoes these same sentiments: "For a debut, we'd like to get near five thousand copies total sold, print and ebooks combined."

- **Midhouse publisher sales for a literary debut with decent buzz:** A third industry veteran agreed that there are so many factors at play that it's hard to cite a number, but for this particular editor, ten thousand copies "would feel really good."

- **Big Five sales for a literary debut with a lot of buzz:** A Big Five editor who similarly preferred anonymity said that although it really depends on the advance, recently the market has been tough, so she personally breathes easier when hardcover sales reach fifteen thousand.

These numbers shouldn't imply that smaller presses only sell five thousand copies of a given book, and big publishers fifteen thousand. "The playing field is a lot more level than that," explains one of our anonymous independent publishers. "Although the Big Five do have an advantage. Their marketing budgets are generally higher, and they have a dedicated sales force who sell their books to bookstores—while independent presses often share a distributor with many other small publishers, with those sales reps dividing their energy across hundreds of titles."

Reading your reviews

There are writers out there who think there is a benefit in reading their Amazon and Goodreads reviews, but we're not going to hear from them because I won't let them talk. Give a little thought to this. How do you spend the rare free time that you have? Do you sit around on a Sunday and think, You know what, I really love my garlic press. It's such an efficient little machine, it's high time I tell the world how much I appreciate all it does. Let me take to the Internet and leave a five-star review of my garlic press. Now my day has really started!

Maybe you're that person. A lot of people are. There's a particular brand of garlic press on Amazon right now that has 693 reviews. But it's human nature—most people don't take to online review forums unless they need to kvetch.

Will you find some glowing reviews of your book online that will warm your soul and encourage you to persevere in publishing? Yes. Will the misspelled, hastily written, and completely dismissive reviews ("I just don't like the title so I'm giving it one star") vastly outnumber the raves? Yes. Will it be the nasty reviews that gnaw at you when you sit down to write something new instead of the nice things that people have said? Obvs.

Listen, writers are already engaged in a totally sedentary activity that will never give us health insurance; do we need to make it even harder by reading other people's gripes?

Read your trade reviews. Read your reviews in magazines. In short, read the reviews of *professional* reviewers. Do not read the reviews of overcaffeinated strangers who just want to vent online.

Understanding (and then never looking at) your Amazon sales ranking

Nestled within the product details of your book on Amazon is a volatile beast known as the Amazon Bestsellers Rank that purportedly tracks how your book is doing—hourly—compared with other books in the same category.

If you're interested in sucking all of the joy out of your book launch, this is the place for you. Watch your numbers go up and down! Watch as your writer friends surpass you! Watch when the media hit you just got doesn't make your number move at all!

For neurotic and competitive people (which none of us are, right?), the Amazon sales ranking can make you feel like you know how your book is performing in the marketplace. But for these same neurotic and competitive people (none of us, again), it can open a veritable vat of worms that will chew up your optimism and self-worth.

The problem is, if you can check your sales rank, you can check someone else's. And because the sales rankings are updated hourly, you could do this every hour for the rest of your book's life.

A lot of us have fallen victim to the Pavlovian cycle of rank-checking, looking for a sign of hope we don't always find. A friend of mine couldn't get away from it, even when her novel hit *The New York Times* bestseller list. "The book was at the height of its sales," she said (let's call her Franca), "and I had this intense anxiety that it was going to slip. I had all this fear about that and it was making me stressed out. When it's good, it's bad, and when it's ho-hum, it's also bad."

At her worst, Franca was checking her ranking each time she was at her computer, about fifteen times a day. "What finally made me stop," she admits, "was when the number seemed so low (high?) that I burst into tears and it wrecked an otherwise good day where I was getting positive feedback about my novel, doing events, etc. I don't even remember what the number was now!"

If you absolutely must check your sales ranking, try keeping it to one day a week, or only check when you've scored a big media hit, and are thus more likely to see a change in your ranking, and are thus more likely to feel good about yourself.

And just like we did with the national bestseller lists, let's get these ranking numbers in perspective. On the website MakeUseOf, tech writer Rob Nightingale breaks the Amazon sales rankings down into ranges that suggest how many books you move per day. I'm using his numbers, but the prose is mine:

> **A ranking of 50,000 to 100,000:** You're selling a book a day. You've got a fan out there!
>
> **10,000 to 50,000:** You're selling between five and fifteen books a day, congrats!
>
> **5,500 to 10,000:** Excellent work! You're moving around twenty-five books a day!
>
> **750 to 1,500:** Whoa there, hot shot. Leave some sales for someone else! You're selling more than a hundred books a day!
>
> **1 to 5:** Hi there, Liz Gilbert! You've moved four thousand books today!

Now that you have this information, forget it, and never, ever, ever check your sales ranking again.

My book's sales are sluggish. Should I crawl under a rock and die?

In the pre-Internet days of publishing, readers had to rely on print reviews and word of mouth to find out which books were trendy. Bookstagrammers weren't uploading pics of the hot new YA title next to a matcha latté; holiday spirit was still possible in December because you weren't getting punched in the ear every hour by a new best-of list; your envy monster couldn't feed on pictures of authors #grateful-ing all over their social media for the accolades you wanted and they got.

Today, it is painfully easy to observe how a book is doing (or how you think it's doing) in real time. You hear the phrase "That book is *everywhere*": people are tweeting and Facebooking about them; tastemakers tout them on morning talk shows; the books make all the roundups, they're shortlisted for every prize.

This tempest of activity can make the authors of the books who aren't "getting all the things" assume that their book isn't selling, isn't being read. The online noise, in particular, has contributed to a phenomenon we touched on earlier: the impression that your book has a finite amount of time to shine or die.

"I really hope that for all of our books, we're not publishing just for the initial hardcover publication, and that's that," says Elisabeth Schmitz, vice president and editorial director at Grove Atlantic, who believes all their books have the potential for a long and healthy life. "You do need to get over this hump idea of 'I've got six weeks on the shelves and then it's done.' I don't believe in that."

Elisabeth has earned a reputation for supporting books whose audiences take time to gather; she goes after the long-term slow burns— not the flashes in the pan. "We're not built to do crash, of-the-moment books," she says. "We aren't set up to do that the way the big houses can. We have books that burst out of the gate and books that percolate and can take time to build."

One example is Dani Shapiro's writing guide and ode to creativity, *Still Writing*. "This is a book with a very long tail," Elisabeth points out. "It didn't hit the bestseller list, but it's now a mainstay of our backlist." Another example is *Peace Like a River* by Leif Enger, a book that had the unfortunate release date of September 11, 2001. "Obviously, it wasn't quite the launch that we expected for our lead fiction title of the season. He got bumped from all sorts of media, his tour wasn't what it would have been." But Elisabeth—and Grove—stood by the book, and the word of mouth about it grew, and never stopped. The book has sold more than a million copies to date and earned its author a devoted following. *History of Wolves* by Emily Fridlund and *Euphoria* by Lily King are two novels that enjoyed exceptional reviews and very good sales early in their respective publishing years, but it was later in their autumn seasons when the best-books-of-the-year lists and prize short lists were released that the books' sales picked up steam again.

"For me, it's never over. It just isn't," says Elisabeth. "First of all, you have the paperback. That's an opportunity to relaunch it. If it doesn't work at the hardcover, we'll change the jacket for the paperback, publish the paperback earlier than usual, and try a different marketing approach. If a book is really good, it's going to last and work somehow. Anything can happen. Books have such long lives! It could win a big prize. Someone with a following could discover it in a bookstore— Reese Witherspoon could pick it for her book club, you could win an award for the jacket art, the book could be optioned, or the film could finally come out. There are so many ways to bring attention to a book latterly. I never believe a book is done."

In my opinion, the best way to weather the rocky period after your book's release is by writing something new, but you have to get your feet under you in order to do that. That's why it's so important to establish your own definition of success before your book comes out—a benchmark you can meet on your own terms, a goal that isn't dependent on how other people's books perform.

You might come into the publishing game thinking that success looks and sounds like one thing, when in fact it ends up being something completely different. After the publication hullabaloo has died down and there is time to reflect, many authors find that the notes they received from readers, the conversations they had with people at bookstores, the proof they were given that their work touched someone, this was what ended up being the most meaningful. More than the prizes that they did or didn't get (because most people do not get them), it was these human interactions that made them want to write again.

Set a realistic and somewhat realizable definition of what success will be for you. It should not be "making a bestseller list." We're about to find out why.

Will your book be a bestseller?

Most people wouldn't run a race without knowing how many miles they had to cover, but lots of authors nurture hopes of making a bestseller list without having an idea of how many books they'll need to sell to hit one.

The tricky thing about determining bestseller numbers is that they're relative to how other books are selling nationwide per week. If you have a book coming out in a traditionally slow book-selling month, like February, the competition's steep, but not as steep as, say, July. If the big books are selling four thousand copies a week, and your book is timely, you might very well be able to match those numbers and make it onto a list.

But in a busier reading period, like summer, the big books might be selling upward of eighty thousand books a week. If you're a debut author and no one's heard of you before, that's an *awful* lot of sales to match!

Let's take an example from another season. Here are the amounts of books you'd have to sell to hit these lists' number-one spot for new hardcover fiction the week of November 26, 2017:

The New York Times: 76,748 copies

USA Today: 76,748 copies (same book. Yep.)

The Los Angeles Times: 52,201

It's worth noting that for all of the above lists, the number-five spot went to books selling in between nine thousand and sixteen thousand copies a week. That's more than sixty thousand books fewer than the number-one spot-holder. But even pushing nine thousand hardcovers a week is a *tremendous* number of books. You'll understand just how many books that is when you spend five hours in a car to drive to a book event where you sell only three.

Anyone who works in publishing will tell you—off the record— that the bestseller lists are a game of smoke and mirrors. This is especially true for *The New York Times* list, whose calculations are heavily weighted by sales in *New York Times*–reporting bookstores, which not all bookstores are. Accordingly, bestseller lists are not always true reflections of how a book ranks on a given week, nor of how many copies a book is actually selling.

Earning the right to claim that your book is a "national bestseller" is equally opaque. "There are no set guidelines," says an editor at an independent press who preferred to remain anonymous. "But there is a rule of thumb: you have to appear on two or more national lists such as *The Washington Post, Los Angeles Times*, or *USA Today*."

Just like with the national print bestseller lists, the "national bestseller" label gives a leg up to the book and its author, cachet-wise, but it's certainly not a guarantee of continued sales, nor is it a true reflection of the book's success. "A lot of books are national bestsellers that don't sell as well as other books that aren't 'national bestsellers,'" admits our anonymous editor. "Often they are sold-in very smartly in a specific week, in a specific region. You could have a book that sells six or five thousand copies that makes the national bestseller list and another that sells twenty thousand copies, but doesn't, because of how it was sold-in."

You can have a healthy and happy career as a published author without coming anywhere close to making a bestseller list. If you *do* make one of these lists, it's true that you get to keep the moniker "bestselling author" forever and always, which is both impressive and persuasive on book jackets, but it's important for writers to remember that the "bestselling" accolade doesn't necessarily mean that a book is a long-term success. Sometimes a book hits a bestseller list one week, and sales cliff dive after that, and the book doesn't actually end up having a successful shelf life after its bestselling peak.

Most writers will not have bestsellers. Most writers do not write them. In order to preserve the joy you get from writing, remember that there is real value to what publishers call "the slow burn." Sustained interest and healthy sales over a long period of time can be just as valuable (sometimes more so) than an initial sales frenzy and crickets after that.

Steady Eddys are real assets to book publishing. There should be a list for them!

How to get your book to book clubs
....

In a later section about people who borrow your book instead of buying it (and why that is sometimes okay), we'll learn how the Canadian author Kathleen Grissom's *The Kitchen House* hit *The New York Times* bestseller list eighteen months *after* its publication, but the teaser is that it had a lot to do with Kathleen's participation in book clubs.

If you're not in a book club yourself, you might not know where to find the good people who are. Below are some ideas for getting book clubs to consider you, all of which require stamina. Book-clubbers prioritize engagement, so don't promote your book to clubs unless you have the time and energy to show them some love back.

Up your discoverability

Book clubs are more likely to reach out to authors who have made their enthusiasm for book-clubbing clear. Broadcast your availability on your website, in your author bio, in a prominent place on your book jacket, in the signature of your email. Many paperback editions feature reading-group guides that you can include on your author website: if this isn't planned for your book, consider adding question prompts to your author website or blog.

Once book-club members have found you, give them an action to take. A digital book-club request form makes it easy for members to contact you, without giving away your personal email address. Some authors include recipes for cocktails, mocktails, and family-style foods to be paired with their books on their website, a consideration that members might be wooed by. On the web page for her debut novel, *Number One Chinese Restaurant*, author Lillian Li includes a recipe for her father's sweet-and-sticky spare ribs for six people, with tips to double (or triple) the recipe for larger groups.

Find your (book club) tribes

Bookstores, local libraries, and book-club bloggers can point you to book clubs; websites like OnlineBookClub, Meetup, LibraryThing, Goodreads, and Book Club Cookbook can be helpful, too. If you're not in a book club yourself, ask your friends who are. Do they know anyone running a club who might be interested in your book? Keep copies on hand for club organizers who aren't familiar with your writing. Some bookstores will offer discounts to local book-club members: politely inquire whether your favorite bookstore does.

Get technical about it

Few authors have the time or budget to travel more than a short distance to visit with book clubs, which is why video call-ins are a great option for writers who want to up their visibility without breaking the bank. In the summer of 2014, the author Nomi Eve posted on Facebook about her 100 Book Club Challenge, writing that she aimed to meet with a hundred book clubs that year. When all was said and done, Nomi met with thirty clubs online and a whopping seventy in person, but video-calling definitely simplified her life. "As the mother of three children," she wrote for *Publishers Weekly* on the topic, "I love how Skype allows me to be at home at bedtime and still be able to be with a book club. Skype book-club visits generally only take around forty-five minutes, and all I have to do is brush my hair and change into a decent top and I'm camera ready."

If you haven't used it recently (or ever), run a test-call before your book-club date. Nothing sours that book club vino like a frozen call.

Be a shutterbug

In the *Publishers Weekly* essay about her book-club challenge, Nomi credits the success of it to the photos that she shared after each event on social media. "The photos helped create connections and spread the word," Nomi explains. "Even book clubs that I didn't visit posted their own photos of when they discussed my book, just so that they could also be a part of my challenge."

Photos are a great way to broadcast your enthusiasm for book-club appearances, and they can go a long way toward reassuring other club members that you will behave well in their house.

Engage even the naysayers

I've done enough book clubs by this point to identify the members who didn't like my book. (Generally, they look like they are sucking on a lozenge made of tar.) Instead of ignoring their discomfort and letting their energy permeate the room, I try—as warmly as possible—to invite them to share their hesitations with the group. Maybe I'm a masochist, but I think a reader's dislikes make for a lively debate. After all, it's rarely as simple as "I just didn't like it." Usually, the reader's disappointment has something to do with character development, a topic in the book that was given too much or too little attention, or pure personal taste. In a 2010 interview with BookBrowse, the librarian Terye Balogh argued that the author's presence is a great way to reorient the book's detractors. "I have seen instances where a visit by an author has completely transformed readers' perceptions of the book," Terye says. "A book that they may have thought of as unbelievable, or a subject too sad, suddenly becomes a book that they adore and cherish."

Handling people who just don't get it

In the early days of your book's promotion, you'll meet good-natured people who will tell you that they just can't wait to read your book, but they are in fact waiting for someone to return it to the library, or that they loved your book so much, they lent their copy to their aunt. What you're going to hear from this confession is that you lost a book sale:

this person, for whatever reason, just isn't going to spring to actually buy your book.

Stress over book sales will ebb and flow during your book's shelf life, but it's important to remember that most readers don't think about book sales. They're interested in the *experience* of reading: they want to learn something, be surprised or shocked, they want a book to bring them joy. If it brought them happiness, it's not only natural but encouraging that they'd want to share that positive experience with someone else. That's how books build buzz!

Let's revisit the publishing experience of author Kathleen Grissom, whose debut novel, *The Kitchen House*, was published as a paperback original for a modest advance, and slowly, thanks in part to the author's tenacious energy and emotional generosity, became a bookclub favorite. "We were watching the sales go from five books a week to fifty," says Grissom's agent Rebecca Gradinger (who is also—fun fact!—mine). "Then five hundred a week. Then *three thousand*." The book gained so much buzz, readers didn't want to wait for the book to return to the library, or for someone to lend it to them; they absolutely had to buy it for themselves.

This slow and steady interest turned into a firestorm. *The Kitchen House* hit *The New York Times* bestseller list after it had already been out as a paperback original for two and a half years. And it stayed on the list an entire year. The point of this anecdote is to have faith in your readers. Be thankful (and happy!) that they liked your book enough to share it with someone else. Word of mouth is priceless, a form of marketing you can't buy, and it's also the most trusted way that readers find new books.

As for the readers you encounter who tell you they only get books from libraries (and thus will be waiting for yours to return to circulation), don't shrug off these readers, and do not hate on libraries! Public libraries are book buyers also, and when they get behind a book, their influence can be mighty. Booksellers, from independents to chain stores, pay a ton of attention to *Library Reads,* a publication that alerts the reading community to American librarians' top-ten picks every month, and it's not unheard of for libraries with hefty circulation to buy up to seventy copies of a leading title. (Recently, a reader reported to me that his local library in Wentsville, Missouri, had seventeen copies of Tayari Jones's *An American Marriage* out—and all seventeen of them were already on hold. Too impatient to wait, he bought himself a copy.) Most hardcovers can only be circulated twelve times before they need to be replaced for wear and tear, so a frequently read book is one that will need to be repurchased, which means another sale for you.

Why aren't my friends saying anything about my book?

So this really weird thing happens when you have a book out. Sometimes total strangers are more vocal about having read and enjoyed it than your own family and friends. I don't think I found out for a full year that my father (who never reads) had actually *enjoyed* my first book, and I found out from his wife, not him. With my second book, I finally cracked six months after its pub date and asked my closest friend if he had read it because he never said a word about it himself. I thought these unpleasant experiences might be unique to me, or that I had B-level acquaintances, but other authors admitted that their nearest and dearest weren't just cagey during their book's publication; some of them were downright hostile.

One writer told me that her own sister, who is a designer, and thus also in a creative line of work, went indecent with jealousy after her author sister (let's call her Lara) published her first book. She went out of her way to not like anything Lara posted about her book on social media, and she derailed a book club that Lara had been invited to (that the sister was already a part of) by changing topics any time someone tried to talk about Lara's book, which was awkward because, you know, it was a *book* club.

Another author suffered through her family's total silence about her book's publication until her brother delivered a backhand compliment about it at the pulpit during their mother's funeral.

So what is going on here? What's up with your friends? The author Tom McAllister has a hilarious essay called "Who Will Buy Your Book?" on *The Millions* in which he answers: not your stupid family. "Before I ever published anything," Tom writes in that essay, "I'd assumed that if I ever finished a book, there would be so much demand from family and friends alone that we'd have to go into a second printing before the release date. But I am here to tell you: most people in your family will never buy your book. Most of your friends won't either."

What gives? Where's the love and generosity? Where's the *R-E-S-P-E-C-T*? It takes such a long time to write and publish a book, it's not like you're asking people to buy a new book every month! ("Relative to the amount of time and anxiety you devote to the project," Tom writes in his essay, "you're really not asking for much.")

Sometimes latent jealousy can be a factor in a friend or family member's perceived snub. After all, it can be threatening to watch someone realize a long-held dream. Even if you are in completely different industries from the friend in question, your success could make them feel like they're not working hard enough to reach their own goals, or perhaps they're worried that every social interaction is going to be about you from now on. It's also a possibility that you're being a pain in the butt about the whole thing. You must always consider the possibility that you are the problem when it comes to publishing.

Jealousy, resentment, a lack of time for reading, all this can play into the loved-ones-not-talking-about-your-book thing, but often it's more innocent than that. Some people simply don't know how to talk to authors about their books. One friend told me she thought it might be "condescending" to tell me that she liked it. That she assumed I knew she did. First of all, we all know what happens to people who assume things, and secondly, you should never underestimate how frequently and fervently writers need to be reminded of their genius.

Books are personal—literally. They're usually written by one person, sometimes two. Accordingly, unlike a film, where responsibility for the magic is spread across a fleet of technicians and professionals, readers assign the burden of their enjoyment solely to the writer. Sure, there were a lot of people behind the scenes who helped to get your book out, but most readers aren't going to compliment you on the quality of your typesetting. Discussing a book with its author is an oppressive prospect—where do you hide your reservations? You can't pivot to discussing the lighting or the cinematography, and wasn't it charming how the stylist fixed up that one actor's hair? . . . There's just the book, the book, the cloister of the book. Even if someone loved it—everything about it!—they might not know how to discuss what they enjoyed in a way that will feel "literary" for you. They might be worried about disappointing you with their feedback, even if it's praise. Be generous with these people. If they bought your book, they're already being a good friend.

If it's really bugging you that a friend hasn't said anything about your magnum opus, you might as well buck up and ask if they've read it. Do note, however, that if your friendship can't survive them not having (1) ever purchased it, or (2) enjoyed it, maybe this is a conversation you don't need to have.

So what do you do with the bad feelings? The resentment, the neediness, the impression that your friends don't actually like you if they don't buy your book? Start by reminding yourself of all the ways these people *have* showed up for you, and if that exercise doesn't go well, flip the tables and consider how infrequently you show up for them. "I admit to having felt betrayed by my friends' indifference," writes Tom in *The Millions*, "especially after the first book, but I remind myself that I do the same thing all the time. I have friends in bands that I haven't seen live in years. I've never been to any friends' improv shows. I skip a lot of readings, even when I know the readers. I have friends with books I haven't bought or read. I have explicitly lied to colleagues about having read and enjoyed their books. The book industry is partly kept afloat by a shadow economy in which the main currency is bullshit."

The takeaway here is that you are probably going to need to attend more improv if you want to sell your books.

When Trump happens to you

No matter how much forethought your editorial team puts into your book's release date, even powerful publishers can't control what Mother Nature and/or shameless dictators do the week your book comes out.

Superstorms wreak havoc on book distribution. Beloved bookstores flood. "Bomb cyclones" see launch parties cancelled; hopeful galleys end up in a snowmelt on an influential author's stoop, costing an unlucky newbie a blurb. It turns out that snow, rain, heat, and gloom of night *can*, in fact, stay your book from slaying. So can botched presidential elections. So can death.

In 2001, author Mike Magnuson's editor at HarperCollins passed away unexpectedly, just when Mike was in the heat of prepublication for his buzzy humor book, *Lummox: The Evolution of Man*. Mike had been close with his editor, and the sudden loss was devastating, but Mike had a string of fall appearances booked on influential television shows like the *Today Show* and *The Man Show*, and he felt like the best way to honor his late editor was to keep the momentum up.

The editor's funeral was on September 10, 2001. Funerals are never a happy occasion, but on September 11, this particular loss was compounded by a national tragedy. Needless to say, none of Mike's shows ever taped, and when *Lummox* finally published, Mike's lighthearted tale of a twentysomething man-boy slacking around Wisconsin failed to resonate with a nation roiled in grief.

Similarly, all signs pointed to go for author D. Foy's second novel, *Patricide*, which had started to garner attention far beyond what its independent publisher, Stalking Horse Press, had anticipated for its October 2016 launch. "It was released to pretty snappy fanfare," D. remembers of the novel's publication. "In some parts of the lit world, it was even considered a 'most anticipated book.' On publication, it began to receive shiny reviews. Things were going as well as I could hope for. I began, almost, to have expectations."

On November 8, 2016, the buzz abruptly stopped. For authors like D., in the middle of a book's promotion, the news of Trump's victory felt like "a cosmic hoax had been executed on the world at large, one to which not a single person could reconcile themselves."

Reviews that had been promised never came to fruition. Interview opportunities fell through giant cracks. "From November 9 up into January 2017, I heard not a peep about my book," D. says. "While I could have taken this personally, I didn't, if simply because what had happened was happening to just about every work of fiction published at that time. The only books I knew that folks were reading were *Brave New World* and *1984*."

For authors who have the misfortune to publish during a presidency that facilitates an anti-intellectual atmosphere hostile to both writers and the reading public, relying on—and collaborating with—your literary community can be an emotional salve.

Author Tobias Carroll was booked for a slew of group readings to promote his novel *Reel* and short-story collection *Transitory* the weeks following Trump's contested election. Happily, Tobias was able to find mental strength in numbers. "There was a pretty amazingly large crowd for one of our events, which I wasn't expecting," Tobias says. "I think it was comprised partially of people who were curious about or familiar with our work, partially of locals who wanted to support art in their community, and partially people looking for art as a catharsis as a response to the events of the previous week. So that was refreshing; it felt like a community in the way that not all readings do."

It's not a good look to bemoan the way a national disaster hijacked your book sales, especially when the emergency cost other people their loved ones, their homes, their sense of safety, their own lives. This being said, a book takes a lot of time to write, and it's hard to accept that its success might have been affected by events you couldn't control.

Regardless of what threw your launch off course, you'll feel infinitely better and more empowered focusing on the positive things that could still come to pass for your book rather than the sea of missed opportunities behind you. You can pitch yourself and simpatico writers for festivals, conferences, and lecture series (or try to hire a speaking agent to do this if you have an elevated platform). You can send the book to influential readers who might connect to your book's message. You can start a literary support group with other authors who got screwed by timing. (My second novel came out during the first summer of Trump's presidency when people were still glued to the news cycle, and my agent liked to joke about renting a Winnebago for all the other women novelists whose summer books had suffered with a big mural painted on its side that said AMERICA: ARE YOU READING YET?)

You can fight to get your book to readers by remaining active in the literary community and continuing to publish online and in print. You can also #resist by writing a new book. Don't forget that sometimes it is an author's third or fourth book that brings readers to their first.

It's worth mentioning that books can still flourish despite—and sometimes *thanks* to—turbulent times. Carmen Maria Machado's award-winning debut collection of queer stories, *Her Body and Other Parties*, took off like wildfire in 2017 and kept burning through 2018 despite the veritable shitstorm that the news cycle was raining around the world. Rebecca Traister's *Good and Mad: The Revolutionary Power of Women's Anger* and Soraya Chemaly's *Rage Becomes Her* both launched in the fall of 2018 when the Kavanaugh hearings saw women across America looking for empowering ways to brandish their rage.

When good books gain momentum because of negative events, authors get apprehensive about their right to share book news. Obviously, you want to be attuned to the cultural and political environment that your book is coming out in, but you don't have to choose between being political and being a writer. "Art is a way of engaging with the world," says writer and disability activist Emma Smith-Stevens, "it produces heightened empathy and even motivation to reflect inward, and promotes a sense of human connection that compels us to act. Nothing related to spreading the word about creative work is beside the point."

Debuting after forty

Like almost every industry except, perhaps, insurance, publishing is obsessed with youth. The twenty-four-year-old ingénue whose six-hundred-page doorstopper earned them a million-dollar advance is the literary equivalent of the world's next supermodel being discovered on a beach.

"Aging is funny in a not-funny way most of the time," says author Amy Brill, who debuted when she was the ancient age of forty-two. "Sagging this, fading that, ha! But within the arts in particular, youth worship is particularly galling. Art cooks slow. Once in a while you get a Zadie Smith or a Jonathan Safran Foer who, at twentysomething, is just on fire, a five-star sauté."

The ageism in publishing even comes accompanied with awards. The National Book Foundation has been running its 5 Under 35 list for over a decade, the New York Public Library's Young Lions Fiction Award goes to writers under thirty-five, and there are thirty-under-thirty lists a-go-go in such publications as *BuzzFeed* and *Forbes*.

So what's a broken-down, used-up, geriatric debut writer to do? Happily, writers are pushing back against the literary cult of youth, a fetish, by the way, that has absolutely nothing to do with the reality of the craft: writing is one of the rare careers that many people can practice into an advanced age. This isn't true of other creative professions, like pole-dancing or ballet.

Author Lisa Ko's award-winning debut, *The Leavers*, came out when she was forty-one years old, about seven years after she started writing it. In 2014, she set herself a goal of receiving fifty rejections a year in order to make sure that she was getting her work out there. On a lark, she submitted her novel in progress to the prestigious PEN/Bellwether Prize for Socially Engaged Fiction. Clever woman, she went to the Bahamas without her cell phone after this submission, and only found out on her return that Barbara Kingsolver had been trying to reach her all week to let her know she'd won the $25,000 prize. *The Leavers* went on to garner major accolades, including being a finalist for the National Book Award for fiction.

In an interview for *Flavorwire*, Lisa credits the superpower of "saying no to things" with getting her novel finished while working other jobs. "Finding time to write was more about getting to the point where I believed I deserved to have time to write," she said. "I also read interviews with writers who took a long time to write their first books, who were in their forties, who weren't wealthy or being financially supported by anyone else. It helped to know that I wasn't alone, and that there's not one right way to be a writer."

As for Amy Brill, she found that her age actually helped mitigate the stress of having a debut out in the world. "By the time I finished my first novel," she explains, "I was forty years old, with a three-year-old daughter and another on the way. My friendships had been cemented by decades; my marriage was strong; I knew who I was and what my priorities were. So in many ways, it was a gift to come into the world, tender as a foal, with this, my first public creative offering, as I approached middle age. I still had my insecurities—who doesn't?—but they were muted by the fact that the things that really mattered in my life were already crawling around on my living room floor, hitting it with a wooden spoon. I didn't have time to stew in doubt or party too hard to function. I had to be very precise with my energy before it ran out at 11:00 p.m. More importantly, I think my age allowed me to take both the success and failures that followed with a little more perspective. I didn't have time to freak out about who made the top ten, top hundred. Fifty Under Fifty, you say? Bring it."

Dealing with disappointment

Regardless of what's disappointing you, stewing in negativity and would-have-should-have-could-haves isn't going to help your book's performance. I'm of the mind that you should give your book a healthy amount of stage time, but when the curtain needs to close, don't stand between the drapes.

Your publishing team can help you identify the things you can do to try to rekindle public interest in your project, but you shouldn't make saving your failed book the goal of your entire life. Set a period of time—maybe three months—during which you will hustle for your book, and then graciously move on.

If you're coming off of a disappointing sales experience, it might be hard to sink into the writing of a new project—you might be filled with doubt. Now is the time to read. Immerse yourself in the love of storytelling that made you want to be a writer in the first place. Find strength in literary citizenship: blurb more books than you normally do. Send respectful fan letters to writers and journalists you admire. Go to readings, buy books from bookstores, buy people's books at readings. Subscribe to some new literary magazines. Share photos of books you're enjoying (or excited to read) on social media. Leave positive reviews on Amazon and Goodreads. Be the good you want to see in the book world, and let your love of reading and writing bolster you until you just can't wait to write.

My publisher turned down my second manuscript. What now?

There are many reasons why your publisher might turn down your second manuscript. Perhaps your sophomore project touches upon the same themes as your first book, and your first book underperformed, so the publisher doesn't have the confidence they need to feel like they can support your work again. Perhaps the manuscript is either too commercial, or not commercial enough, for their particular imprint. Maybe it represents a genre that they don't usually sell. Perhaps the manuscript is such a hot mess that your editor doesn't feel up to the task of getting it into publishable shape. Maybe there was friction between you and your publishing team, and they're not keen to work with you again.

Other times, your publisher might offer to purchase your second project, but for less than you would like. This happened to author Chloe Benjamin (with whom, in the spirit of disclosure, I shared an editor for my first two books). Chloe wrote a candid essay for *Poets & Writers* about the peculiar journey of her second novel, in which she explained her conviction that she was sitting on a manuscript that was worth more than the modest advance her original publisher offered her. "It wasn't just that I hoped for more money so that I could build a more sustainable life as a writer," Chloe explained. "I also knew I'd written a novel that was better than my first. Just as my agent was my advocate, I had to be my book's advocate, and I didn't want to foreclose the chance of finding a publishing house that felt as strongly about it as I did." Chloe amicably parted ways with her first publisher, freeing her to seek another editor. Her instincts proved correct. *The Immortalists*, her second novel, was fought over at auction and eventually earned Chloe an advance generous enough for her to leave her day job.

Sometimes there is a happy medium to be reached with your publisher regarding the project you're trying to pitch. An author I know (whom we will call Charlie) always imagined her debut novel as the first book in a trilogy, although it wasn't sold as such. Secretly, though, she continued thinking of—and writing—her second novel as a sequel. This came as news to her publisher when she tried to sell it on proposal. "We pitched it to the publisher a month before my debut was released.

They came back to say that they couldn't take on the sequel, which was crushing," Charlie admits. "They did offer a lot of encouragement, though, saying that they were committed to my career as a writer, offering suggestions as to how I could make the sequel more of a standalone novel, and strongly reassured me that they wanted to publish my next book; it just had to be something different."

Publication does not always beget publication. This is a hard truth to learn. There is a reality that exists in which your second project doesn't find a home, even if your first book was well-received, well-reviewed, etc. Most writers have been writing long enough by the time they secure a book deal that they're used to rejection, it's a familiar location for them, it's the place they lounge. The chummier you are with rejection, the easier it is to remember all the times you decided to keep writing anyway, despite the nos, the not-reallys, the just-not-right-for-us-at-this-times. Writers are persistent. And kind of mulish. The world tells us they don't want our material, and we refuse to agree.

Dealing with success

When it's coming at you full force—especially if it's unexpected—success is in fact a situation that you need a game plan for.

Writer, editor, and cultural critic Roxane Gay was already an accomplished and prolific writer before her first essay collection, *Bad Feminist*, became a *New York Times* bestseller in 2014. In the years since, she published two other bestsellers, started a Black Panther comic-book series with Ta-Nehisi Coates for Marvel, became a contributing opinion writer at *The New York Times*, edited anthologies, toured extensively, sold a major two-book deal, remained engaged with her 500,000-plus

Twitter followers, *and* continued teaching English at Purdue University. Does she sleep? Not really.

Roxane hasn't even had time to figure out how to keep up with her achievements. "In terms of coping with success, I am still trying to figure that out," she says. At the time of writing, Roxane has a research assistant handling her professional Facebook presence, while Roxane manages her own email and Twitter. She has a hearty publicity team to support her: two publicists at HarperCollins, one at Grove Atlantic, and one at Marvel, along with two speaking agents who handle all the travel and booking logistics related to her numerous speaking engagements, but finding a day-to-day personal assistant is a challenge because Roxane's personal voice is such an integral part of her brand. "I'm a control freak," she admits. "So I need to allow myself to take full advantage of an assistant once I hire one. It's a little overwhelming how much nonwriting work comes with writing success."

Anthony Doerr already had four books under his belt when his second novel, *All the Light We Cannot See,* set the reading world on fire. When asked how he initially handled the attention, he said, "I was so convinced it was all going to go away the next day, and I'd go back to being the guy who showed up to a Barnes & Noble in Tampa to read to eleven people with a really loud cappuccino machine roaring in the background."

In the beginning, Tony tried to answer all of his electronic and written correspondence from fans. "I was determined to be grateful for every reader and every postcard," he says. "And I am! But it gets to a point where you're just not physically capable of doing that."

Tony thought about hiring an assistant, but he never did. Instead, he came up with policies to help him decide, quickly, what opportunities to say no to. "For blurb requests, I only give them if you've been a student of mine in the past," he explains. "For correspondence, I always write back if it's a kid." Tony tries to accept speaking engagements that won't require him to spend too much time away from his family, and, reluctantly, he's had to make it harder for people to get to him.

"I changed my personal email about seven months in," he says. His website lists contacts for his publicist and lecture agent, so there are multiple barriers to entry before he sees any requests.

Film and TV options

Film and TV options can come at any point during a book's life cycle. Sometimes a project is so exciting, optioning starts before the book is even written, on a pitch alone. Other times, books are optioned when their book deal is announced publicly, or after a book has started to perform well in the marketplace. And there are tons of examples of books whose interest from Hollywood came years after they were written: Annie Proulx published the short story "Brokeback Mountain" in *The New Yorker* in 1997. The film version came out in 2005. Michael Punke wrote the novel *The Revenant* in 2002, and the film came out in 2015. Margaret Atwood published *The Handmaid's Tale* in 1985, and it became a hit television show in 2017.

True to its definition, an *option* means that someone—usually a production company or a director—is purchasing the option to turn your writing into something else. The most common options are for either feature-film or television adaptations, but books are also optioned for musicals, theatrical productions, and short films. So are articles. So are podcasts. Writer, hope abounds!

Many of the big agencies like William Morris Endeavor, United

Talent Agency, or Creative Artists Agency will try to attach in-house talent to a project for competitive purposes, a practice known as "packaging." For an author watching the wheels spin, this can feel like the agency is sacrificing the project's momentum for a heftier commission. The dealmakers, on the other hand, believe that packaging gives a project its best chance. "The dream is to package something really well with a great showrunner and actor and producer and send it out to the world like that so people fight over it," says Priyanka Mattoo, a Los Angeles–based producer, director, and writer who used to work for William Morris Endeavor and United Talent Agency. "We are in the business of sales," Priyanka continues. "Selling projects and actors and writers. I'd rather call a producer and say, 'I have a project and Danny Boyle wants to direct it,' than, 'I have a Word document coming your way!' If they know someone else is already interested, they'll put it at the top of their reading pile. Otherwise, it's a recipe for getting ignored."

If your book is optioned, the amount of money you will receive will depend on both the appetite for the book (is it a new release? Is there a lot of competition for the project?) and the financier's resources. Film agents have sold options for as much as $35,000 (or higher!), but many authors—even bestselling ones—frequently accept options in the $2,000 to $10,000 range.

Although it's nearly impossible to estimate what kind of option money you can expect, Creative Artists Agency film agent Michelle Kroes says that while TV traditionally paid less than features in the past, with the advent of streaming, things are quickly changing in TV land. "You have more buyers to go to now," explains Michelle. "The ability to sell is better."

Though most financiers prefer an option of two years, the average duration for an option is either twelve or eighteen months. It's a leasing program, basically. If the option runs out, and the film or show hasn't been made yet, the original optioner can pay for an extension, or you and your agent can put it back out on the open market.

Options are great because they're basically free money: you're getting paid for the big fat maybe of your book's adaptation reaching the silver screen. To be clear, the likelihood of this happening is slim. (Slim like dental floss.) According to Michelle, it would be optimistic to say that only 10 percent of optioned projects actually get made. But it can happen. And with video-streaming services producing more and more original entertainment, producers and screenwriters are desperate for fresh material. We very well might be living in the golden age of optioning. So feel free to cross your fingers, as long as you don't mind having them crossed for a long time. As Ernest Hemingway once said of his experiences in Hollywood, "Drive to the border of California, throw your book over the fence. When they throw the money back over the fence, collect the money and drive home."

Amusing as this sentiment is, Priyanka considers apathy the enemy of empowerment. "I'll never understand the giving over of control," she admits. In the next section on screenplays, we'll include her advice for adapting your own material, but on the option front, Priyanka urges writers to be protective of their work and try packaging it themselves. "Mine your own network," she advises. "Which actors do you know, which writers, which directors. Creative people know creative people. Take charge a little bit! If you want to attach someone to your project, go right ahead. If the agency wants to attach someone, approve them before they talk to other people. Personally, I love talking with authors during the optioning process. I want to get to know the person who created this particular world."

Adapting your own book

Author Matt Sumell was suffering through a serious bout of postpartum book depression after the publication of his critically acclaimed debut when Hollywood came calling. "I was desperate after *Making Nice* came out. I didn't have another book, I didn't have a job. I watched my advance disappear. Hollywood gave me encouragement and an office on the Warner Bros. lot," he said. "I was thrown into a new project that stopped me from thinking about the old one."

A newbie to screenwriting, Matt had to learn the ins and outs of script writing quickly. "It's a completely new muscle," Matt admits. "You have to think of the whole story first. You can't meander. There aren't interesting discoveries along the way. It's much more collaborative. There are outlines, beat sheets, approvals throughout the process."

Matt's experience adapting his own book followed a traditional trajectory: he was approached by a studio, and there were signed contracts at every checkpoint. But until your TV or film options sell, you own those rights. Which means you have the right to adapt the book yourself.

"I have so many writer friends who say they want to get their books optioned," explains the producer and writer Priyanka Mattoo, whom we met in the section on film and TV options. "They're racing to a five-thousand-dollar check. Great, so now you can buy coffee for a year. Who cares? Adapt your own stuff. Be a screenwriter. It pays more!"

One author who went the DIY route is Teddy Wayne, who wrote a screenplay for his third novel, *Loner*, so that he could have more weight at the negotiating table.

"I studied screenwriting in college and wrote a bunch of screenplays hoping that I would sell one," Teddy explains. "But shockingly, my eighteen-year-old self could not write a screenplay. But I focused on it, read a lot of books and watched movies with the eye of a screen-writer." At twenty-four, Teddy dropped his screenwriting ambitions and switched to writing novels. "Writing novels was less daunting than writing screenplays," he admits.

Teddy's experience trying to get other projects made taught him that things move quicker if you have a script. Through a combination of luck and personal connections, Teddy's book ended up in the hands of a well-respected director and actor who really liked it. When word got out that Teddy had a script ready, the actor-director (let's call him Famous Stevie) agreed to meet.

To date, Teddy has continued discussions with Famous Stevie without a contract in hand. "I'm going on good faith," Teddy says, "and if it isn't made with him, I know I have a screenplay." This is a risky move because without a contract, there isn't any promised money, but Teddy still believes that forward motion matters. "The option money is so little you really want the movie made. I got a sit-down with an actor-director because I had the script in hand, which wouldn't have happened otherwise."

For authors looking to adapt their own work, Teddy says to make sure it's adaptable first. "If the main appeal is the language, it isn't a candidate for a movie. It shouldn't be deeply interior, or the very least its interiority should be able to be expressed through interactions. It should be a well-paced story that fits into a neat three-act arc that has a protagonist that we either identify with or root for." Slow-moving, highly intellectualized memoirs, for example, would be difficult to adapt because "nothing really happens."

Teddy's main advice for newbie screenwriters is to have low ex-pectations. "Assume it will never work out and be pleasantly surprised if it does." Author and screenwriter Benjamin Percy agrees that lack of expectations can protect you—as can a day job. "If I was a screen-writer exclusively, I think I would drink Drano and leap off the nearest skyscraper," Benjamin says. "But it can be—every now and then—an exciting and lusty thing to chase on the side."

If your book becomes a film

When author Daniel Wallace was getting ready to submit his first book, *Big Fish*, to editors, his agent asked him how much he thought that they should ask for. "A pony ride and all the Fanta I can drink?" he said. "And one dollar more than my sister," who had recently started publishing books, too. Daniel got twenty thousand dollars from his publisher as an advance. Expectations weren't terribly high. But the book caught the attention of a well-respected screenwriter who just hap-pened to have the Hollywood go-ahead to make any project he pleased.

"I absolutely never thought my book would make a great movie," said Daniel. "Just as I never thought that someone could turn it into an automobile." *Big Fish*'s road to the silver screen was a story of friend-ships and connections as so many Hollywood stories are: the project's screenwriter asked his buddy Steven Spielberg to take a look at it. With Spielberg's stamp of approval, the film was as good as made.

Daniel never dreamed of playing any role in the adaptation him-self. He met the screenwriter only once, at an anonymous Virginia road stop that was equidistant between their two residences, where they dis-cussed the project over dismal pizza. Other than reviewing the script from time to time, Daniel was thrilled to watch the wheels turn from afar. "For a project to proceed," he says, "it has to have new owners. It can't just be an imitation of the source material."

Although the rights to author Simon Winchester's breakout book,

The Professor and the Madman, were sold to Mel Gibson in 1999, it took twenty years for the movie to go into production. Reflecting on this experience during a 2018 lecture on the subject, Simon sighed. "I used to think it was going to be made into a movie, and I was a relatively young man." The project has had a number of different actors, and originally Gibson wanted to play the madman, but was told that people already saw him as a madman, so they cast Sean Penn instead.

The film went into production in 2017 in Dublin with a crew of nearly four hundred, which Simon went and visited himself. But right before the crew was set to depart for a three-day shoot in Oxford that would effectively wrap the film, the notoriously difficult French producer Nicolas Chartier decided that he just didn't want to pay the half a million budgeted for the Oxford shoot. Irate, the stars moved onto other projects. Both Sean Penn and Mel Gibson shaved the beards they'd worked so hard to grow for their respective roles. Only several months later, the cost of the Oxford shoot had climbed to a million dollars, and Gibson, intent on seeing the film finished, filed the first of many lawsuits the film is now embroiled in. Although Simon was promised that the film would see completion in 2018, he's not holding his breath. "I think I'll be long in my grave," he says. Happily, Simon has remained levelheaded through the experience, even bemused. "Every time there is a row, my book sells a few more copies."

Revisiting awards

Just as there are prizes and fellowships for emerging writers, there is financial support to be had for authors with one book to their name, or more. These prizes vary in size and in significance. For the best-known ones—the Pulitzer Prize, the National Book Award, the Man Booker

Prize, the National Endowment for the Arts grant, or the National Book Critics Circle Award, just to name a few—your book has to be sent to the juries for consideration, and an application has to be filed or they won't come to you. Others—like the MacArthur "Genius Grant"—change the lives of people who didn't even know that they were nominated, but these recipients are few, far between, and exceptional at what they do.

Big prize committees charge entrance fees in the fifty- to seventy-five-dollar range for applications. Publishers who can afford to do so will often submit their lead titles for major prizes, irrespective of these titles' chances at nabbing the award.

Regardless of your publisher's size, it's worth putting in the leg-work to identify which awards your book might be a realistic contender for. If your book appeals to special-interest groups or communities, identify them. (If it deals with environmental stewardship, for example, perhaps it has a chance at the Sierra Club's Rachel Carson Award for environmental journalism. If it explores Islamic–Jewish relations, look into what awards are being given by the Jewish Book Council that year.) You should also keep your eye on critically acclaimed books that share your subject matter: keep a running list of what prizes they've been nominated for or won.

If there's a prize you really want to go for, be vocal about it. If your publisher won't submit the book for whatever reason, save up for the admission fee, and send it in yourself. Even the Pulitzer committee accepts entries from authors.

Welcome to list time!

My first novel came out in the summer, which is a hot season for lists. The 10 Books You Absolutely Need in Your Beach Bag (along with a really big beach bag), Five Cool Books for a Hot Summer, *The* Fall Book That Will Cool You Down. I was prepared to either make these lists or not make them, because I'd been exposed to such lists all my life, usually in a physician's office filled with backlist *Redbook* and *Better Homes and Gardens* magazines.

What I wasn't prepared for, however, were the "best of" round-ups that set the Internets on fire three times a year. If you're not "the best" of something, you can be "notable." There are lists for the X number of books that everyone is most looking forward to in the coming year. Then, once you're halfway through that year, there are lists about which books are the best so far. At the end of the year, there's another list about which books were the very best of the whole year.

These lists are unavoidable, unless you stay offline. ("I don't even have a book out this year and the year-end best-of lists are stressing me out!," tweeted author Melissa Febos in the list-heavy month of December 2018.) Newspapers run them, magazines run them, online magazines do, too. It's even become fashionable for writers to compile their own best-of-the-year lists for their social media. Don't bother scanning the big lists for your title; if your book was on them, you'd already know. If you make a list, congratulations, you now have extra accolades to put on your paperback. If you don't, have faith: the unlisted are the majority. As author Elissa Washuta replied to Melissa's December tweet, "There's too much pressure on the publication year. Momentum can build later."

III

....

When the show goes on the road

Although the majority of authors won't have publishers willing—or able—to foot the bill for their book tours, most authors do hit the road (or the subway) to promote their books in some way. A lot of wonderful—and less wonderful—things can happen while you're out there doing public events and interviews for your book.

Avoiding overcommitment (or: learning to say no)

If you're not careful—and you say yes to everything you're offered—you could be promoting one book for the rest of your adult life. In the year after author Nathan Hill's bestselling *The Nix* was published, he spent 174 days away from home, slept in 68 different hotel rooms, took 95 flights, did 106 public events, and gave 143 interviews. (Nathan is a devoted fan of spreadsheets, which is why these numbers are precise.) "After being sort of ritualistically ignored by the publishing world for about a decade," Nathan explains, "I was mostly just so surprised and touched whenever I received an invitation to anything that I always said yes. Yes every time."

Nathan's marathon year offered a pleasant change to the solitude of the writing life, and he was grateful for every interaction with readers and other writers, but his promotion schedule did come with its downsides. "There is no doubt that touring is difficult—and not only logistically, but also biologically," he admits. "There are just basic physical requirements that go unmet: quality food, exercise, sleep. The longer you're on the road, the more drained you feel—and then one day you have to get up at 4:00 a.m. to go to one of the TV morning shows and attempt to match the host's improbable enthusiasm. There's just no way."

Nathan is home now from his year of touring, with an extra fifteen pounds as a souvenir. He was so blown away by the success of his first book that he wouldn't have said no to the things that he said yes to, but in hindsight, he would have said yes differently. "You have to build in time for your mental and physical necessities," Nathan says. "I didn't do this for my tour—I didn't want to be a diva, didn't want to be a pain in the ass—but what I ultimately realized was that if I didn't ask for these things, then they wouldn't appear on the schedule, and I wouldn't get them. Because here's how the schedule is put together: the venue will ask for you to show up at a certain time, and your publisher's travel department will want to get you there as cost-effectively as possible, and your publicist will want to set you up with local media during your time there, and so on and so forth. Everybody's doing their own job really well, but nobody's really responsible for thinking about what *you* need, what your mind and your body require to be able to continue touring for weeks or months on end: regular healthy meals, a daily exercise routine, generous amounts of sleep, some quality time on the phone with a loved one. So insist on these things, build them into the schedule, make them a priority."

"You have to say yes to enough things that you end up regretting taking part in to learn when to say no," says poet and translator Rosa Alcalá, who travels to promote her own work, and the books she translates for others, too. Rosa is also a full-time teacher, mother to a nine-year-old, and married to an academic, so deciding what to say yes to has taken her a decade of trial and error. "It's especially hard with social media because you can see how people arrange their tours," she says. "You know, you see these people doing five cities in three days, and you think, I should be doing that! I should be booking this, I should be going everywhere."

Ultimately, in order to stay on top of her teaching schedule, to advance in her own writing, and to enjoy downtime with her family, Rosa had to take an inventory of who she is as a person, and what that person needs to be healthy and fulfilled. "I've had to stop measuring myself against others," she admits. "I don't feel good when I'm doing three trips a month, or traveling back to back. I have to decide what is a workable schedule for me: what makes me feel okay physically and mentally. And what allows me to keep writing, which is ultimately my goal."

Rosa has come up with meaningful criteria to help her judge what to say no to, and this includes not just invitations to reading series and festivals, but to employment and grant opportunities, as well. "I've set an objective for the year," Rosa explains. "Everything I do ultimately has to give me more time to write. So if a fellowship is going to buy me a year off from teaching, it is worth the monthlong investment to prepare the artist's statement."

Rosa admits that as a woman from a working-class background who doesn't have an agent, it was very hard—still is—to advocate for herself. "I had to get comfortable with having uncomfortable conversations," she explains. "For example, if I'm visiting somewhere, I want to know what is expected of me up front. Will I be asked to meet with students, will there be a Q&A after my reading, will my books be for sale, am I expected to go to a dinner or a cocktail? Initially, I felt like an asshole, frankly, for asking these kinds of things, but the way that these questions are responded to can help me gauge whether I want to do the event at all."

Whether or not your publisher is footing a countrywide, two-week tour, you've Kickstarted a road trip with other author friends, or your book tour is just you reading at your local library and then heading to your best friend's apartment for some party snacks, after book launch your mental and physical well-being will depend largely on the amount of free time you allow yourself. And having free time means saying no to things.

So here is a simple guide to help you understand whether you should say yes to everything you're invited to because you have a book coming out:

1. Do you have anything that depends on you to keep its heartbeat going? Like a child or a pet?
2. If you answered yes to the above, do you have someone or someones who can help keep those heartbeats going in your absence without begrudging you too much?
3. Are you already working on a new project, or have something that you're excited to start?
4. Do you have trouble sleeping when you're away from home?

If you answered yes to any of the above questions (except for the one about having people to help you out, it's great if you answered yes to that, it will be a key to your success), you are the kind of writer who should say no to some of the things, especially if you already have an idea of what you want to write next. Fame, glory, and the occasional comped drink is great and all, but the fame flame is going to extinguish if you can't nurture it with new work.

If you can pull it off logistically and financially, I think a good rule of thumb is to say yes to most things in the five weeks after your book launch. Allow yourself to be stuffed to the gills with interviews and events, and don't feel too badly about unopened email and your dying plants.

After that period, only say yes to things that you're really, truly excited about: Are these events taking place in cities you want to visit? Are they high profile, or do they pay really well? Make sure you have some weekends off. During my second book's publication, I was horrified to realize that I'd left myself without a single summer weekend that was free of book events.

If your book has been out three to four months already, take a seat. I mean, sure, keep on saying yes to the fancy stuff, but come home already. Water your damn plants. Are you traveling so much because you're petrified that you don't have a second book in you? You're being avoidant. Get back to your desk, turn off the Google alert with your name, and find that second book.

The DIY book tour, three possible tracks

1. The DIY tour (solo)

Author Laura van den Berg's first story collection came out with a small press that didn't have the resources for a publicist, so she planned her book tour alone. While on that tour, a number of empty-chair events taught her to prioritize accepting reading invitations in places where she knew people. "If you don't have a local audience where you're headed," she says, "try to join a local reading series, or partner with a friend who is publishing a book around the same time."

Although teaming up with other authors can draw bigger crowds to your events, for Laura, what that collaboration really guaranteed was companionship. "Book tours can be lonely," she attests. "You want to build in something that can alleviate the stress and loneliness of the tour."

Companionship was particularly welcome when Laura and fellow author Jessica Anthony decided to call up local Barnes & Nobles to see if they would have them in to read, because both authors had recently been selected as part of their Discover Great New Writers program. "Smartly," Laura recounts, "most of them had no interest in hosting us." But a few said yes. Many of their events were underattended, or not attended at all. "The low point occurred in Warwick, Rhode Island," Laura laughs. "Only two people were there, teenage girls. And Jessica and I thought, Hey! We don't know these people! This has potential! But it turns out they'd only docked in the chairs to text, and they soon drifted away."

Two other people did come to their event: one was the author of a science-fiction manifesto that he wanted Laura and Jessica to edit, and the other was an elderly man with a medical bracelet on who was looking for a date. "It was horrible, but after that, we went out," Laura says. "We danced, we had fun. Fun looks different for different people, but there is space for fun on book tour."

In addition to collaborative readings, Laura had particularly positive experiences reading at universities. With few exceptions, they covered her expenses (including lodging), paid her an honorarium, and helped her get to local bookstores to sign stock. Laura used most of the money from these university readings to pay for her book tour. "This was in 2009," she said. "Kickstarter wasn't really a thing then."

Fast forward to 2015, when it was very much a thing. Author Sarah Gerard raised $10,000 on Kickstarter for an ambitious cross-country book tour for *Binary Star* that saw her mostly driving, but occasionally taking planes. Sarah was working as a bookseller and was on the masthead of *Bomb* magazine at the time, so she made good use of her contacts in the industry to arrange places to read. The magazine contacts especially came in handy when it was time to distribute gifts (Kickstarter funders receive gifts for different levels of funding). Top funders received subscriptions to literary magazines that her editor friends donated.

Although Sarah originally envisioned touring with other authors for certain legs of her trip, ultimately she found that trying to coordinate her travel schedule with other people's slowed her down. "It was much easier to pair up with writers who lived in the cities I was going to," she recalls.

Sarah toured for a month throughout America, Canada, and Mexico, and in hindsight, she found it far too long. "Publicity is important, but most of us writers are introverts. I felt very exposed. A month is exhausting—I couldn't get any writing done."

For the publication of Tanaïs's (née Tanwi Nandini Islam) debut, *Bright Lines*, her publisher hadn't planned to tour her outside of the New York area. It was important to Tanaïs, however, to go on a national tour. "After spending ten years working on something," she wrote for *Catapult* in an article about debut-author book tours, "shouldn't I give it a chance to reach audiences across the country?"

A friend put her in contact with the literary advocate and publicist Kima Jones at Jack Jones Literary Arts, an agency that partners predominantly with women writers of color who have been historically underrepresented in publishing. Working with Kima, a seven-city tour quickly took shape in which Tanaïs would be paired with a veteran author at each stop.

Some of the events were packed, many were not. But after her first disappointing turnout, for which she felt "a sticky mix of hurt and embarrassment," Tanaïs quickly moved to a place of gratitude where the conversations she was having with her fellow authors and readers were what counted most. After one event, to which only one person showed, both Tanaïs and her coreader, the poet Tarfia Faizullah, ended up feeling like they'd all had a really meaningful discussion, even if it had just been them, one audience member, and a scented pumpkin candle that the bookseller had put out for the event.

"With these things, it's better to just accept what it is," Tarfia said to Tanaïs on their drive home after the event, "and give it everything you've got, each time."

2. The DIY tour (en masse)

The founder of the independent press Short Flight/Long Drive Books, Elizabeth Ellen, has planned—and been part of—numerous group book tours for her authors. The first one she ever planned was in 2012. Called the Southern Summer Comfort Tour, it consisted of four other women authors: Mary Miller, Chloe Caldwell, Brandi Wells, and Donora Hillard. They raised $1,300 dollars and traveled to Austin, Houston, New Orleans, Oxford, Tuscaloosa, and Atlanta, with special literary guest stars joining them for certain stops.

One thing Elizabeth has learned from planning group tours is that you can't predict audience turnout. For example, during the Oxford, Mississippi, stop on their road trip, they had five audience members, which isn't a lot when you have five people reading.

Like Tanaïs, Elizabeth advises writers to focus on the quality of their interactions at events, not the number of people in the folding chairs. She also advises DIY tourers to favor small cities and large towns over huge metropolises for their road-trip stops. Personally, Elizabeth is a fan of house readings, which tend to be more intimate and better-attended than bookstore events. "Sometimes they even pass around a jar for you for gas money!" she remembers.

And finally, Elizabeth thinks it's critical to travel with people who have the same gastronomical inclinations as you. She has nothing but fond memories of her Summer Comfort Tour cohorts grazing on Combos and Rolos and "massive quantities of coffee" with her, and was thus vaulted into despair when she next traveled with authors who preferred hard-boiled eggs and digestive walks to taking a load off after a reading with bourbon and cigarettes.

3. The local-haunts tour

This is a smaller scale version of the DIY effort that sees you involved in readings in your local area. Your publisher might have assisted you with organizing these events, and might even cover your travel expenses. If not, save those receipts for the tax accountant that you hired during prepub.

If you don't have a publicist, make sure to confirm with the event organizer that your books will be available for purchase. As crucial as this detail is, it's one that can fall through the cracks, especially when you're organizing events yourself.

Local event promotion can take a lot of time and energy, but it doesn't necessarily require cash. Here are a few things you can do to leverage your local events:

- Create a simple flyer with your book and headshot advertising the event and distribute it to the places you are reading for their store window. (Okay, this one takes a little cash. Alternatively, you could email the JPEG of the file to the location's event manager and hope they print it out.)

- Create Event pages via Facebook for your local events, and (gracefully!) encourage your friends to share news of your shindig on their personal social feeds. Once again, do not invite people to your book events if they have to take a plane to get there. Be realistic when you are asking people to go to bat for you; respect people's time.
- Reach out to local book clubs. Your local library is a good way to find out who's running book clubs in the area. Local bookshops should be able to give you some intel on book clubs, too.
- Pitch your event to local radio stations: a pitch of this nature would include the date, location, and time of your event, and a reason as to why strangers should drag themselves away from whatever Netflix show to hear about your book.
- Submit your event to local event-listings sites: local papers will draw from these listings when they're suggesting things to do each week.
- With their permission, put up flyers about your event at local libraries, bookshops, and cafés where bookish people hang out.
- Wear a sandwich board around advertising your event until the event in question. Step out of the sandwich board, with assistance, at your event.

It's worth noting that there is a whackadoodle thing called "bookstore co-ops" that sees publishers paying bookstores a certain sum (between $100 and $400 on average) for an author event. This sum helps to keep the bookstore's doors open: it covers costs for staff, food, beverages, printing, and the like. Co-ops are the reason you should not go planning your own events all willy-nilly over town. Communicate with your publisher about the places you'd like to go to make sure no one is hit with a surprise bill after the event.

The full-court press, national tour

Because of the significant expense, the nationwide book tour is a dying beast. If your publisher is touring you, take comfort in the fact that they really have your back. If you're a debut author, it's worth having a conversation with your publisher about their expectations for your tour before you leave. For my first book, I imagined that the point was for me to sell a boatload of hardcovers, so when audience turnout remained modest night after night, with book sales in the single digits, I was crushed. My agent assured me that the tour was about exposure and relationship-building with booksellers; the beginning of a foundation to support the rest of my career. Was she just being nice to me? Let's ask.

"The book tour doesn't always bear fruit right away," agent Rebecca Gradinger repeats. "It really is about planting seeds, making connections. Even if you had five people at your reading, maybe you had a great conversation with the bookseller who is going to hand-sell your book. The thing is, sales are out of your control. What you focus on is opportunity. People who use the opportunity of having a book as a way to build more opportunities build their own success."

One way to manage expectations during tour and keep the home crowd satisfied is by daily check-ins with your publicist and/or editor via email. I'd write these in the morning after my events. I'd always start out positive: what special efforts the bookstore had made, whether I'd noticed any signage. Then I'd let them know what the turnout had been like, and around how many books I sold. I was honest with these numbers, even if they were disastrous. There's no point in lying; although not every store reports to BookScan, most bookstores' events coordinators will update the publicist after the event, so you don't want your sales account to vary much from theirs. I was also honest if the event had been a bust because publicists need to know which booksellers will play ball if they send their authors (promoting the event ahead of time, placing the author's books in store windows, talking the event up on social media), and which booksellers roll over and play dead about it, like the bookseller—who will remain unnamed—who put up a poster about my book event *after* the event was done.

I'd always end these check-ins with a glowing rave about my accommodations. If there was anything wrong with the establishment, I wouldn't mention it unless it might impact the experience of other authors. Petty complaints are for the hotel management, not your publicist. Broken air conditioner? Tell reception. Is the hotel undergoing a drastic, noisy renovation that makes it hard to sleep? Find out how long construction will go on for and give your publicist those dates, so they can avoid sending authors there until the work is done.

Book tour FAQs

Do I need to pay for my own meals?

If your publisher is sending you on tour, they will have a reimbursement policy: ask them what it is. Many publishers will cover food and beverage up to a certain amount per day, and will reimburse you at the end of the tour once you present all your receipts. You shouldn't feel ashamed to send in these receipts. A debut-author friend of mine told me she never sent hers because she felt like it was already such a privilege to be sent on book tour. This is true, but it's also true that you wouldn't be eating a burrito supremo in the Tyler Pounds Regional Airport if you weren't on tour.

Be sensible about it. If you have to order breakfast in your hotel room one day because you have a 6:00 a.m. flight and nothing else is open, that's an appropriate expense to invoice. If you buy a round of drinks for your MFA buddies after a reading, that's not.

Wow, the hotel room my publisher got for me is GIANT! Can I show it off on social media?

You can—once—but you don't need to boast about your hotel rooms every night. If you're on a national tour, giddiness is understandable, but you don't want to be a show-off. Remember that most writers don't get sent on tour. They might never stay in a hotel that's paid for by their publisher or take an airplane on someone else's dime, so be sensitive to that. All the same, you have every right to be excited, so be excited. Just do it in good taste.

What should I pack?

For my first book tour, which was nationwide, and thus involved a lot of different climates, I crammed a checked bag full of outfits that complemented my then-aesthetic, a diaphanous attempt at nonchalance that was three parts resort and one part fallen socialite: picture Lucille Bluth in a caftan.

But when you're changing cities daily, checked luggage is a pain. And it turns out the gauzy chiffon maxi dress that worked so well in Los Angeles leaves you freezing in Chicago. And one weird thing I discovered was that when you are truly at loose ends, and have been traveling alone for weeks (albeit in a very public way), you don't want something that's all loose and flimsy and diaphanous, you want something that's *tight*.

Or at least I did. For my second book tour, I did away with the checked luggage, got a roller carry-on, and established a touring uniform. I was only going to wear navy. I basically bought three of the same form-fitting, stain-resistant dress. I had one outfit for the plane, and it involved Lycra and running shoes, which allowed me to run around the block a few times when I arrived at the hotel, which was all the exercise I ended up having time for. Although a nationwide book tour appears glamorous from the outside, from the tourer's point of view, it involves gastric problems from too much fast food and a lot of sleepless sleep. Pack a bottle of Woolite because your hotel sink is the closest you're going to get to doing laundry while you're gone. You can't even use the hotel dry-cleaning services—unless you've got a rare day off from traveling, there won't be enough time to get your clothing back.

What do I do if I can't remember the name of the person I need to sign a book for?

This is called Signing-Line Amnesia, and it gets really bad when an author is nervous or jet-lagged. As we mentioned in the section on book launches, the best way to combat this is to ask one of the booksellers (if your publicist isn't present), to hand out little Post-its for the book buyers to write their names on. Sometimes book buyers will refuse to do this, because it's only been eighteen years since you last saw each other; of course you know their name!

Your third-grade music teacher not being able to fathom a world in which you can't remember their name is the reason why you need to come up with an emergency-signing solution. I recommend choosing a clever line that you write inside of almost every book. (By way of example, the author Jill Santopolo wrote, "Sparkle on!" inside of her children's book, *Sparkle Spa*.) You'll also want a generic salutation you can use in lieu of the person's name in case you can't freaking remember it. You might try, "To a true friend."

Why do dudes keep asking if I can publish them? Isn't it clear I'm not an editor?

No, writer, it is not. As someone who is literate and sitting on a stool, to some people, you will represent the publishing industry at large. No book tour is complete until some person (it's usually a white man in a disheveled dress shirt, this author knows not why) gets up during the Q&A portion of your book event to ask you how he can publish his nine-hundred-page epic memoir about his grandfather who used to sell ice out of a wagon, and can he meet your agent, can he meet your agent now. Don't let this person derail your event—if there is no one else available to ask a sensible follow-up question, ask the audience a question, ask yourself a question!—do whatever you can to get the event back on track. Ice Wagon will be the first person in the signing line, by the way, and he's not going to buy your book. In order to make way for the people who will, refer Ice Man to the "writing reference" section in the bookshop where he can find this book. Do not give this person your agent's name: he'll never leave her alone. If the dude will just not let it go, if he just needs *closure*, give him the name of your publicist. She'll forgive you, in time.

What if no one comes to my reading?

If this happens, the event organizer will usually give you the choice of reading to an empty room (or to one of the booksellers), or canceling the event. Definitely let your publicist know about the event fail so they can get on the phone with the event organizers to gauge what went wrong, promotion-wise. Spend the evening telling yourself, "It's not me, it's them," and take comfort in the fact that you have now experienced the essential rite of passage known as the audience no-show.

Will my books be for sale?

If you've been asked by a bookstore, a university, or some other entity to do a reading from your book, it's reasonable to assume that your books will be for sale at the event. Dear writer: don't assume this. Whether you have two publicists with a Big Five house or you're DIYing your first book tour, always verify that your book (or books) will be for sale at the place that you are reading, and, if possible, that they are being sold by someone who is not yourself. In many cases, you will not be paid for the time you spend reading at this outlet, nor will you be reimbursed for the way you had to get there, so selling your book(s) is a bare minimum gesture of respect for your energy and time.

If the event organizer asks you to bring your own copies to sell, this might seem like a cool idea because you can pocket the cash from any sales. It will seem less cool when you are trying to negotiate a set of subway stairs in your fancy dress shoes with a heavy box of unsold books.

Some book tour tales of woe

As eager as publicists and bookstores are to fill up folded chairs with engaged audience members, event fails do occur. Misery loves company, so let's hear from the flops.

The event was a disaster

When memoirist Jessica Lamb-Shapiro was asked to return to her alma mater of Brown University to do a reading, she was thrilled until she saw only two people sitting in the audience. Or rather, make that one. "When I started reading, one person left," Jessica remembers. "Turned out he was just sitting there to sit. I asked the remaining person if I could buy her a beer instead of reading to her. Fortunately, she said yes."

There is no shortage of author horror stories from the open road. I once heard of a poet who had won a major award and was asked to give a reading in a giant auditorium. There was one person in the audience, and after the host introduced the poet, the host turned to the poet and said he had to go. The poet read for a while, utterly befuddled, until the audience member asked him, politely, if the poet could keep it down a little because he was trying to study.

The novelist Jessica Anya Blau once received a memorable invitation to a nudist book club in Maryland, and bravely, she accepted. When she got there, she had to wait for "nude yoga" to end before everyone joined her to discuss her book. Jessica read for the nudist book club, clothed, while everyone else was naked, and all of the photographs from that evening were intensely cropped.

It's true that book tours can change an author's life. When memoirist Elissa Altman was working as an editor at HarperCollins, she had an author who was served divorce papers by a lawyer waiting in the signing line.

The call is coming from inside the house

Make no mistake, book tour snafus don't just happen to writers. Sometimes it's the authors who behave like wildebeests with an expense account.

Ellen Gerstein was working as a marketing director at a major publishing house when she was tasked with managing a difficult debut author because, in her words, "I was good with toddlers." Among other larks, the author claimed he never saw his driver at the Seattle airport so he felt entitled to rent himself a Hummer. He also used the company credit card for emergency cosmetic dental work while he was on tour.

Author Patty Chang Anker was the publicist for an author who missed his connecting flight in D.C. and decided to take a taxi from D.C. to "Charleston" without specifying to the driver that he, rather incredibly, wanted to be driven to *South Carolina*, rather than West Virginia, which was where the car initially took him, until the author gazed out the window at their destination and said, "No, the other one." "This was way before cell phones and GPS," explains Patty, "so our publicity team had no idea where he'd gone and had to track him down via airport security and taxi dispatchers and his editor had to meet him in the middle of the night in Charleston, South Carolina, with fistfuls of cash for the driver."

An audience of hellcats

Not to be outdone by the authors or the event organizers, sometimes it's the *readers* who kick up trouble during your event. After driving nearly three hours to attend a book club, author Karen Shepard enjoyed hors d'oeuvres and chitchat with the affable sixtysomethings who had invited her to one of the member's homes. When it came time to discuss Karen's book, one of the members raised her hand. "Would you like to know what I really didn't like about this book?"

In addition to going out of their way to point out how your work disappointed them, the authors I interviewed said you can look forward to readers scrapbooking, eating takeout, guzzling open milk gallons, shouting obscenities, intoxicating themselves, stealing cheese, and catching up on sleep during your events. Even if they only show up once, or show up and go comatose, these rabble-rousers will haunt your future readings. At every event I do now, I still see and hear him: the elderly gentlemen snoring through a sex scene I was reading, fast asleep in the front row of my first-ever event.

Last but not least, sometimes it's the fans' own fandom that takes down an event. Publicist Carrie Bachman was at a signing for her client, the celebrity chef Emeril Lagasse, who was speaking to a standing-room-only crowd at a Barnes & Noble when a female audience member passed out from the heat. Medical aid came quickly, but she refused to be taken away by the paramedics until she had her book signed. Emeril actually had to enter the ladies' room to sign this woman's book.

Things you should pack for book tour that you might otherwise not think to pack

....

- Tea, if you're a tea drinker, because no one gives a f*ck about us in hotel rooms, it's a coffee-drinker's world
- A wide variety of sleeping pills in varying dosages
- A laundry soap bar (and a Ziploc to store it in)
- A bullet vibe, to take the edge off
- A talisman that makes you feel good in case a negative review comes in
- Band-Aids
- Stamps*

Prepping for live events and interviews
....

Regardless of the scope of your book promotion, most authors will be called upon to talk about their book in front of an audience. Whether this involves reading a book excerpt, going on a podcast, or being interviewed at a panel, it's important to learn how to discuss your book in a selling way.

---

* It's a nice practice to thank the bookstores who welcomed you for events, and you're more likely to get that handwritten note out if you do it from the road because when you get home, everything except marathon viewings of your favorite television program will feel Olympic-level impossible. So pick up a packet of thank-you cards at one of the bookstores that you've visited and make use of those stamps! Do you have to send a note to *every* bookstore that hosted you? (Even the one store that not a single person came to?) Yup! You still want them to sell your book, right?

Choosing your book excerpt

Most bookstores will allot forty-five minutes for a book event and Q&A, with time afterward for signing. If you haven't been partnered with a moderator or another reader, that's a lot of time to fill. IMHO, your reading should run between eight and twelve minutes maximum—modern humans are manufactured with attention deficits, and their heads will explode if you read longer than that. Steer away from excerpts that require setup. If the audience needs instructions in order to enjoy your reading, your book is going to sound like too much work to buy.

Bookstore readings are generally intimate events—if you chat with the public before you share your excerpt, it won't feel like you're reading "at" them once you start. Share what you like most about their town; talk about the origin of the book that you're promoting. Warming up the room *before* your reading will also help the audience feel more comfortable asking questions during the Q&A.

Should your crowd turn out to be a tough one, try asking the *audience* a question. What do they love most about the bookstore? What other books are they reading now? Be inventive, keep them captive. If things get weird because there aren't any questions, there's always hope that one of the audience members will go in for the pity buy.

Sharing reading recommendations with the public

As a published author, you'll be asked what you are reading by a variety of outlets. Not everyone is going to agree with me, but I think you should lie. Because here is the thing: whether the question comes from a magazine, a podcast host, or an audience member, every time you're asked what you are reading, you've got a chance to impact another writer's sales.

Most readers are aware of the big bestsellers: while these books are worthy of your attention, they don't need your help in the way that underdog projects (short-story collections, books with independent presses, poetry collections) do. It's a nice practice to keep a list of three to five quiet titles that you're excited to put your weight behind and name-drop them on tour. If you're reading (and enjoying) a commercial bestseller, that's awesome, but again, maybe don't mention that book first. Challenge the audience to venture outside of their reading comfort zones and show love to backlist titles. Use your power for good!

Staying on message during live interviews

Seeing that you wrote the book you're going to be interviewed about, you might assume there's no need to prep for interviews. You came up with the plot and the characters, you revised the book painstakingly, what is there to rehearse? Alas, your ability to speak about your book intelligibly can go out the window when something is at stake—and something is at stake during live interviews.

Author Brendan Matthews experienced panic at the steering wheel when he was interviewed by Lulu Garcia-Navarro for NPR's *Weekend Edition*. Everything was going swimmingly until Lulu asked Brendan to summarize *The World of Tomorrow*'s plot in thirty seconds or less— essentially asking him for a logline that he hadn't worked out yet.

Though he made it past this roadblock gracefully, his confidence was shaken. As Lulu went on to inquire about his research process and the book's characters, Brendan felt his answers running long. He managed to touch upon his book's main themes—the immigrant experience, political violence, redemption—but when the interview was over, he worried that he had glossed over the novel's joyful, madcap side. Although Lulu assured him that he'd done a stellar job, Brendan nevertheless vowed that he would be better prepared next time with a logline, and shorter, livelier answers that "would give someone some-thing to take away."

Although the format of interviewer and interviewee confuses this, you *can* control the conversation if you think about your messaging beforehand. What are the main points you want to get across? What do you think makes your book enjoyable? Is there anything that reviewers aren't picking up on that you'd like to tout yourself?

Book events are great practice for media interviews: readers often ask the same questions as radio and podcast hosts, so you get practice under your belt. Don't worry if it feels like you're churning out stock answers—unless you have a super fan or a particularly supportive part-ner, most people aren't listening to you promote your book night after night. At the end of the day, people want to know what your book is about, and whether or not they'll like it. This actually has very little to do with whether or not they like *you*, so do try to keep the conversation linked up with your book.

If you're doing a live radio interview, it's worth noting that most studios won't let you bring any food or drinks into the recording studio, so soothe your voice (and hunger pains) with some snacks before. If you're taking back-to-back calls on the merry-go-round known as "the satellite-radio tour," make sure you have what you need on hand to sus-tain you between phone calls, but don't crunch or gulp on air.

Authors from marginalized communities revisit their experiences on the road

There is so much positive energy around the release of a debut, nobody wants to rain on your parade by bringing out the storm clouds. It's my belief, however, that if you have an idea of the things that can go awry during a book release, you'll be better equipped to handle both the ups *and* downs.

You don't get to choose who reads your books, who reviews them, who comments about them online. Along with people who get you and respect you, you and your book are going to encounter readers whose value systems includes prejudices, bias, and stereotypes. If you publish something melancholy as a woman, people are going to want proof that you are happy in real life. If you're a mother, you'll be asked for the rest of your career how you juggle "motherhood" with "writing." If you're over forty, you'll be asked what it feels like to publish a debut at your age, which is a veiled way of asking what the hell took you so long. If you're a person of color, you might encounter white readers who want their own feelings prioritized when they talk about your work. If you're queer, you might find your book branded as a saucy detour from "normal" literature.

While a conflict-free, gratifying, and empowering book release is what you deserve, you can't control the kinds of people who come to your book events, nor the opinions that they bring. Writers from marginalized communities have had to become particularly adept at navigating affronts, cultural misunderstandings, and tensions during their book releases. There are ways to handle BS should tension arrive.

Extraordinary bodies

With the pressures on contemporary authors to be all of everything in person and online, it's no wonder that the writers who don't fit inside neat boxes encounter major challenges. The writer and cultural critic Roxane Gay has written extensively about her difficulties touring as a fat person.* In a profile for *The New York Times*, Roxane relayed the

---

* At the time of writing, "fat" was a word that many body-positive activists were reclaiming, and thus we are using it in solidarity here.

time her segment on an Australian podcast was introduced by the female host with the following teasers: "Will she fit into the office lift?" "How many steps will she have to take to get to the interview?"

Roxane, who is vocal about making room in cultural conversations—literally and figuratively—for all different kinds of bodies, was understandably outraged. The incident brought attention to the kinds of accommodations large people require to feel comfortable, while also revealing how condescending some event organizers can be about providing them. (Regarding the Australian podcast incident in May 2017, Roxane tweeted, "Am I supposed to be grateful you provided a sturdy chair? Why would you tell me this? Is it that arduous? Come on.")

Although they're making inroads, the publishing industry is still learning how to value, promote, and celebrate the work of writers with extraordinary bodies. This is especially true for disabled writers, whose individual accessibility needs can make the already difficult act of book promotion unnecessarily strenuous.

When I asked writer, editor, and queer disability activist Alaina Leary about the kinds of assumptions nondisabled publishing professionals make about disabled writers, she responded: "That they're aren't any disabled writers out there at all. That they're not publishing. That they're not worth the time and energy and effort and marketing. Or that they're a one-trick pony. A blind kid writes a memoir about what it means to be blind but he couldn't *possibly* write YA."

The American Association of People with Disabilities programs manager and writer Carrie Wade runs a column on disability and queerness at the online magazine *Autostraddle*, where she tracks what it means, looks like, and sounds like to engage with disability. She's candid about the fact that this journey began with her trying to downplay her cerebral palsy around—and for—her able-bodied friends. "Disabled people rarely have the privilege of space," Carrie writes. "You're doing disability right as long as no one can see or be inconvenienced by it. You earn all different kinds of praise for playing it down, staying in line, and knowing your place. Even our workplace laws only cover 'reasonable' accommodation—so you better hope your body's not 'unreasonable.'"

As mobile, articulate creatives with jobs, apartments, and platforms for their writing, both Alaina and Carrie acknowledge that they are privileged members of an underprivileged population. Nevertheless, they've both experienced—and continue to experience—the entitlement, ignorance, and prejudice of the able-bodied toward their own bodies and minds.

"I was given an exorcism on the train," says Carrie. "A woman came up to me with a tray of votive candles. People ask me all the time, 'What happened to you?' I used to be more accommodating until I woke up and got angry."

In addition to being treated as if strangers are owed an explanation for their nonconforming bodies, disabled writers are also expected to inspire total strangers with their everyday heroics and ability to overcome. "I've lost count of the number of times that I've been approached by strangers wanting to tell me that they think I'm brave or inspirational," said comedian and journalist Stella Young in a 2014 TED Talk on inspiration porn. "And this was long before my work had any kind of public profile. They were just kind of congratulating me for managing to get up in the morning and remember my own name."

"When people think of disability, they think of an insurmountable challenge," adds Alaina. "Able-bodied people see a *New York Times* bestseller get up on stage in a wheelchair and they think, 'What an inspiration! If she can do it, imagine what I can do!' But I prefer to be an inspiration to other marginalized people, or to queer writers. So they realize someone like them exists."

In an industry that is already starting from a place of exclusivity and privilege, disabled writers have to work ten times as hard to get their work seen and shared. But the standard tools of self-promotion aren't always accessible. "People incorrectly assume that everyone can log onto Facebook," says Alaina. "For low-vision and blind readers, screen readers are a big way that they access social networks, and a lot of websites aren't built that way. Twitter is notoriously inaccessible. They only recently added a way to manually add captions to images."

When it comes to online writing and social networking, Carrie admits that disabled writers have to be especially attentive to their emotional and physical needs. "There's an online mindset that you're only worth reading if you're prolific and putting stuff out there," she says. "That there's no way you're going to make it if you don't put in 24/7 engagement. It's unhealthy and unnecessary for anybody, but it's especially true when there is stuff going on that complicates your energy level. You have to rejigger the way you do your creative work. I know people who can only write every once in a while because executive functioning or sensory-processing challenges make that work very hard."

When it comes to physical promotion—touring, giving readings, participating in panels, and conventions—the need for self-advocacy and self-care becomes even more essential. As a cane user, Alaina has a particular empathy for disabled writers who participate in book conventions. "You're going from panel to panel, it's exhausting, and it's loud. You have a fan stopping you every two minutes to talk and take a picture with you. It's hell for anybody. I can't imagine it for someone who doesn't have a disability ... and then to add a disability on top of it?"

The physical book tour—already a luxury for able-bodied writers—is far from being part of the standard publishing package for disabled authors. "A lot of time smaller publishers don't have the capacity to support things that cost extra money," explains Alaina. "So it's: you have to get there, but we can't pay to get you there. With that kind of budget, no one is going to pay to hire an ASL interpreter."

Woke publishers exist, of course, and authors such as Leigh Bardugo and Jen Wilde have had positive tour experiences backed by editorial teams eager to understand and accommodate their needs, but both women are high-profile authors with books that performed well commercially and critically, so there was a budget to match their publishers' good faith. So what happens to the emerging disabled writers whose publishing partners have the enthusiasm and contacts to support their work, but no marketing budget?

"That's where the gap is for most marginalized groups," says Alaina. "The New York City–based group People of Color in Publishing has done a lot for industry diversity. I'd love to see something similar started for disabled people in publishing. But as a community, disabled people tend to be lower income. Nobody has the extra time and resources to start a group like that."

Travel awards such as the Ohio Arts Council's Artists with Disabilities Access Program help disabled writers attend literary events and conferences, writing retreats are adding scholarships that celebrate marginalized voices, Hachette U.K. launched an inclusivity initiative called the Future Bookshelf to educate newcomers about publishing, and We Need Diverse Books offers an internship grant program that includes (but isn't limited to) disabled applicants.

Many publishers are based in urban centers where the larger conferences and conventions also take place. Accordingly, writers outside of city centers work against geographical barriers that some conferences are easing by offering transcripts and videos of their events, some of which are accompanied by ASL interpreters. At college campuses and bookstores, event organizers are learning to talk disabled writers through the accessibility options of their respective locales long *before* the event, so that the unexpected staircase is an effrontery of the past.

Of course, there's still a long way to go. For emerging and established voices, "more writing workshops would be great," says Alaina, "as would more conferences that provide scholarships to help with accessibility." For people interested in working in the publishing industry, remote internships, flexible work schedules, and generous medical-leave policies would go a long way toward empowering disabled people to excel in roles traditionally held by the able-bodied.

Equally important, however, is conversation and engagement. Brianna Albers, the founder and former editor-in-chief of the literary magazine for disabled women and nonbinary people, *Monstering*, suggests that disabled writers start looking for publishing resources and allies through the website Disabled Writers, or by searching (and using) the hashtag #criplit and #ownvoices on Twitter. "In my experience," Brianna says, "disabled writers are often eager to promote the work of other disabled people, and there's something special to be said for spreading the word through the community."

Able-bodied publishers, editors, and event organizers should work to understand how they can better promote and support the voices and perspectives of disabled writers, too. "Engaging with disability is risky," Carrie has written of these conversations. "It is delicate. It is excruciatingly personal. It is everything you fear it could be. That doesn't excuse you from trying."

Queer as (not all) folk

The poet Bryan Borland, who founded the LGBTQIA-championing Sibling Rivalry Press, says that for himself and his authors, touring as a queer writer can come with surprises—some of them quite pleasant. "You're going to be all over the place," Bryan says, "and you don't know the types of audiences you'll have and how receptive they will be to the queerness of your work. But one thing I have learned is to never underestimate or prejudge your audience."

Bryan remembers when Sibling Rivalry was at a Memphis book fair in 2015, placed between a children's book publisher and a religious outlet. "This man starts walking toward all of our tables. He goes to the other ones first, but then he comes to us. He was a biker guy. You could *feel* his masculinity. We had some publications with provocative imagery, provocative covers. And then he picks up this literary journal we have for queer women, *Adrienne*, and says, 'I want to buy these. All of these. My daughter is a lesbian and she loves poetry.'"

Again and again, Bryan has seen his LGBTQIA colleagues encounter positivity and respect in the most unlikely places. When Holy Cross College in Indiana banned Bryan from reading on their campus, his event was relocated to a nursing home for retired nuns. Tough audience? "They were *the best*," Bryan gushes. "I sold so many books!"

Bryan's best advice for queer authors heading out to promote their work is to focus on connection. "If you connect with one person—if your work builds a bridge to that person, or gives them tools to build a bridge outside of themselves to where they need to be, it doesn't matter if you have twenty people or ten people or one person at your event, then you have done your job."

For author and poet Garth Greenwell, his experience promoting his bestselling debut novel *What Belongs to You* was also full of surprises. Garth was fortunate in that his editorial team at FSG gamed out the challenges of promoting a "gay book" with him well before his pub day. "My publicist had this very frank conversation with me," Garth remembers. "'How do you feel about putting it forward as a gay novel? Is there another way you'd like to package it?' I appreciated that he let me be part of that conversation; I know from a lot of friends that that wasn't their experience, or won't be their experience."

Accordingly, Garth set out for his book tour feeling like he knew where the resistance would come from, but he ended up finding support where he least expected it, along with pushback from some of the very people who were purportedly championing his work. In one of his first major interviews in the U.K., the interviewer asked Garth why he would open his novel with a sex scene in a bathroom after gay men's lives have been reduced to sex for so many decades. "You know, there's this mixture of debut-novelist feelings," Garth says of that conversation. "One: you feel totally powerless; two: you're grateful to have a major interview; three: you wonder, How aggressive can I be in pushing back against this?"

Garth's book takes place in Bulgaria, where he taught at the American College of Sofia for four years. Given that Bulgaria isn't known as a bastion for gay rights, Garth was apprehensive about this leg of his tour. "I expected it to be especially fatiguing because there is groundwork laid for the legitimacy of queer lives and queer fiction that we take for granted in the United States that there isn't in Bulgaria. But I had this brave publisher—they held the book launch in the National Palace of Culture, just steps from where the bathroom scene takes place, and the event was filled with these gay men telling me what it had been like cruising bathrooms in Soviet Sofia. In some ways, the place that I had anticipated as being the hardest place to release the book was the most wondrous."

The haters came for Garth, of course, but Garth says he was prepared for vitriol online. What he was less ready for, however, was the way that some readers pressure minority writers to tell a certain kind of tale.

"At one point during an event in San Francisco, a man stood up—he was so angry, he was shaking," Garth remembers of this moment. "He said, 'I don't understand why your narrator can't be an out and proud gay man.' This floored me for a lot of reasons—my narrator is an out and proud gay man! At another event, someone asked, 'Don't you think it's important that we have happy gay stories? Why didn't you write a happy gay story?' On the one hand, you don't want to deny people's experience of the book, or their desire to experience a certain kind of story, but on the other, you have to push back against the pressure put on writers by readers who want to be represented in a particular way."

Much like the bristly journalist he locked horns with during a British interview, Garth also experienced hostility from heterosexual readers who didn't see the value in certain stories being told. "It's fatiguing when you feel like you have to do the groundwork for people, and in some ways, these interactions were more fatiguing than the ones that I expected to be difficult, like when I went on a ladies' afternoon talk show in Bulgaria, and they said, 'So, you're gay? That must be very hard!' "

Nasty women

Being a female author is like handling a chainsaw in public—people are gobsmacked when they realize you are practiced at your craft. I recently had a conversation with a man who, when I told him my first book was written from a male point of view, asked, "Are you sure?" On Twitter, I'm often blessed with input from total strangers who write to tell me that my books "are not without their charms," and my own mother asked me "if I had friends there" when I published an op-ed in *The New York Times*. The author Lauren Groff was told by a copanelist at a literary festival that "she sells lots of books because she has an attractive author photo." And then there was the infamous *Entertainment Weekly* article about writers' huge advances in which a top editor acknowledged that an author's looks can impact her advance, but that a certain title was so incredible, and its author so promising, "We would have paid her the same money if she weighed five hundred pounds and was really hard to look at."

Yikes.

In our current cultural moment, women have to work harder, produce more, and be better groomed than their male colleagues in order to be taken seriously. It's not enough for us to write a book—we're also expected to look attractive, dress well, and have our eyebrows waxed. If any female writer I know submitted an author photograph of themselves with oily hair, dehydrated skin, soiled clothing, and insomnia eyes, their publishing team would think they'd suffered a psychotic break. Google Karl Ove Knausgaard, though, and see how such photos worked out for him.

Women aren't only expected to *look* nice, they're expected to *be* nice, too. For some reason, before I signed my first book contract, it was exceedingly important to me that my publishing team understand that I was not the kind of woman who baked. "Put something in my contract about me never making cupcakes," I said to my poor agent. "I do not want to be thought of as the girl who shows up with baked goods."

Certainly, this wasn't very kindhearted of me and was probably an earful for my agent, but my fighting heart was in the right place. Writing a book is hard work. Selling it and promoting it is exhausting. Summoning up the energy to also be this Mother Goddess who brings homemade cheese crackers to her book events and stitches needlepoints of gratitude was just not in the cards for me.

Be gracious, ladies. Be forthright. Be generous. But you don't need to be fake. Contrary to what it's going to feel like, you do not need to be all things to everyone.

Don't carry their cross

In a powerful piece that Mira Jacob wrote for *BuzzFeed* called "I Gave a Speech About Race to the Publishing Industry and No One Heard Me," she recounted the time a prominent radio producer asked her to edit the novel excerpt she was planning to read on air because some of the ethnic names were "confusing," and also, could she please say "Asian Indians" instead of "East Indians" because no one knew what "East Indian" meant. The racism here was casual and professionalized—the producer was trying to "protect" Mira from being too confusing for "his" audience.

Writers of color have seen someone else's face used for their author photo at events, they have been publicly complimented on their "good English" even though it's their native tongue, they've been told during Q&A sessions that an audience member's relative is dating someone of their particular heritage, leaving an ellipsis hanging there, apparently for applause? Several Asian American writers told me that white men have asked to have their photographs taken with them at events "because their brother/colleague/neighbor is dating someone Asian."

As if this wasn't creepy and infuriating enough, writers of color are often expected to write deep, enduring, incredibly important work about pain and oppression, rather than the coming-of-age novels and romantic comedies that white writers can publish without fearing that their readers will chastise them for writing something "light."

The author Tanaïs, who is of South Asian descent, wrote movingly for *Catapult* about several of her experiences as a debut author. At one of her first book events, she remembers a black friend asking, "We're in very violent times right now. What do you think our work must do in this moment? What do you think your work does?"

"While my friend posed his question out of love and respect," Tanaïs recalls, "I knew that I'd need to prepare myself for the discomfort of answering strangers' questions in subsequent readings during my tour."

These questions soon came, and Tanaïs, whose debut *Bright Lines* features mostly Muslim Bangladeshi characters, realized there was a certain ennui toward fiction dealing with the immigrant experience. At another event, an Asian American audience member asked, "We're familiar with stories by Asian writers—you know, a family story, a return home to their country of origin. How is your novel doing anything different?"

"Why can't people of color live nuanced, complex lives?" Tanaïs found herself thinking. "Why can't we just eat, pray, love? Does everything have to depict well-worn tropes of arranged marriage, honor-killing, strict parents, slavery? Why must we suffer?"

Author and journalist Porochista Khakpour (who was once reported to the program director of the low-res MFA she teaches at for tweeting that Joan Didion was overrated) has written extensively about her experiences as an Iranian American for such outlets as *The New York Times* and CNN. In her own essay for *Catapult* in which Porochista describes her transformation from avoiding writing about identity to earning praise for her work on the subject, she documented the dorm politics during her MFA program that saw her fellow students saying their dads paid for her to be there, along with her earning the erroneous title of "first Iranian American novelist" by a journalist apparently uninterested in opening his eyes, or at least another web page. "Who can even tally who they ignored before you?" she asked.

Porochista's advice for people of color who are about to have a book out is the following:

1. Remember that you don't need to be any more appreciative, grateful, etc. than white writers.

2. Figure out who your allies are. Former professors, people on-line who have been encouraging, idols. Remember you can write people notes without asking for anything. I often have students reach out to me telling me they like my work and es-pecially if they are POC, I respond. When their work is out, I cheer it along.

3. Talk to other writers of color. Commiserate, share, and scheme with them. I often have several email threads going at once with POC. Not surprisingly they are often there to vent!

4. Figure out who to avoid. Toxic people, especially toxic white writers with power, are everywhere. Figure out how to navi-gate them.

5. Do events with other POC. First of all that means you won't be the only token POC, but that means you get to not be alone and depend on your own people to fill a room. It also means allying yourself with others you love. Partnering and grouping always makes things better.

6. Formulate for yourself how you want to be discussed or framed or shelved even. Do you identify as POC first and foremost? Or queer? Is intersectionality your thing? Make sure you tell inter-viewers, publishers, publicists—basically anyone who will be dealing with your book being sold in some way or another—how you want to be thought about. This is your choice and while not everyone may respect or observe it, at least you know you tried.

7. Look out for residencies, retreats, events, etc. with other POC. It makes all the difference in the world.

8. Don't let people get away with disrespecting you. If any inter-viewer messes up your identifiers or makes a racist or xenopho-bic comment about you, correct it. Social media is your friend.

Especially Twitter, which I find is where POC run the dialogue the most.

9. Remind yourself that you are more than just a POC. You didn't get this because of some affirmative action. You are not a token. Don't go down this dark path.

10. Self-care. If you are POC, you will need it more than your white colleagues and friends. Take breaks. Nap, vent, space out, do something else. You deserve to be off as much as you are on. Your identifier is not your burden alone. You don't owe anyone anything. You've already done more than enough. Love yourself. You have a book. Not many people can say that. You are now in the business of dreams. Let it feel like that more often than not.

IV
....

Postpublication
(or: life after your debut)

If you know what you're doing next creatively, or did an exhausting tour for your first book, you might enter the postpublication feeling tremendously relieved. But most of us writers will stumble across the threshold from publication to postpub harboring disappointments that we don't know where to put, all the while knowing that the clock is ticking for our second book. But how is it possible to write a second book when you haven't digested the experience of publishing a first one? How do debut authors deal with the pulsing neon question of what's next?

The Great Big First-Book Comedown
....

The initial month after your book's publication is a speedy joyride. You have reviews coming out—actual people are writing about your book!—and total strangers are Instagramming it next to fair-trade cappuccinos. You're being notified, retweeted, liked, mentioned, and you're feeling pretty fine.

But something odd happens about four weeks into your book's

publication. People start talking about other books online. Your book's only been out a month, so you still have a little dignity. You use it to remind yourself that it is irrational—unseemly!—to expect the Internauts to talk of nothing but your book. People have a right to read books you haven't written, you say to yourself while deciding whether or not you have it in you to floss. *People have a right to read books you haven't written,* you repeat, instead of flossing. You know this is true, because you have been reading those books your entire life.

But still, you think. But *still*. What you'll do is call your agent. She always makes you feel like number one. But surprisingly, her assistant says she's on another phone call. This is weird, because the person she is speaking with isn't you. Is it possible that she has other priorities than you and your first book? You spend the rest of the week Googling yourself in bed.

By week five, the thumbnail of your book cover that your editor used to display underneath her email signature has been replaced by the new book that they're supporting. Of course, of course, this is the way of publishing, you think to yourself from the bed you need to get out of. Of course your editor will go on to publish other books. You just never dreamed that it would happen so soon.

The Great Big First-Book Comedown will hit full force by week six. Unless you're, like, Colson Whitehead or something, what you're going to find yourself with six weeks postpub is the double-edged gift of time. If you have exceptional willpower and a second project you're already excited about, you might use this time to write. If you're mortal, and fallible, you might use that time to, say, research how other books are doing in comparison with your own, read your Amazon reviews, monitor your Amazon sales ranking, incessantly refresh your social media feeds, overeat, overdrink, maybe cry a bit.

It doesn't matter if you published a bestseller, a total sleeper, or just a respectable debut; at this point, editors and journalists and readers are going to move on. And regardless of whether you are feeling manic with satisfaction or completely dashed, you need to move on, too.

Let's spend some time understanding how to do this.

The stress of the sophomore project

The existential ups and downs of the debut publishing experience can unmoor even the most grounded personalities, and this vulnerability is intensified by the fact that everyone's asking you the same question: What's next, what's next, what's next?

Literary agent Monica Odom suggests that authors find a safe harbor in their first book's place of origin: the book contract. Depending on your option clause, you could find yourself in one of several scenarios. You might already be under contract for a second book. You might have an idea for a second book, but you haven't started writing it. If your book was a hit, you can sometimes sell the second book on a pitch alone. Most fiction writers, however, will have to write about fifty pages, or three chapters, of a new project before they can submit the manuscript, while nonfiction writers will have to share a hearty proposal with sample chapters and comp titles. Your last publisher will always have the right of first refusal on your second book, unless your new project is in a different genre than your first one. (For example, you might not be obligated to show your publisher your new memoir if your first contract was for fiction. Check your contract to make sure.) If your publisher turns your manuscript down, you and your agent are now free to submit to other houses.

A lot of authors are sitting on collections of short stories or essays, waiting for the right time to hatch them. Now might be the time. Some publishers prefer to publish such collections after an author has already published a book or two so that they have a better chance of bringing readers to their project. Talk with your agent about whether polishing up your short-story collection is a good move right now.

There's another option, of course, and that is that you don't have any manuscripts a revision away from stardom, nor do you have any $&!@ idea what to do next. "A lot of my job is figuring out if a person has a next idea," says Monica, "and to read between the lines if the idea is coming from a sense of urgency, or if it has the same magic and intent that their debut did."

Monica admits that the stress of the sophomore book is real, especially if your book experienced underwhelming sales. She urges the idealess to take some serious time off. "Often, the client conversations I'm having involve me pulling someone out of the muck of what they *think* they should be doing," Monica says. "Go do some other things that are definitely going to make you money. Steeping yourself in the publishing landscape is the worst way to come up with a new idea."

In order to maintain your audience while you're searching for inspiration, Monica suggests starting an engaging email newsletter or podcast as a side project, while also participating in the gig economy so that you can pay your bills. "I love talking to Uber and Lyft drivers," she says. "They're often so creative. The first thing I do when I get in is say, 'Tell me about you, tell me what you're working on.' I believe in the side hustle. They can bring incredible opportunities that weren't there before."

The world is going to want a novel, but you don't have to give it one

Whether you're a poet with an ice-sculpting business or a hedge-fund manager who ditched it all to go into stand-up comedy, if you can write in complete sentences and you have an interesting life story, publishing professionals will think you have a novel. (You don't have time to write a novel, you're doing stand-up comedy!) The thing is, this novel is inside of you. You might not be able to feel it, but the publishing professionals can.

The pressure to produce a novel is nearly reproductive in its fervor. If you try to sell a short-story collection, you will often have to promise that there is a novel coming behind it. If you publish a risky essay online that gets a lot of views, you will be contacted by literary agents who are en route to your domicile to find your secret book.

Here is the big secret: you don't have to write a novel. (Unless you're under contract to do so, friend.) Absolutely, novels tend to come with bigger advances than collections or novellas, so it is tempting to pursue the novel track. It's good work if you can get it, and in an age where social media makes it look like career authors are cheerfully pumping out a good book every two years, it's tempting to think that you can work on the same time schedule, and happily at that. I'm hearing more and more from authors that they're being given a year to write their second books. If the world is not enough, then a year *definitely* isn't. It's enough if you're James Patterson, and you have a stable of writers helping you meet deadlines (and a housekeeper, and a chef . . .), but it's usually not enough for the rest of us.

Take a breath before starting your next project. Lots of writers switched gears to keep their morale and energy up with projects that were a total departure from their first books. Deb Olin Unferth debuted with a novel, and has written short-story collections and a graphic novel since. Tim Federle started writing cocktail books for adults at the same time that he was publishing novels for children. Lydia Davis translated freaking Proust, and after the success of "The Love Song of J. Alfred Prufrock," T. S. Eliot started penning cat poems to his godchildren, which would eventually be adapted into the Broadway favorite, *Cats*.

If you do decide to switch genres for your second book, be aware that your current editorial team might not be able to support your creative change of heart. When the author Alexi Zentner turned to writing thrillers and mysteries after feeling burned out by the publication of his second literary novel, his publisher feared that Alexi's regular readers would be disoriented by the change of style. Accordingly, Alexi and his agent decided to publish his thriller manuscript *The Hatching* with a different publishing house under a pen name. Coming at a time when Alexi was exhausted by publishing in general, writing under a pen name felt liberating and fun. "I liked the Old Testament sound of Ezekiel Boone, and I was eager to not have a last name like 'Zentner' that would land me on the far bottom shelf of a bookstore," Alexi says of the new pen name they chose.

Although this might feel radical in a culture focused on hyper-homogenized personal brands, your second project does not have to be a book.* The aforementioned Tanaïs runs her own fragrance and beauty company called Hi Wildflower that often features artists of color as its models; Emma Straub opened up the independent bookstore Books Are Magic in Brooklyn; authors Heidi Sopinka and Claudia Dey run the fashion label Horses Atelier together; and I founded the learning collaborative The Cabins in between my first and second books.

Whether your sophomore project is something that you can hold in your hands or an offering to the community, take the necessary risks to make sure that the act of writing retains its creative mystery and its joy. It is, without question, better for your long-term career to work on smaller, less commercial projects until you have a great idea for a new novel than it is to force yourself to write an uninspired second book. Bad second books will harm you much more than patience will.

---

* Unless you already have a second book contract. Then your second project does, in fact, have to be a book.

Tips on entering the academic market

You've got a first book out, you either do or do not have an idea for a second one, and in the meantime, you need to earn a living. If you're thinking about entering the academic market [insert scared emoji face], godspeed!

By this point, you may have enough teaching friends to have a sense of how crazy-making the academic market is. Recovering academic Lisa Munro has called the academic job search a "bizarre slow-motion hazing ritual"; writer Rebecca Schuman has dubbed it "Byzantine." If you type "academic job market" into Google, it will proffer "market depression" and "stress" before any other search term.

Many applicants spend up to six years in the academic job market before they find a stable (or semistable) job in a place that they can stand to live in. Some candidates end up with tenure-track positions; others end up as visiting professors who never know when the hiring committee is going to yank the welcome mat from under them; everyone knows that they must publish, publish, publish, else they sink into oblivion.

Stay nimble as all get-out

The academic market favors candidates who can travel—literally and figuratively—without a lot of baggage. If you are in love, like your current home a lot, are attached to your friends, or have dependents, the job hunt is going to suck harder for you than it will for your colleagues who are single or practice nonattachment. With every year that passes, the writer, teacher, and mother Ramona Ausubel finds the prospect of moving her family out of Boulder, Colorado, where they're happy, to a question-mark city where they are question-mark content less and less appealing. For many years, she only applied for teaching jobs if the

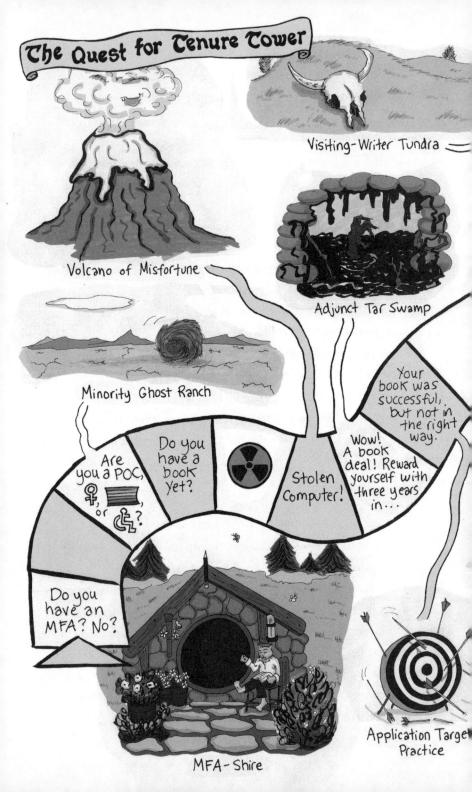

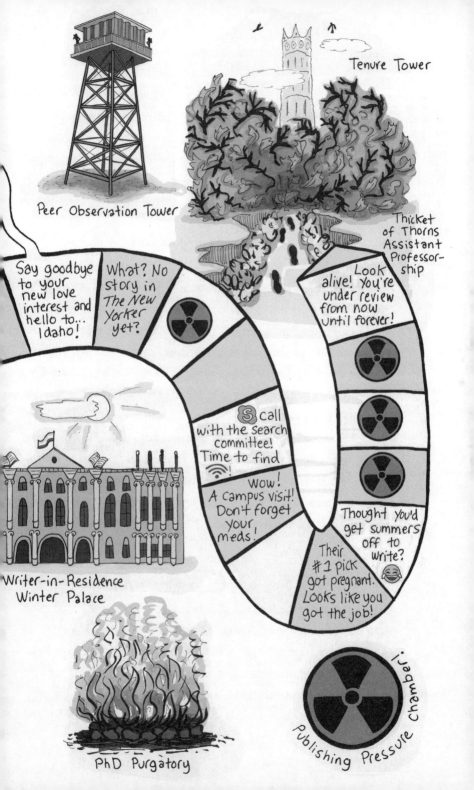

commute was within an hour of her home. Although the stars aligned for Ramona after five years of job-hunting, she's the first to admit that her rigid geographical criteria and consideration for her family's needs kept her from being more competitive in the academic market. "I put family first, and that's part of why it took me so long to find a full-time job," she laughs.

Keep track of your good news

The academic job hunt will require a Herculean level of organization and paperwork, both virtual and physical. The minimum ask for most creative-writing applications is a cover letter, three letters of recommendation, a teaching portfolio (composed of recent teaching evaluations and a one-page statement of teaching philosophy), sample syllabus, a writing sample, a diversity statement, and an updated CV. To combat these requests effectively, you'll need to keep your materials up to date. Every month, revisit your accomplishments: Do you have new publications? Have you participated in any noteworthy speaking events? Been accepted to a fellowship or a residency? Do you have a new book deal? Have you met someone recently who could give you a recommendation? Have you slighted someone who has recommended you in the past? How will you make this right by them? DON'T MESS UP YOUR LIFE!

Write like your career depends on it (it does)

Good news about the Internet: it's made it easier than ever to get your work published and read. So take advantage of that World Wide Web. Certainly, you want to be picky about where you're publishing (admissions committees will probably balk at a byline in *My Little Brony*, for example), but the playing field is wider than it has been in the past. Top-rate literary magazines like *The Paris Review*, *The New Yorker*, and

The Atlantic have online components where it's easier to get your work published than in print, but you still get to enjoy the prestige of these magazines' fine names and reputations. The pitch, acceptance, editing process, and publication of an article or story in a reputable print magazine can take a long time, so it's worth supporting your print bylines with some online ones each year.

Know the hidden costs of moving . . . anywhere

"I decided to live in New York through a complex, sober, careful deliberative process," jokes author and translator Rosalie Knecht. "No, of course I didn't. I decided to live in New York because I was fresh out of college, and I felt that D.C. was too hot, and Boston was too clean, and Philadelphia contained a recent ex-boyfriend. So if I'd been more tolerant of muggy summers or more able to handle my exes with grace and class, I would have gotten an MFA at one of those not-in-New-York programs, and then it would have made sense to teach, and I would be teaching now."

Save for the independently wealthy, very few people can live on a beginning teacher's salary, and if you can live on an adjunct's salary in a city like Manhattan . . . ? (Come on, admit it. You totally have a trust fund.)

Before you go applying willy-nilly to jobs in cities that excite you, do your research on the city's cost. What are rent and mortgage averages? Will you have a commute, and how much will it cost to have a car and car insurance? What's the cost of childcare? (Research this even if you don't have kids, or don't plan on having any. Listen! You never know.) Do you currently have a lease, and if so, when's it up? Do you plan on having any dental work done in the near future? (If the answer is yes, you cannot be a writer! Have you read Martin Amis's memoir about the financial repercussions of his wonky teeth?)

Look beyond the U.S.A. for teaching opportunities

The United States is not the only country that offers teaching positions in creative writing. (Although it might be the only one whose educated masses think they can make a living doing so.) The United Kingdom, New Zealand, Australia, Canada: there are a lot of places that seek lecturers and visiting professors in creative writing for English speakers, and if you speak a second or third language, the world is your oyster to apply to. Check out the websites of Teach Away, Go Overseas, or World Teachers to get a feel for what is out there in terms of jobs and benefits. (Make sure the school assists with visa administration unless you want a fast pass to the third circle of hell.)

Your MFA program and undergrad program can also help you connect with teaching programs and opportunities abroad. If you are an American citizen and you decide to fly the coop, please file for an absentee voter ballot before doing so!

Stay connected to the community that you want to employ you

There are two major conferences for academic networking in the United States. The first is the Modern Language Association (MLA) that takes place annually in the fall or winter, and the second is the Association of Writers & Writing Programs, which happens in the early spring. Both conferences offer ample opportunities for networking, research, and interviews—the problemo is that they're both held in a rotating cast of cities, and unless your MFA program offers generous travel stipends, you are going to be paying out of pocket to transport, lodge, and feed yourself while there.

If you live outside of a major urban center with a strong literary community, you'll have to work extra hard to schmooze. Look into the local colleges that have literary magazines; show up to their readings. Keep on top of academic conferences that are coming through your town: the website PaperCrowd will be helpful in this regard, as will Conference Alerts.

In the academic job market, last-minute efforts never take the cake, and this holds true for networking, as well. Keep in mind that most job openings are posted in the fall. For the lucky few who make it that far in the process, campus visits are usually scheduled around January, with offers sent out in March. This makes a conference such as AWP—which is traditionally held in February or March—helpful only for the proactive: the discussions you're having at a spring conference can't bear fruit for another year.

The stress of the academic job market is a hot topic at the moment, so the community of writers and reporters covering this subject are a mere click away. Although it's specific to the U.K. market, *The Guardian*'s education department is doing thorough coverage of academic-market concerns; the websites *Inside Higher Ed* and *ChronicleVitae* are constantly publishing informative and varied content, and Karen Kelsky's handy book *The Professor Is In: The Essential Guide to Turning Your Ph.D. Into a Job* will educate (and entertain) tenure-track job seekers as well as those just starting out on their teaching paths.

Should I take this weird-ass ghostwriting opportunity?

In 2010, author Mira Ptacin was approached to ghostwrite a children's book about a celebrity animal while her agent was trying, with little success, to sell her first memoir. The agent thought the project would be great for Mira because the interest in her memoir just wasn't there at the moment, and Mira, who was working in a Brooklyn bakery, really needed cash.

"I didn't really have any credentials to ghostwrite," explained

Mira. "I had a master's degree, I had some articles published, I ran a reading series. My agent really sold me to the animal's owners. She said that I was this fantastic writer, the right person for the book."

Mira was paid $3,000 to write a proposal. Happily, a mass-media company purchased the proposal for the big-ass sum of $150,000. Unhappily, her agent wasn't able to negotiate aggressive terms. Mira was granted 14 percent of the advance money: about $20,000. After paying off grad-school loans, taxes, and 15 percent to her agent, Mira remembers, "I had enough money leftover to buy some makeup and a hair brush."

The book went on to become a number-one bestseller in the children's book category. But Mira wasn't given credit for her ghostwriting, nor was she thanked in the book's acknowledgments. A writer's dream, and a ghostwriter's worst nightmare, she had to watch the animal's owners go on *Oprah* to talk all about the experience of writing a book that she had written for them.

"I learned a lot about writing a kid's book," Mira says of the experience, "and it was relatively easy ... it was only a thousand-word book. But it was a very complex experience with a lot of tension. I wouldn't do it again."

I once heard of a successful novelist who was paid $100,000 to write a novel for an even more successful novelist, and I was told that he used that money to escape to the Caribbean to pen his second book, but my efforts to contact this author to corroborate this did not bear fruit. (I don't think he gets very good service on his island.)

I myself was approached once to ghostwrite a romance novel that took place on the *Titanic*. This sounded like fun until I read the terms: regardless of how the book performed, or whether it went on to be a movie (as romances that take place on the *Titanic* are wont to do), I would receive $10,000 and never a dime more. "Show me the money!" I shouted.

"Show me a little more!" Though the publisher didn't increase their of-fer, they did say they'd put my name somewhere on the book jacket, but I cannot—at present—deposit book jackets in the bank. The money-to-work ratio just wasn't worth it. That ship did not sail.

If you're going to ghostwrite, make sure you have a contract that respects your creative worth and time. And by all means, lobby for a writing credit, preferably somewhere noticeable, like on the book's front.

OMG my inbox: handling your email

Although it would be nice to live in a world where the only emails we get from strangers are complimentary ones, this is not a reality that most writers know. Once your work starts to gain a certain amount of attention, it's a good idea to set up a separate email address for your friends, colleagues, and family that trolls can't use or find. If you have an agent or a publicist, you can list their email addresses on your web-site, and/or you can always use an email contact form. You are not obligated to make it easy for strangers to contact you. But many writers do feel a responsibility to their readers, and they feel guilty when they leave nice notes unanswered.

Accordingly, one thing you might consider doing on your public-facing email account is to create an autoresponder that includes both a thank-you-for-writing message and some helpful FAQs. For example, if you've written a viral essay about beating an addiction, perhaps in-clude some of your favorite addiction-recovery resources in your auto-response. If you wrote an op-ed about how great and affordable college is in Canada, why not include some hyperlinks to your favorite schools in that good country? You don't have to anticipate the questions that readers will be asking you; once you've had a popular piece out there for a couple days, you will know what most of these questions are. Be candid in the autoresponse: let the sender know how grateful you are that they took the time to write you and how you wish you had the chance to write everyone back personally, but . . .

As for the daily handling of your inbox, writers tend to fall into two camps: those who deal, and those who just cannot with all the email. In the "dealing" camp, entrepreneur and writer Rebecca Soffer swears by Streak, an easy-to-use tool that automatically pulls Gmail conversations into your customer-relationship management system. "It's a terrific tool for people working on books with multiple contributors," Rebecca explains. "It's how I managed communication with the forty-plus contributors to *Modern Loss*, since we were dealing with multiple drafts and email brainstorms for each piece." Rebecca also transitioned from responding to emails as soon as they came in to setting aside two hours every day for her digital communication. "When it comes to book writing, you can't get much done if you're fanatically checking your inbox. I'm usually the kind of person who responds to emails immediately, but I realized I was sending a sign that I was perpetually accessible," she says.

Paul W. Morris, executive director of House of SpeakEasy, and the former vice president of membership and outreach at the Authors Guild, maintains different email accounts for the various roles that he takes on. "I have them all forward to my Gmail where they arrive coded by color and tags, and presorted for folders. It knows which ones are more important than others generally, and unread ones get the higher priority, broken down across three categories. Also, I swear by the Boomerang plug-in, which is a handy reminder and email scheduling tool that affords me a lot of flexibility, not to mention efficiency."

You receive a lot of email. Try to remember that reality when you email someone else. "With a toddler," writes author Miranda Beverly-Whittemore, "I have only about twelve dedicated hours of paid-for childcare every week, which is not nearly enough time to write and read anything for myself, which means I basically ignore my email. I used to feel very guilty about it, but I just can't anymore."

In order to prioritize her creative work, Miranda has started to come down harder on flippant or disrespectful asks. "With limited time, it's very easy to tell the difference between an email that invites me to be included in something and one that is strictly about that person getting something from me," Miranda says. "A book launch, a recommendation letter, or a blurb request can fall into either of those categories, actually—it's really all in how the invitation/request comes in, and the clarity with which that person defines my role in the process (what they need from me, when, and why I'm the person who they've come to instead of anyone else out there). I am much more likely to respond and be eager to help someone quickly who is warm, knows what they want, has a specific ask, and understands that my time and resources are limited. That my helping them in this way would be worth something. I'm at a moment in my life when any work I'm putting out into the world—especially if it's taking away from my creative time (even if it's just an email!)—has to feel like it has meaning to it."

Hiring a speaking agent

If your book was well-received critically and/or commercially, or is on a zeitgeisty topic, you might find your inbox swelling with speaking invitations well after your book's publication. If it gets to the point that your invitations are becoming numerous, lucrative, and unmanageable by your lonesome, it might be time to find a speaker's agency.

There are three different partners for writers who are already receiving paid speaking invitations: in-house speaking bureaus at commercial publishers; independent corporate speaking bureaus; and speaking agencies. The major difference is that bureaus book speakers for their client venues, whereas with a speaking agency, the *authors* are the clients.

While speaking agencies tend to be more collaborative in terms of pitching authors, not all agencies will work with emerging talent. "Although I leave a certain amount of spots open for up-and-coming poets and writers that I can book for under three thousand dollars," says the head of a leading speaking agency, who preferred to remain anonymous, "a lot of agencies won't speak to an author or handle an event unless it will bring in at least ten thousand dollars."

Much like literary agents, speaking agents don't get paid until you do: the industry standard is a 20 percent cut. If building your speaking career isn't your long-term focus and you just need someone to help you through your book's promotion, you might be better served by a personal assistant or a freelance publicist instead. After all, you can't get a speaking agent just because you want one; they need empirical evidence that you can woo a crowd.

In order for the author–speaking agent relationship to be fruitful, the agency has to have a clear idea of the topics you're passionate about and a blueprint for how to connect your message with the appropriate audience. You'll be building a personal brand together, and in order to do this, you'll have to know the brand you want to build.

Author Elizabeth Rosner felt like she was ready for a speaking agent well before she actually secured one. She considers public speaking to be one of her strengths: whenever she gives lectures or appears on panels, people would compliment her on her presence and her oratory skills. But Elizabeth felt that if she had to reach out to a speaking agent, instead of the other way around, it reflected poorly on her. "I'd gotten gun-shy about looking around," she says. "I felt convinced that I needed someone to come looking for me." But when her fourth book (and her first memoir—she'd published three novels and a poetry collection before) achieved critical success, landing her both on *All Things Considered* and in *The New York Times* for the first time, she decided to be more proactive about putting herself out there.

After a successful appearance at the revered Pittsburgh Arts & Lectures series, Elizabeth went on a walk with one of the organizers and asked for her professional opinion: "I want to do more public speaking," Elizabeth told her. "What's the secret?"

The organizer said that she would personally recommend Elizabeth to two agencies she enjoyed working with. One of these agencies set up a call with her after receiving the recommendation email: Elizabeth has been working with the EMT Agency ever since.

In addition to removing her from time-sucking back-and-forth emails about logistics, Elizabeth deeply enjoys not having to talk about money anymore. "I get that it's a business and it's part of the business, but I'm not good at that stuff. I'm not good at saying no and standing up for myself, nor am I good at walking away from something if it feels like they aren't valuing me enough."

For nonfiction writers, deciding which topics they're knowledgeable enough to lecture on is fairly simple: they can talk about their book's subject. For fiction writers, the path's more circuitous, but general lecture topics can be unearthed with some careful thought.

Author Rebecca Makkai, who often incorporates historical research into her novels, has become an ace at putting a nonfiction bent on her lectures and presentations. Rebecca's second book, *The Hundred-Year House*, was a generational saga told backward with a fictionalized Chicago artist colony at its core. Based on her experience researching and writing that book, she now gives lectures on the history of the arts in Chicago in the twentieth century. "I found cool slides," says Rebecca. "I talk about the history of artist residencies, which isn't something a lot of people know about. I discuss real figures that I fictionalized for the book, and I share quirky anecdotes that will hopefully lead people to my novel."

Regarding her third book, the award-winning *The Great Believers* (which deals with the impact and aftermath of the AIDS epidemic), Rebecca concedes that she isn't the person people want to hear from about the latest breakthroughs in AIDS treatment or barriers to care. "But I can give a talk about how I incorporated and conducted historical research in Chicago, and what I learned from people in AIDS research," she says.

Rebecca keeps a spreadsheet of her craft talks and lecture topics that she updates regularly with any changes she has made. "When an organizer comes to me saying, 'We need a seventy-five-word description,' or, 'We need a talk targeted to grad students or senior citizens,'" Rebecca says, "I can cut and paste written pitches right from there."

Whether you are applying through your own publisher to be part of their in-house speaking bureau or your agent is reaching out to independent speaking agencies on your behalf, be prepared to hear "no." Many writers think they're ready for a speaking agent because their book's been well-received, when the reality is that it takes far more than a good book to fill a room.

"The time to get a speaking agent is when the market asks for it," says Andrew Wetzel, a senior agent at the Lyceum Agency. "Not when you're 40,000 words into your projected 90,000-word novel, or when the book's months from coming out."

Andrew says it isn't necessary for writers to rush their quest for a speaking agent, nor do most writers need one. "Anything that is bringing in less than $5,000 is the kind of opportunity we would usually pass on to the authors themselves," continues Andrew. "This is where the emerging author will find most of their opportunities, with professors and smaller programs who love what the respective author is doing on a sentence-by-sentence level." Speaking agencies, on the other hand, can't be "micro" in their affection for a particular writer's style. "The people we have added recently are either wildly popular, or they're offering something really meaty off the page," says Andrew. "They represent huge topics that are pertinent to campus: environmentalism, homelessness, social-justice issues."

For writers interested in seeking speaking representation once they're more established, Andrew suggests keeping an updated CV. Include a "Speaking" tab on your author website where you can share video clips, testimonials, topics you're prepared to speak about, and places you have spoken in the past. "Self-agent for a while," Andrew encourages. "Don't list your prices on your website, but do have a standard range in mind so you can push for fee integrity."

Do I need to go to parties?

Author Maggie Shipstead is both successful (her books have garnered her placement on *The New York Times* bestseller list and won her the Dylan Thomas Prize) and rarely home. She moves around a lot for her side career as a travel journalist, and she's never been one to force herself to go to parties she doesn't want to attend. "I think it's worthwhile for first-time authors to genuinely and purposefully consider what feels authentic for them and then protect that," Maggie says. "I don't mean 'authentic' in an Instagrammy #authentic way, but more like, what feels natural? What feels comfortable, uncomfortable? What fills you with eagerness, dread?"

Don't like social media? "Forced and tepid tweets will not make your book appreciably more successful," Maggie says. Hate attending shindigs? "The same is true for going to book parties or participating in the scene, which sort of requires you to live in New York and so isn't even an option for lots of writers. If you want to go to parties, great! Have fun. If you don't, your career probably won't benefit much from your unhappily hiding behind a potted plant and texting. Yes, you might miss out on making a few contacts, but I think that's counterbalanced by the advantages of leading a more diversified life. Sometimes getting in too deep with the literary world—i.e., paying too much attention to what's happening to other people's books and careers—breeds anxiety and erodes perspective and possibly even stifles creativity. Writing can be a job, not a lifestyle. It doesn't have to take over your social life and become the only thing you care about."

On the flip side, the aforementioned Paul W. Morris—literary advocate for organizations such as the Authors Guild, PEN America, the National Book Foundation, and other cultural organizations—believes there are tangible benefits to attending literary events. Readings, festivals, and fundraisers can help you better understand the landscape you're trying to be a part of. What cultural issues are being written about and discussed? What industry initiatives have people buzzing? Who are the kindred editors and publishers you might turn to when you've written something you're really excited about?

"Of course, being able to participate in an organic and unscripted conversation is a big factor, too," Paul says. "In our current age of social media and screen addiction, so many of our online interactions can be cold and dispassionate. Too often, writers allow themselves to be anonymous in ways that can hinder and hurt their careers in the long run. Writers traditionally work in isolation. It's part of the job description. And writers have also been known to be shy, hesitant to engage socially, or just uncomfortable in large groups. Maybe this apprehension is what led them to become a writer in the first place, but getting outside this comfort zone feels like a prerequisite for a writer hoping to build a career that is part of a larger publishing ecosystem."

Whether forcing yourself out of the house yields a conversation by the coat check with your future publisher or a shared elevator ride with a curator who will one day help you reach hundreds of readers by paneling at their literary festival, face-to-face interactions give authors the opportunity to articulate their work in a way that they might not be able to do online.

Many of the larger parties and conferences take place in urban centers like New York or Los Angeles, and not only do many writers not have the financial or physical means to make it to these cities, accessibility issues can make attendance for some writers—especially the disabled—near impossible. Some of the larger conferences, such as BEA (BookExpo America) and AWP (Association of Writers & Writing Programs), are held in different locations annually, and they tend to announce their scheduling up to two years in advance, allowing literature lovers to gauge when a major conference is coming to their region. These two conferences are also working to address accessibility concerns in order to make it easier, and more comfortable, for disabled people to attend.

As exciting as it can be to meet a writer or editor you admire, Paul cautions partygoers from expecting industry interactions to bear fruit right away. "Be real, be honest. Be who you are, not who you think someone wants you to be. If the connection doesn't emerge right then and there, that's okay. Not everything needs to connect in the short term. You never know the ripple effect that serendipitous encounters can have!"

Do I have to blurb? (And how, exactly, do I do it?)

If you experience a modicum of success with your first book, editors and publicists will start sending you review copies of new books for your endorsement. "Endorsement" is an industry euphemism for "blurb." Some of these books will be in the genre that you write in and cover topics and themes that concern you, other books will come your way because you grew up in the town that the author is writing about, others because you share something in common with the author, i.e., a cervix. If you're famous, you will receive all of the books in the whole world. You won't have time to read them. They will fill up your domicile and make neighbors think that you're a hoarder. You're not a hoarder, you are a respected author living in the blurbing world.

Authors who receive a lot of blurb requests often come up with a rule to make it easier to say no. Some only blurb work by former students or current colleagues; others prioritize members of communities marginalized in (or by) the publishing industry. Some writers come up with an arbitrary number: they'll give four blurbs for every one person who blurbed their book, or they'll blurb one book a month. Others only blurb the books they really, truly like.

Unlike other aspects of life where I think honesty behooves us, honesty has little place in blurbing. When a publicist follows up with you about a book you didn't like, the answer is always, "I'm sorry but I did not have time to read it, but good luck with its publication," and never, "You know, I did read it, and I really some reservations about the way that character *X* was developed, and I also felt like the sex scene on page forty-three was ..."

Nope. Why risk offending an editor, a publicist, an editorial assistant, an author, and all of the countless other people who have their hopes built into this book when you could stay silent? You never know when the publicist you offend will replace your own, so lie. You are busy, you appreciate their thinking of you, you wish the author the very best in life. If you have to blurb the book for political reasons but you want the world to know you didn't like it, simply say that the book in question is "keenly observed."

Let's fast-forward to a future in which you have agreed to blurb a title, and now that blurb is due. You've received endorsements in the past, so you assumed that you could write one, but now you feel incredulous as to what a blurb actually is.

Blurb length

If you are super famous, you can get away with a one-sentence blurb. You can even order people around! (As in, "I loved this! Read this book right now!") For the rest of us, blurbs should hit the forty-to-sixty-word mark. If they are longer than that, they'll begin to eat into real estate reserved for other blurbers.

Blurb structure

Although blurbs stroke an author's ego, they have a deeper purpose. Book buyers, sales agents, book scouts, festival organizers, and many other professionals read blurbs with an eye to the year ahead, in terms of what they will be buying, promoting, and organizing. Knowing this, it gives the author a leg up if you sneak a minisummary into your blurb. Hint at the predicament in which the heroes/antiheroes find themselves; offer up the book's central, burning question without giving plot away. You also want to create a sense of urgency for the reader: an unignorable reason as to why *this* is the book the reader needs right now. In general, a winning blurb (as in one that is both industry and consumer facing) will look something like this:

[Introduce situation or setting], [emphasize the mood]. [Compliment the writing and the book's main themes]. [Finish with a call to action about how incredible the book is].

Applying this formula in the real world would look something like the sixty-two-word stunner provided to Carmen Maria Machado in 2017 by the author Karen Russell:

> Carmen Maria Machado's *Her Body and Other Parties* tells ancient fables of eros and female metamorphosis in fantastically new ways. She draws the secret world of the body into visibility, and illuminates the dark woods of the psyche. In these formally brilliant and emotionally charged tales, Machado gives literal shape to women's memories and hunger and desire. I couldn't put it down.

Infuse your blurb with style

Karen's blurb isn't just a testament to the quality of Carmen's collection, it's also an example of how well Karen writes. It makes people want to read *both* Carmen's and Karen's books—a truly winning blurb! Remember that it's a privilege—and an opportunity—to have a blurb on someone's book. If the book in question becomes a bestseller, your name is going to be in a lot of people's hands, so don't write a throwaway quote that doesn't do justice to your aesthetics.

Take credit

When you send your blurb in, make sure you specify how you want to be credited. Most editors will default to citing an author's latest book, so if there is a past or forthcoming book you'd prefer attached to your name, be sure to mention it. Generally, because of space concerns, you'll only be able to list one of your book titles.

What do I do with all these galleys?

Galleys are rough printed proofs of forthcoming books and *ARCs* (standing for either "advance review copy" or "advance reader copy" or, if you are me, and no one corrects you for an embarrassing amount of time, "advanced reader copy") are like galleys, except with fewer typos and a nicer cover. Although galleys come before ARCs in the production timeline, you'll hear these terms used interchangeably, with readers talking about a "galley" that is actually an ARC, probably because it sounds like you're barking at someone when you say "ARC" out loud.

Galleys will begin to fill your mailbox like spores postpublication. You will have neither the time nor the inclination to blurb every galley you receive, but there are still a lot of ways to show these books support.

- Share a picture of the book—or books—on your social media with the hashtag #galleybrag. Tag the author and their publisher. Other hashtags you might consider using: #amreading #bookstagram #newrelease #bookhaul #booklove
- If you start receiving an impressive amount of galleys, follow the example of *Book Riot*'s Liberty Hardy, who posts celebratory pictures with all the advance copies she's received on the floor next to her cat, which works well because Liberty gets great books and has an exemplary cat.
- Galleys can't be sold, nor can they be put in a circulating library, so don't post them on eBay, Amazon, or include them

in the Little Free Libraries popping up around the country. In a ShelfTalker essay for *Poets & Writers*, bookseller Josie Leavitt encourages the galley-laden to put bookplates stating the "can't be sold or circulated" disclaimer into their review copies before donating them to schools, prisons, hospitals, and charitable organizations such as the Ronald McDonald House. This move will be appreciated by the books' recipients and unappreciated by the writers whose prefinal words were meant for your eyes alone.

- Although you won't feel good about it, most review copies can be recycled. Binding, coated covers, and string binding can complicate the process, so call your waste hauler if you'd like to get the whole recycling thing right.

- In an industry where social media builds buzz, a picture is better than no picture, but keep in mind that it's bad form to post photos of a galley when the finished book is available. And do not bring a galley to an author's book event to get it signed unless you also buy a copy of the published book while there.

Publishing your paperback

If your book came out in hardcover and performed admirably, it will probably come out seven to twelve months later in paperback.

The paperback edition gives the world a second chance to meet a title in a lighter, less expensive format. Your editorial team might decide to freshen up the cover by changing its design, and paperbacks will proudly host all of the nice press you've received thus far, along with the titles (and stickers) of any rewards it may have garnered.

With few exceptions, most books get the most attention when they debut in their original format. Paperback releases receive far less press than hardcover debuts, and the outlets that do cover them (*People, Entertainment Weekly, The New York Times*'s Paperback Row) are difficult to land.

Accordingly, a paperback release can be a milestone that arrives with curiously little fanfare. The earth shakes when you publish your hardcover, and social media shimmies. With your paperback, the world doesn't slow down to notice that your book has come out again. As with all things publishing, your pride in a job well done must live alongside the realization that most people will never understand or care about your work as much as you do. The physiological effect of these two emotions can be bittersweet, so plan something nice for yourself that doesn't involve the Internet on your paperback pub day.

(It should be mentioned that some writers *do* set the earth to shaking with their paperback releases: they hit bestseller lists; they go on paperback tours; they start book clubbing a-go-go. Say it with me: #goals.)

Reevaluating your professional relationships after your debut

When the dust has settled, and your first book has been out in the universe for a while, you'll want to take stock of all that passed to discern whether you'll go back in with the same team for round two.

It's true that writers are lucky to find agents, and even luckier to find publishers. Ditto for the writers who get to work with film agents, translators, and so forth. But it's also true that these parties make money off of us, and in that sense, we are allowed to ask ourselves if they're doing a good job.

Think very specifically when you're considering your disappointments. If your frustrations are linked to elements that nobody could control (your book published during a political scandal, your publicist had a family emergency right before your launch), you probably had an adequate publishing team and some rotten luck. But if you have real concerns (books weren't sent to people they were promised to, opportunities weren't followed up on, edits weren't sent in time, important calls or emails were rarely returned, or, in one incredible case I heard, your editor adopted a fake publishing-assistant persona complete with a faux company email address to "deal with" your tricky questions), maybe you have a couple of weak links in the chain. If the fault lies with your publisher, you don't have to work with them again unless you're under contract to. This being said, keep in mind that your book still belongs to the publisher and lives inside their house. If you part ways, try to do so as amicably as possible. When it comes time to promote your backlist, you want a fond ex on your side.

If the issue's with your agent, this is slightly thornier. Put in some reflection before you ask your agent for a meeting. The author and etiquette expert Henry Alford suggests that you send high-voltage emails to yourself first and wait twenty-four hours to read them, in order to better gauge what it would feel like to receive such a message out of the blue. Once it's sent, it's sent—so it really is worth sensitivity-screening your sentiments before you take to your computer.

If you live close enough to do so, take your agent out for a meal so you can discuss things face-to-face. Like with any conversation that is going to involve your criticizing someone, start by telling them all the ways that they did a stupendous job. Make sure you come prepared with specific examples of times they disappointed you or didn't take your interests into consideration. Don't be vague and say, "I just don't feel cherished." That won't get you anywhere.

You'll probably know from the tenor of the conversation whether or not you two can continue working together amiably. If so, congratulations. If not, the nature of your sophomore project will determine what happens next. It isn't unheard of for agents to suggest colleagues who might be better suited for their current client than themselves. A friend of mine is about to put out a book that is vastly different from her first one in subject matter and genre, and her first agent is spearheading the effort to find her a new agent because she doesn't feel experienced enough representing this book's particular genre.

If you do decide to part ways with your agent, and you already have a book—or books—out, it's worth remembering that your ex-agent will always be the agent of record on your book. That means that royalties on the books they agented will continue to flow through to them, even if you're not on speaking terms. This awkwardness is usually alleviated by the fact that your new agency will happily handle the discussion of (and forwarding of) these royalty statements, so that you don't have to.

But what happens if your film rights never sold, or the book wasn't translated outside of the country it was published in? What's a writer to do if they feel like there are unexploited opportunities for their past books? "If publication rights in the book have already been sold," explains agent Veronica Goldstein, whom we heard from in book one, "the author would give a period of notice for the fired agent to wrap up their ongoing foreign/film submissions. After that point the author could request that the agent officially releases all unsold rights in the work to them and then the author would be free to pursue those rights with their new agent." Most times, the fired agent agrees to release the unsold rights because it's highly unpleasant working with someone who has fired you.

If you've had a rocky publishing experience, you'll also want to leave room for the possibility that your agent might be the one who wants to do the parting. "You can't hold someone's work hostage," says

Veronica. "You want an agent who is passionate about your work and engaged with it. If they're not, then something is broken."

It will feel scary to leave your agent (or be left by them) without another one lined up, but it's better to cut the cord earlier rather than later. If you already think you're going to end the relationship, don't have your agent submitting essays for you or assisting you with pitches: that isn't forthright behavior, and animosity will accrue. If you're too terrified to make a clean break without a safety blanket, be careful and discreet. Use the cooling-off period of postpublication to do reconnaissance. Do you have author friends who have agents they really, really trust? Like, trust enough to have lunch with you to talk potential representation without blabbing to everyone in the industry that you're two-timing your current rep?

Be kind as you begin your new agent search: be generous and professional. In discussions with potential agents, you can say you have a different working style than your current one; don't call your agent "inept." The agent world is a small one, and you don't want other agents thinking you might one day bitch about them, too. As with everything publishing related, take your time and be deliberate. Truly good writing will find representation. You know what the best way is to find a new agent? Write something great.

Should I move somewhere remote?

When the advance money is spent and the cushy teaching position denied, you might find yourself reevaluating the zip code you live in.

Urban centers offer countless advantages for writers: cities are filled with bookstores, bookstores have events, cities have colleges and

MFA programs that you can attend or teach at; in short, there are people making literary love all over town.

But cities are expensive. Housing in cities is expensive. And as romantic as it was to be writing your first novel in a five-story walk-up with suspect accordance to building codes that you shared with three (or sometimes five, depending on sleepover guests) aspiring writers, it can get tiresome to share a shower when you're thirty-five.

"I had lived in New York City for fourteen years—it defined and delineated every aspect of my life," says author Sarah Gerard. "I will always have an abiding love for New York City, but it had also started to grind me down. It's expensive to move, and saving money is difficult in New York. My partner and I wanted to move to a city where we had the best shot at being happier."

Poet and New York native Robin Beth Schaer also considered the city central to her identity, but with a husband who was also adjuncting, finances were getting tight. "We paid for our own health insurance, at times had none, never knew if our adjunct contracts would be renewed, and barely made ends meet," she says. "Because the city was so desirable, the competition for full-time teaching jobs was tremendous. But being in New York felt vital to us as writers for the community and inspiration, so we soldiered on."

Jay Babcock, a conservationist and the cofounder of the counter-culture magazine *Arthur*, was traveling around the West Coast looking for funds for his ailing publication when he fell in love with the landscape and the community of Joshua Tree, California. Although he felt a strong connection to the desert town, Jay's eventual relocation there wasn't influenced by a desire to find a more affordable place to make art. "Moving somewhere with a lower cost of living with the idea that you will be able to sustain yourself off of only your art seems like folly to me," Jay says about his move. "As the musician Robert Fripp pointed out years ago, you pay to work. Find the money. Don't expect the art to fund your life."

Meanwhile, back in New York, Sarah and her partner were creating a spreadsheet of potential new cities judged against criteria like the threat of natural disasters, ease of transportation, and the politics and culture. For many reasons, Sarah's hometown of St. Petersburg, Florida, proved the place to try. As for Robin and her husband, after the birth of their first child, the financial strain of New York living had become untenable. "We couldn't afford childcare," Robin remembers, "and we had no time to write, or see friends, or take advantage of the city. Stripped of the benefits, sacrificing ourselves for New York no longer made sense." Robin's husband, the writer Anthony Tognazzini, accepted a three-year visiting professorship at the College of Wooster in Ohio—and they headed to the Midwest.

If Jay is contented with life in his new home, Robin, Sarah, and their respective partners are still see-sawing a bit. The benefits of their moves are undeniable: both writers have more time, more space, more energy, and they feel healthier, too. "I can't overstate what a difference it makes in my attitude to see plants and animals everywhere I go, and receive a steady dose of vitamin D each day," says Sarah. The peace and quiet has also been an unexpected boon for Robin. "Leaving the city felt like unwinding myself: loosening, quieting, opening," she says. "Being aware and curious in my daily life is vital to being a writer, yet I had stopped inhabiting the world that way —I'd stopped collecting ideas and noticing images, because I'd been so overwhelmed and exhausted in New York."

But the cons of remoter living gnaw at these writers, too. There aren't a lot of creative-writing positions in St. Petersburg, and the adjuncting jobs that do exist pay as little as $2,000 a semester. Sarah and her partner (who is also a writer) are still struggling to stay afloat financially. For Robin, the physical and mental exhaustion of a big move to an area where she didn't have any contacts has proved tougher than expected, as has the homogeneity and political and religious conservatism that she was unprepared to face. To combat this, Robin is using her Midwestern exodus for creative research. "I've been trying to seek out the usefulness of this experience to find what I can learn from this place and its particular culture and history, and figure out how to use that knowledge in my work," she says.

If you're going to move somewhere new, it's crucial to research the hidden costs of your potential town—both financial and emotional. I myself moved from New York to the Massachusetts Berkshires in 2005, and I thought the only thing I'd have to budget for was my mortgage. Color me surprised when I realized that our fixer-upper log cabin cost $600 a month to heat because it was so poorly insulated; that firewood cost $150 a cord; and that snowy driveways are very, very expensive to have plowed. I was also sure that I was never having children, so when I did have one (whoops!), I found myself living in an area without a school, daycare, or a place to buy milk. (Hell, our town was so remote, the *post office* was for sale.)

Photographer Alissa Morris-Hessler has a guidebook to remote living called *Ditch the City and Go Country* that can help you avoid city-slicker screwups such as mine. Another useful resource is the Chamber of Commerce of whatever town you're flirting with. They can send you relocation packets that will outline the location's demographics, and you'll get a list of the cultural, religious, and professional resources available, as well.

If you do move somewhere rural as a self-employed person, get ready to abandon all preconceptions about what you "do" for work. Since moving to the countryside, I have been (among other things) a not-very-good barista, a publicist for a theater company, a failed entre-preneur (I tried to start a branding company for farmers but everyone paid us in raw milk), and a press-release writer for a religious cult. My husband—an independent filmmaker—has worked as a grave installer, a tennis instructor, and a trade-show convention salesman to get by. And firewood has gone up, by the way, to $175 a cord.

The new face of rejections

Publishing is built upon a system of acceptance and rejection. All writ-ers are accustomed to being rejected . . . a lot. But something funny happens when you start to publish books. The rejections aren't faceless anymore. Suddenly they're coming from your colleagues, they're com-ing from your friends. When you're just starting out, Editor von Editor is just some name in your inbox. By the time you have a book or two out, that editor might be someone you've shared a drink with, maybe even a meal.

Your professional acquaintances will leave you off of best-of-the-year book lists; they won't invite you to literary festivals; they won't ask you to join a panel; they won't accept your short story for publi-cation; they won't publish your op-ed; they won't review your book; they won't give you good books to review; they won't send you galleys; they won't put you on the guest list of the hot party they're in charge of; they won't post Instagram photos of your galley when they get it . . . when you're a published writer, literary rejections become shape-shifters. There are a myriad of new ways to be snubbed.

It isn't accurate, really, to call these snubs "rejections," but rejected is how your heart and mind will feel. The best way to get past these slights is to not know that they're happening. When your book has been out for a while, try to stay offline. Trust me, if something exciting has happened, you are going to find out. If you can't distract yourself from your hurt feelings with another project, stay busy in another way. Put yourself in other people's shoes—literally. If you join a party-planning committee you'll realize how easy it is to leave good people off a guest list. If you edit for a literary magazine, you'll realize how often great things are rejected. If you share your own book recommendations, you'll soon see how impossible it is to mention (or even *remember*) every single book you like.

And most importantly, read. Read writing that is better than yours. Read writing that is different. Read the kind of writing that makes you burn to write.

Will my second book be successful?

I'll never forget a dinner I had with my friend, the cookbook author Alana Chernila, whom we met a little earlier. I had just gotten back from book tour for my second novel, *Touch*, a book for which I'd received a tremendous amount of support from my editorial team at Putnam. But a month into the book's life, the sales just weren't there. "I don't know," I remember saying at that dinner. "It's timely, it's funny, it got wonderful press." Alana passed me some of the gooey, cheesy appetizer she'd ordered for us to share. And then she looked at me with the sweet but unshakeable wisdom that is so uniquely hers. "Didn't anyone tell you that second books always flop?"

Well, no! Right up to its publication, I assumed my second book would do at least as well as, if not better than, my first. I simply did not make room in my brain for any other outcome. So when my second novel underperformed in comparison with my first one, I was shocked.

Second books are tricky, especially if your first project got critical acclaim and/or media attention and an expectation was set. In author Chloe Benjamin's *Poets & Writers* article on the subject, she has an inspiring lineup of well-known authors whose second books were duds: fans of Donna Tartt's *The Secret History* were irate that her second novel, *The Little Friend*, wasn't a knockout like the first, and Zadie Smith's second book, *The Autograph Man*, was a silent follow-up to her cacophonously received debut, *White Teeth*.

The good news about second books is if you've put the hard work in to write, revise, and publish two books already, chances are you'll go on to publish more. "I think there is also a renewed feeling among certain publishers that it is important to recommit to authors over the longer term," says literary agent Dorian Karchmar in Chloe's article on second books. "If you'd given up after *John Henry Days*, you wouldn't have gotten *The Underground Railroad* . . . if you lost faith after *About Grace*, you lost out on *All the Light We Cannot See*."

Your second book might do exceptionally well. It might do far better than the first. But as in everything with publishing, think of your second project as another achievement in what will hopefully be a long and enjoyable career. And if it flops, find a good listener willing to share her cheese appetizer with you.

Writers, it can happen to you

Remainder letters

No one tells you about this horrible milestone because all publishers hope it never happens, but it happens a lot! When your publisher was a little overzealous with your print run, they can find themselves with too many leftover copies of your book. The remainder letter is a depressing notice that gives you the opportunity to buy back a little dignity by purchasing the leftover copies of your book at a competitive price. If you don't purchase them, the fine print lets you know that they'll be pulped. Before you're tempted to share your home with three thousand copies of your hardcover, realize two things: lots and lots of writers get remainder letters, so don't feel too badly about this notice. It is not the end of the world, your career, or the environment if the books are pulped.

This being the case, it's useful to have *some* extra copies of your books on hand. Drive around with several in your car's trunk: give them to libraries, give them to prisons—prisons are desperate for good books! Leave them for your Airbnb hosts when you travel. You can make those extra copies your personal calling card. Just don't go into debt buying back your own book. Note that there are usually twelve hardcovers to a box. Give some thought to how many boxes you can realistically fit into your dwelling (and keep away from moisture and rodents) before you place your order.

Uncashable royalty checks

At most publishers, royalties are paid out twice a year: in the fall and in the spring. You receive a royalty check if you have earned back your advance, period. If you haven't earned out, you don't get a check.

Some writers will start touching royalties quickly: the lower your advance is, the fewer copies you have to sell to earn back your advance. Other authors—with either very modest advances or very popular books—can earn their advances back before the book even publishes thanks to prepublication audiobook-rights sales, foreign sales, film or TV options, and other tasty treats. Earning royalties is wonderful news, and it's something you should be proud of. With royalties reflecting international sales and multiple formats (ebooks, paperback, hardcover), there is a future in which you can be receiving surprising little bonus checks twice a year for quite some time.

But royalty checks can be depressing. And depressingly low. Based on past sales of my first novel, I entered March of 2019 thinking that I'd receive $2,000 in royalties, and I got $323 instead. That same month, the author Allison Amend shared a photo of her royalty statement on Instagram: she'd earned $5.93, but as the publisher couldn't cut checks for less than $25, she wouldn't be receiving it. "No fancy latté for me!," she wrote.

Pregnancy

Even though we touched upon this topic in book one, I think it's important to revisit it because things might have changed during the course of this book's reading (it's a long book; maybe you were involved in a conception between page 83 and now?), and people's opinions on the child question fluctuate with time.

Personally, I think that having a child has brought depth to my writing, but if I didn't have a place I trust to put my daughter during the workweek, the writing would not get done. This is why I remain convinced that writers shouldn't reproduce unless they have the savings to protect their writing time.

The time-for-writing question is one that keeps most creative, potential parents up. The author and playwright Sarah Ruhl eloquently discussed her fears regarding motherhood and creativity in *100 Essays I Don't Have Time to Write*. "When I looked at theater and parenthood," she wrote, "I saw only war, competing loyalties, and I thought my writing life was over." Three children later, Sarah decided that "life intruding on writing was, in fact, life."

For bestselling author Jean Kwok, having children actually forced her to realize her dream of publishing a book. "I am a person filled with fear," Jean admits. "I fear failure, I fear success, and I fear everything in between. However, when I was a mother with two young children, I was consumed by my greatest fear: I would never be a writer because I now had every excuse in the world to not write. It would be legitimate. I honestly had no time to write."

All day, Jean was parenting two young ruffians (Jean compares her children to "super affectionate Velcro monkeys on cocaine"), and in the evening, she taught classes at a university. "So that was when I pretty much gave up sleeping altogether and finished my debut novel," she says. "Because I was terrified that I would indeed, never become a real writer. I think I'm not alone in this. I know many other writers, especially women, who wrote their debut books in this insanely busy, hectic time. Perhaps the stress spurs creativity; perhaps we grow so much through the intense experience of motherhood; perhaps we know that if we stop writing, we will lose an integral part of ourselves. "

If you decide to have children, congratulations! Make the most of your new family and write down the funny things your children say so that you can use them in a memoir someday when you have time.

If you decide not to have children, congratulations! You don't have to listen to poop talk, and you have a lot more time to write.

Depression

A writer's work is intensely private, but book publication is public. A book's rejection or acceptance is also public, and the long-term stress of living and creating within these two different extremes can take a toll on your mental health. Many writers (myself included) find talk therapy to be a crucial form of professional support once their books are in the world.

Therapy can be expensive, so it's important not to engage the first person who is recommended to you, but to do some homework instead.

If you have health insurance, your insurer can provide you with a list of therapists and counselors who take your specific plan. Once you have these recommendations, you can use *Psychology Today*'s therapist database to look up a specific person's profile and their specialties. Next up, you'll want to schedule an informal telephone call with potential therapists: these introductory calls should be free. During the call, ask the provider whether they have a sliding scale for artists—some therapists do. Other mental-health workers will also provide a steeply discounted rate if you pay in cash; it saves them a lot of paperwork. (Note, of course, that you can't be reimbursed by your health insurance if you pay in cash.)

If you don't have health insurance, or the therapist's hourly rate is prohibitive even with a sliding scale, options still abound. Online counseling services like Talkspace are a legitimate and affordable alternative to in-person talk therapy, and might even prove preferable for those who would benefit from daily interactions with a professional rather than an hourlong meeting once in a while.

The mental-health resource website Psych Central has some great ideas for therapy on a restricted budget. Local colleges and universities often have training clinics in which psychology grad students (who are supervised by licensed mental-health professionals) will counsel patients outside of the university community for free. Likewise, if you are part of a congregation, the religious institution itself might offer counseling, or they can help you find a way to pay for therapy. Your state government's website should have a "human services" section where community mental-health services will be listed: these clinics should either be low cost or free, and you can also find free moderated support groups in your area focused on the issues that you are struggling with.

Psych Central also urges therapy seekers not to ignore the body, and as someone whose second novel is all about the negative effects of touch deprivation, I heartily agree. The occasional massage, Reiki session, chiropractic visit, acupuncture, or body-work session can do an immeasurable amount of good for your emotional and physical health.

If you're starting to feel unbalanced, anxious, or overwhelmed, talk about your worries with trustworthy family and friends. You'd be surprised how many people are struggling—in silence—alongside you. Once you open up about your difficulties, not only will you have a group of caring individuals who can help you find the support you need, you'll probably find yourself with deeper, stronger—and more honest—friendships, too.

V

....

Readying the gangplank

*Publishing professionals and authors
share their best advice for debut authors*

Though a book is as unique as the author's journey to publish it, every author has experienced the mind-bending weirdness of having something deeply intimate turn intensely public. From the household-name authors to the up-and-comers, no one is ever safe from book-related doubt. But veteran authors have the gift of hindsight: they have been there, they have done that, and with time and practice, they have learned what truly matters when it comes to having a book out. Walk on through the wind, little author. You are part of a writing family now. You will not publish alone.

Author Daniel Wallace

Enjoy it as much as you can. You only get one first book, and no matter how well the others do, no other book compares to the first. When my first book sold, I was so happy, I thought I'd never be unhappy again. I have been happy ever since, not a moment of unhappiness!

Author Angie Kim

Plan something special with a good, supportive friend for your publication day to make it special. In Anne Lamott's *Bird by Bird*, she talks about how disappointing and depressing pub day can be, how you expect pomp and circumstance, but usually, nothing much happens. With this in mind, I took out a local debut author friend for lunch on her publication day and then escorted her around half a dozen D.C.-area bookstores, signing stock and taking pictures, and we had a blast. On my pub day the following month, she and another friend did the same with me during the day, and another close friend (with whom I'd shared the Anne Lamott anecdote) held a champagne-and-sweets celebration at her house that evening. It made my publication day an amazing day I'll always remember.

And for the blues that will inevitably hit in that postpublication period, I recommend keeping an Awesome Stuff email folder. Any fun news you get, whether it be your book making a great list, a heartfelt email or review from a reader who loved your book, or an invitation to that cool literary festival you've always wanted to attend, put into that Awesome Stuff folder to read whenever you're feeling sad.

Author Anthony Doerr

The only way I'm really happy is if I'm living my life, reading something I like, and writing something new I like. You have to keep that going. If you're reading reviews of your work, they will mean less to you if you're working on something new.

Author Maggie Shipstead

Be yourself, but don't be self-indulgent.

Author Emma Smith-Stevens

A writer friend told me to always consider whether you're in it for the long run, and then to never lose sight of that. Everything isn't riding on one book. It's one book in a long career. I have friends who had gigantically successful novels and saw the pressure that follows that. Personally, for me the most meaningful thing is getting correspondences from strangers. People for whom the book really meant something. You have to be tuned in to stuff like that and not just care about awards. It's about the people who read books.

Author Michelle Hoover

As much as possible during a tour or any event, try to enjoy the people in the audience as diverse individuals who you'd otherwise not have a chance to talk to and exchange ideas with—an opportunity for a true human connection. This made my running around here and there seem all the more meaningful for me, that I wasn't just out there touting myself but was searching for that connection, bringing together a group of strangers for a communal experience. It helped to tone down my nerves in front of big groups—reach out, see faces, try to understand who they are, stop thinking about yourself—as well as placate my ego when only stragglers showed up—here's your chance for a real one-on-one. But of course, the tour, the events, all the face time with the public, that's not the real thing. You'll probably find yourself yearning to get back to your desk and work—yes, that same desk you were cursing before, where you wrung your hands, praying to just finish the damn thing. You'll want to be back there working, not signing books. And for me, that's the mark of a real writer—the one who prefers the act of creation over any possible adulation, however large or small. Get done with the marketing already and write. For me, that's the mark of a writer who will keep getting better and may just produce something astonishing.

Author Mira Ptacin

Dry shampoo is your best friend.

Author and editor Morgan Jerkins

What I'd urge debut authors to do is lean into their anxiety. Don't fight it. It's going to be there, and it will mount as buzz grows for your book. Acknowledge it, but don't let it consume you. Surround yourself with friends and family who knew you before this moment, those with whom you feel comfortable sharing all your fears.

Author Matt Sumell

Worry about the only thing worth worrying about: what is on the page. Instead of looking up at the writers who got a million dollars for their books, compare down so you can feel grateful for your shit and not be measuring stuff to other people who have done better. Keep busy. After my first book, my agent wanted my next thing, and I was busy having a nervous fucking breakdown.

Author Andrea Dunlop

My biggest piece of advice for debut authors, having both been through it myself and seen dozens of authors through the process, is to enjoy it! I find that so many authors get so nervous and caught up in expectations and comparing themselves to other authors that they lose sight of the fact that this is a moment they've been dreaming of for years—maybe all their life—and they let it pass them by. Give yourself absolute and total permission to purely celebrate on the day your book comes out, definitely have a party of some kind and just try to soak it up as much as possible. There's nothing like the first time, and it only happens once!

Publicist Alyson Sinclair

Book promotion is a collaborative process. If you're not sure how to be helpful, even if you don't know who your publicist is yet, find out

if there is a list you can start building. And fill out your author questionnaire! Don't think of it as a throwaway thing, it really is helpful. If
you're hiring a publicist, it's good to know anything that isn't Google-
able. That you're friends with so-and-so or went to school with so-
and-so. Be collaborative, share the information you can share. And if
you're not comfortable with certain things like social media or going
out on tour, know what areas you *are* comfortable in and at the very
least, build a website. I don't want my client's first online result to be
some professor they used to have!

Author Iris Martin Cohen

Make sure all your quotes are in the public domain. Virginia Woolf
isn't. That gave me last-minute heart attacks times a thousand. I had no
idea permissions take months, and I almost had to write a new ending
in the last two weeks before production started.

Agent Nicole Aragi

Be nice to booksellers, they are your friends and allies and they work
hard! I'm always astonished when I hear of rude or high-handed behavior at readings, etc. And stay away from fast food at airports while
on tour. Waiting-at-the-gate boredom leads to snacking, but it'll wreck
you. My gang calls it "tour fat," and it's hard to shake.

Author Teddy Wayne

If you get under $100,000 for your advance, expectations will be modest
from the publisher's viewpoint and you should recognize that beforehand. There should be some pride in a book not taking off, because—I
don't want to sound like sour grapes—but for 99 percent of the books
that "break out," maybe it's not the greatest book. Acknowledge that
your book's life after publication is distinct from its life beforehand.

Be happy about the work you did on it. After it is published, it is out of your hands.

Agent Mollie Glick

My best general advice for an author being published is to be specific in your asks. If you don't like the proposed cover, come back with designs and concepts you do like. If you aren't sure that your team is doing enough promotion, come back with specific ideas of pitches to publications or places to market.

Author Weike Wang

Work on something new, consider working on something new, work on something new. Once the book is out, you will find yourself engulfed by that book, and who you were when you were writing it. You will sometimes become terrified to write again, or even too busy to write again. But mostly terrified. You are scared of not being about to reproduce what you made before. Maybe this is just how I felt. When my book came out, I felt like I was being drawn back into a black hole (a good black hole) but talking and thinking about the book again made me nervous that I would never write something like that again. Working on a new project helped me push past that. The point is not to write the previous book again, but to write a new one.

Author Wayétu Moore

We all know the saying, "It takes a village." Growing up, my parents abided by this and were very strict about who my siblings and I spent our time with. It used to infuriate me, but later I understood their wisdom, and that they were only trying to protect us from the heartaches that stem from bad company and influences. I would honor their methods later in life—the care they took in choosing their friends and those they let into our home, and their circle. This circle, this village, has power. The members of this group give counsel, and bad counsel can sometimes lead to devastating outcomes. You're pursuing a profession that is competitive, stressful, and to be honest, downright hard. None of us become writers to become rich. This may perplex those closest to you who aren't writers or artists. For them, the question is, "Why pursue something with no guarantee of monetization?" Those who are around you will either be your greatest encouragers, pushing you toward that extra page or chapter, or be the reason why you abandon those stories in that unnamed desktop folder. Choose them wisely and choose them well.

Author Jess Walter

The advice I would give is to create a ceremony in which you put your own book on the bookshelf. Twenty-two years and eight books later, it's still my very favorite part, holding that first copy in my hand, walking around, looking for just the place to put it, stacking and restacking the book shelf (maybe I'll organize them by color this time) . . . You wrote a book! You're holding it in your hands! No prize or reward can beat that.

I also learned pretty quickly not to spend too much time checking to see if bookstores had my books. Because there are only two possibilities: (1) The book is there (it's not selling!), and (2) the book isn't there (they're not stocking it!).

Author Lindsay Hunter

Most importantly: expect *nothing*. No life change, no windfall, no salivating Hollywood queue. It's just you and your astonishing achievement. It's just you and your work, always. For better or for worse. Once that thing is out in the world, you cannot control how it's received. You can only return to your passion for it, which, when you inevitably ask yourself *why*, is all the reason you'll need.

Author Kristopher Jansma

Remember that "author" is always only a temporary job description. It is a role you play when you step out to talk to readers, booksellers, critics, or whoever about your latest work. It might be a role you play for days or weeks or months—one you slip back into now and then when called upon. But it can't and shouldn't be a permanent state of affairs, because your permanent job description is "writer" and that's what you are even when no one else is looking.

Most of the stress you go through while being an author is really about worrying that if you don't perform well enough, you'll somehow have to stop being a writer. But you were a writer before you started being an author, and you will still be one afterward.

Author (and this book's editor) Julie Buntin

I didn't anticipate that publicity would change my writing or my relationship to writing, but as I went on, and that quiet, internal voice got smaller and smaller . . . really, that's the most precious thing. It's a kind of trauma, making that part of yourself public. Being a writer in the world, it's a privilege, but it's not gentle. It's a really heavy experience. It's important to check in with yourself and make sure you feel like a writer, and not just someone who is talking about writing.

Author Jimin Han

I'd been waiting for publication for so long that when it happened, I was intent on being earnest and enthusiastic every single step of the way, and it can be exhausting and, to be honest, not necessary. The overriding lesson learned: lighten up! Don't sweat the small stuff. Look to what's ahead and not behind you. Have a sense of humor. And trust the organizers of your event! They're truly nice folks who are confident about having invited you and will make sure everything runs smoothly. And if it doesn't, so what? The number of people who show up is not a reflection on you or your book.

Author and translator Jennifer Croft

For events around the release of your book, I recommend renting outfits from somewhere like Rent the Runway. I've had an unlimited subscription for a few months now, and it has saved me so much hassle. Also: when you do read, try to find the shortest possible passage, or involve others to stage your reading so that the audience doesn't get bored.

Author Benjamin Percy

Always be deep into another project before your book publishes. Because the interviews (some awkward and uninformed, some robotic, some fun and engaging), the guest blog posts (that no one reads), the events (both exhilarating and depressing), the reviews (good and bad), the social media promotion (that everyone finds annoying and has a questionable impact on the numbers), the sales figures (confusing and ultimately not up to expectations), the awards season (you will not win anything—let's be honest) can all blender your brain and make you feel untethered and short-circuity. If you're already working on another book—and committed to its plot and characters—then you don't stress out as much about the current one. When that lousy review publishes in the *North Central Eastern Arkansas Gazette*, you're like, "Well, I wrote that thing like a year and a half ago. I'm so much more awesome now."

Also: be your publicist's best friend. Send them wine and funny emails.

Author Tobias Carroll

If you don't have a Square Reader, I'd highly recommend picking one up.

Author Lincoln Michel

One thing you'll learn is that publishing is sloooow. One to two years will probably elapse between selling your book and its appearance on bookstore shelves. By the time your book does come out, you may feel deflated. You wrote it years ago, and you've already had edits, a cover reveal, galleys, and early reviews. But publishing a book is an amazing thing, so don't wait for publication day. Celebrate every small step along the way.

Poet Joanna Hoffman

Try not to be detailed about what quantifies as "successful." Don't compare yourself to other people, "Oh, that person had that many people at their book-release party, I had less at mine." Think about what success means to you, what makes you feel like your book has made a difference. I still, once in a while, get notes from gay teenagers in the Midwest saying that my book meant something to them. That's what makes me feel successful, more than winning an award.

Translator Elisa Wouk Almino

When publishing a translation, you might run into one of two fears: that your work will be invisible or intensely scrutinized. The greatest solution to coping with either problem, I've found, is publicly speaking about your translation process. By sharing the thinking and research that went into your work, you will not only prevent misunderstandings or misreadings, but also make your crucial role as translator more apparent.

Author Elizabeth Crane

Back in the ancient times of publishing, an editor took me to lunch, prepub, and gave me some fancy gold pencils and a big eraser for the editing process, and he told me to "save everything," which honestly, no one needs to tell me personally to do, and I'm not sure now is such good advice whoever you are. (Let go of everything! Isn't that better advice?) Print coverage of books was still abundant enough that I easily filled the archival scrapbook my dad bought me—I had a nominally splashy debut, at least as story collections sometimes go. Five more books later, with what seem to me like wildly varying degrees of attention on each one, it's hard for me to find a through line besides, "Things change and then they change again."

Author and bookstore owner Emma Straub

Be grateful. Try to honor all of the time and effort that you have put into making this happen. Do so by saying, "Thank you," over and over again, to every single person you encounter. Here are some people who are making your dreams come true: your agent, your editor, your publicist, your marketing person, your local bookseller, your sales rep. The more you know and love these people (and the more they know and love you), the better your books will do.

Make friends with other writers. Make friends with booksellers. Be kind. Be generous. Write blurbs. Write thank-you notes. Ask people's names.

Even if you have a space to write at home, go write other places, too, where you won't be tempted to do the laundry.

Author Rachel Khong

For a while after my book came out, I couldn't do very much. I felt exhausted and spent—often in a good, happy way, but still. "Publicity is part of your job" is something you'll hear over and over again. And yet, for me, it was a part of my job that was hard to get satisfaction from; it never came naturally to me, and it never felt like a job well done. Writing is my main job, and the job I love. But during that time, I was also utterly incapable of writing. I didn't have the energy or time, and my brain wasn't working properly; it felt like it was wrapped in Bubble Wrap and that I was just poking helplessly at it. If you are feeling that way, too, try not to worry. This is temporary, and you *will* feel normal again. In the meantime, for as long as you need, GIVE YOURSELF A BREAK. It's okay to not be working; it's okay to just be a human in the world—that's part of your job as a writer, too. If you must work—and I understand this impulse all too well—do work that is simple and gratifying: Read. Research a vague idea you have. Make lists of people you are grateful for, then thank them one by one.

Another tip: I was constantly ravenous on tour, and sometimes I'd be stranded in a city, running from place to place, snackless and bereft. Only somewhat late in the game—i.e., this year, at age thirty-two—did I discover the convenient miracle that is Babybel cheese. It's not like it's the best cheese in the world, but you can take it places, and that is important on a book tour.

Editor Masie Cochran

For a first book, it's hard to stay sane and balanced because it's all consuming—what has been private is going to be public. My advice is don't expose yourself to the idiocy of other people, don't read the comments section in places where you've placed essays, don't read your Amazon or Goodreads reviews. Have a trusted friend send the good ones to you. Reading the comments section is like being in high school and sitting in a stall with your feet on the toilet seat so nobody knows you're there, and listening to what the girls are saying.

Author Alex Marzano-Lesnevich

I'm not an athletic person at all, but any form of exercise that was so intense that I couldn't think turned out to be really useful. I'd recommend CrossFit, but it gave me a concussion.

Author Porochista Khakpour

Use agents. Trust your agent. If you can't trust your agent, fire your agent and get a new one. Write, as much as you can. Read even more. You will never be paid enough for what you write. If you teach, it will be the same. No one will ever read you as much as you want. You are in a profession where nothing adds up: not enough money, not enough readers, not enough time. You are not even enough. What you want to do is too big. Just keep writing. And reading—more. Also: Live. Have friends, lovers, pets, other things to do. Go places. When you are there, talk to people. Love people. If you hate people, maybe you should not be a writer. You are in an audience-based profession. Without readers, there is no writing. Readers matter more than writers. Hopefully all writers are also readers, but readers don't have to be writers. They win.

Author Justin Taylor

If you say yes to a given thing, and it turns out you don't enjoy doing that thing, don't ever say yes to it again. Ultimately your peace of mind and comfort in what you're doing is worth more than any amount of press, exposure, etc. Some writers know in their gut they don't ever want to write a book review, or do a "The Story Behind My Novel" guest post, or what have you. That's okay if that is you, and don't let your publicist tell you otherwise. But most of us figure out what we're up for, and what works, via trial and error.

Author Edan Lepucki

1. Start a new book.
2. Whatever you're feeling, it's normal.
3. Go cry.
4. Congratulations!

Author Laura van den Berg

A book coming into the world involves asking people for a lot of favors, you have to do a lot of outreach. It's important to try to give as much as you're taking. For me, I try to be an "in-combo" person, someone that bookstores can pair another reader with, partly because it's enjoyable, and partly because it's something I've asked people to do for me. In this way, I can help replenish the system.

Book scout Cathrin Wirtz

Don't talk to negative people. As a person who has made themselves vulnerable and put blood, sweat, and tears into writing a book, you deserve the benefit of positivity. Keep the flame of pride alive. You wrote a book and someone is publishing you, and no one can ever, ever take that away.

Author Jean Kwok

Buy your domain name: yourname.com I didn't think *Jean Kwok* was a common name but there are twelve of us on Facebook. It's a pain if someone else owns your domain name and has put up a website selling vacuum cleaners on it. That means you'd have to improvise by using variations, like yourname.net or yournameauthor.com, which is not the end of the world, but it's nice if you can get your own name. You can register that name, usually for less than twenty dollars a year, and it'll be waiting for you when you sell your first book and need to build a website. I also own common variations of my name, like jeankwok.net, just so that no one else buys them and puts porn on them.

When you choose your social media name, I am a big fan of simply using the name you publish under if it's still available. If it's not, I would just add on the word *author* or *writer*. Of course, it's your choice. If your Twitter username is something like @Iloveartichokes, that's great and will probably make some people smile, but remember that later on, people will tag you using your username for book reviews, awards, articles, and events. This is an important type of publicity. Other people who see those posts will not necessarily know who you are if your username doesn't contain your publication name. Those who don't already know you would have to click on your tag and go to your page to figure out who you are.

Author Mike Scalise

Define your limits. Communicate incessantly and openly with your people—publicists, agents, editors, your boss at your day job, your romantic partners, your friends helping you—about what your promotional expectations are, but just as importantly, when you'll need rest. I categorized pre- and postpub in terms of yes time and no time. My publicist and I shared a calendar, then identified the months when I was open to interviews, events, readings, and conferences, but also when I needed to hide away from everything, locked in my apartment, watching minimalist travel-packing videos on YouTube (look: they calm me). We ended up with a ratio of about three months of yes time to every two months of no time, spread out over about a year and a half, which worked for me. Figure out what ratio works for you. Stay open to changing the ratio if it's not working. Be kind to yourself. Book promo should be a victory lap, not a gauntlet.

Author Ottessa Moshfegh

Stay grounded to the people you love. Watch out for ego exploitation, as it will turn your success into a wall behind which you will be very lonely. Be kind. Keep working and searching beneath yourself for more. Stay off the Internet. And don't drink.

Author Sarah Rose Etter

Get great at reading your work out loud in front of an audience—it matters. Interview writers you want to be in conversation with to find out more about their process and what makes them tick. Punch above your weight—apply for a hundred residencies, and expect to be accepted to none. Enjoy the one you go to. Imagine the most impossible thing you could have—and then go after it. It's going to take many years, many stories, many books to get where you want to go. If you're in this for the short term, find something else to do. If you understand how long this is going to take, how it will take five years, ten years, fifteen years, to become the writer you really are, then work hard, keep asking, keep seeking.

Author Patty Yumi Cottrell

Be aloof, distant, and kind. Start generating new work to get distance from the first book. Meditate. Sleep eight hours. Drink green tea. A wise friend told me not to post links on social media to every piece of press or good news. That advice stayed with me. Resist talking incessantly about your book to anyone who listens. The truth is, not many people care. You'll write more books. You'll appreciate the people who care. You should read more often than you write. Ask your friends how they're doing and what they're working on. Stay away from writers who glance around a crowded room as they evaluate who is the most successful, who they should talk to next. Distance yourself from writers like that. Their books are boring. Take the long view. Robert Walser had no idea his work would be read with such admiration and envy sixty years after he died in the snow on Christmas Day.

Editor Vivian Lee

Aside from the business of publishing, it's so important to cultivate a supportive writing and literary community. Having mentors is great because they can help guide you through the process, but I can't stress enough how rewarding it is to also champion writers who are also just starting out. Sharing advice, commiserating with each other, and shouting out other incredible writers and lifting them up opens you up to new friends, of course, but also new ways to think about your own work and career as a writer.

Publicist Britt Canty

Don't get too fixated on reviews in the sought-after publications. Publicists are responsible for getting their authors' books into the right hands, and then the rest is left up to fate. The mention of fate might seem bleak, but as confusing and frustrating as this aspect of publicity might be, it's this inherent element of mystery that can be the most exciting part of the process, especially if you embrace it as such. It allows for a kind of alchemy to take place and bubble to the surface in remarkable and unanticipated ways. It can be a beautiful thing, a creative thing.

Poet and translator Rosa Alcalá

So often we have a fear of saying no because we don't want to miss out, we don't want to offend, we don't want to disappoint. But you know what's going to happen when you say no? Nothing. For the most part, there are very few things related to your literary life where if you say no, your life is going to collapse. People understand, they've been in the same position. The carrot of "more success" and "more recognition" is exciting, but you also have to ask yourself, is this what I really want?

Author R. O. Kwon

Work on other things, perhaps a project that isn't all yours. I know everyone says to begin the next novel or collection before publishing the first one, and I'd entirely agree with that, but sometimes the run-up to the first novel feels so hectic I can't consistently find the quiet I crave for fiction writing. I've started dreaming up an anthology, and it's both energizing and calming to be able to put time into bringing other people's writing into the world.

Author and teacher Rebecca Makkai

I would encourage people to start (or join) a small and private Facebook group of writers that you know, writers that you trust. Whether it's ten or fifty writers, it should be a private forum where you can ask each other questions about finances and business things and other things that would be tacky to put out there in the public in some way.

Author and editor Kelly Luce

My advice for writers who've just signed a book deal? After bursting with pride and telling everyone you know, become humble and worship at the altar of copy editors. Your manuscript will come back to you at least twice, slashed by different colored pencils, an unrecognizable beast. You'll think there can't possibly be that many errors or things to fix. There will be. It may seem tedious and joyless because you just want your book to be out already, damn it. But bask in it: take joy in the fact that someone read your book carefully enough to notice that a character's January birthday actually equates to a different sign in the

Chinese zodiac than you thought, because Chinese New Year is in February. Or that that department store didn't exist yet in Chicago in 1985. Or that Blue Öyster Cult is spelled with an umlaut.

Author and artist Kristen Radtke

The thing that surprised me most about publishing my first book was how truly *strange* it felt. On some days after its publication I was proud of what I had done and excited that I'd reached a step I'd been aspiring to for a decade, but on others I felt more exposed than I'd expected. I didn't understand how weirdly vulnerable it would be, but also how detached I was from a lot of it—I'd started writing the book so many years earlier, and talking in interviews and at events over and over about something so far from me now often felt performative and a little inauthentic. I'm seven or eight months out of the book's publication at this point, and I like how I feel now better than how I felt when it first came out. Now it's just a thing I did. I'm working on—and doing—other things. I have more space in my brain for the art, rather than the sales and the media and whatever else I'm supposed to be concerned with.

My main advice is to keep room for the art, every day, even when you're answering one hundred emails and behind on six interviews and coming up on too many deadlines. Erase "I'm sorry" from all your emails when you're saying no to unreasonable asks. Also: know that it's just one book, and you will have more books. It's okay if you weren't brave enough or ready to write what you really needed to write. You will be next time.

Agent Regina Brooks

Build up your endurance. Writing and publishing a commercially viable book requires stamina. And believe me, not everyone has the constitution for the long run. Fortify your mind. Stay focused on your original motivation for writing: Was it a story you had to get off your chest? Was it a book to help extend your brand? Was it a movement you were trying to start? No matter your motivation, keep it front and center in your mind because it will keep you inspired.

Author De'Shawn Charles Winslow

I once heard from other writers that the time shortly after selling a book is the best time to start another project. So, about a week after my agent sold *In West Mills*, I opened a blank document and began to write. But after reading the first page—I'd only written three—I discovered that *In West Mills* was still too fresh on my mind. I'd just spent two weeks obsessing over its potential future, its potential lack of a future, its characters, etc. My advice to someone who has recently sold a book is to consider waiting a while before actually sitting to start another big project. Naturally, you'll think about it. But let it simmer. And in the meantime, celebrate the hard work you've just done.

Writer and editor Haley Mlotek

There seems to be this notion in the publishing industry that there is a game at play; that if you know the rules and hit certain key touchstones on the publishing board, you'll have a bestseller. But it's not a numbers game. There are probably seven writers on the planet that get to do whatever they want. There are a lot of romantic things about being a writer, but the truth is, you are going to struggle your whole life. That's what you're committing to. We will always be leaning too hard on one side or the other: "These are my art years," versus, "These are my paying-the-bill years." That is a privilege in so many ways, but it doesn't make it less hard or less difficult. In fact, struggling to find that balance between art and commerce can lead to some great work and some great thinking. If it did work out like a game board, if you published a viral essay and went right to the pot of gold, you would miss so much. It makes you so much stronger and smarter to hold low-level day concerns at the same time as these very admirable dreams and goals about contributing to the field we all want to be a part of.

Author and teacher Juan Martinez

My first long summer away from teaching, I was convinced I'd crank out a major chunk of novel revision but just fell into this funk of inactivity and despair. Like, I'd wake up full of hope and then somehow it was afternoon already, like close to four, and I had not taken a shower, or left the house, or done anything except freak out about novel revisions without actually doing the novel revisions. I need structured time. Teaching provides that structure, and it also forces me to carve out the spaces in the day where writing happens. What I learned during the Summer of Despair and Late Showers is that I have to get up really early and write and revise before I psych myself out or before anyone's done anything interesting on Twitter. So that's my giant piece of advice: wake up early and get your own writing done. Teaching, email, whatever service work you're expected to engage in—you can take care of all of that, and you will, but write first. Or revise first. Make a chunk of the morning wholly yours. Also, be aware of your luck, if you happen to be teaching: it becomes tremendously easy to take a teaching career for granted, and it's also relatively easy to focus on its frustrations and difficulties, but it's a huge gift. Every day I wake up early and I write, and then I get to go and talk to people about that process—to share what I've learned, to read what my students are working on—it's a rare and lucky way to earn a living.

Author Etaf Rum

It takes a really, really long time to publish a book; but creating something from scratch using only words and emotions is the most rewarding thing I've ever done; nothing else can compare. At times you will doubt yourself—before, during, and after—and that feeling never really goes away. But writing a book, creating something so intimate, changes you for the better, always.

Author Lillian Li

Something I didn't quite understand until the six months before my first book came out was how important, and how impossible, a sense of scale and perspective would be. I would be up at night, picking over my publication fears, trying to discern which ones were real dangers and which ones were just fabrications of a neurotic mind. I think it's useful looking back to know that a lot of my issues were simply with the unknown—I'd never published a book before, so I had no idea what to expect. Reaching out to other debut authors helped, if not to resolve the issues then to know that I wasn't alone in freaking out. But also, reaching out to authors who have already debuted (though not so long ago that they've forgotten those first-time freak-outs) helped me figure out what were actual problems I needed to address and what were simply anxieties that I needed to process. So know this: you might not yet have a sense of scale in this brave new world, but you will build one, slowly and surely, and we are here to help.

Acknowledgments

In second grade, I had a teacher named Mrs. Vicidomini who announced that we were going to learn about the art of "book making" one week. We were given a few days to perfect our stories back at home (I swear I can still smell the wood of my father's desk and see the dust mites floating through the room I locked myself inside to do this), and on the big in-school production day, Mrs. Vicidomini rewarded us with a table full of book-making instruments and an art director's verve, gussying up our written efforts with wallpaper dust jackets boasting "about the author" sections. At seven years of age, this publishing session was the closest thing I'd ever come to intoxication. The fruit of my imagination now had weight, and heft, a little rubber cement bleed-through—I had a real book! The message to my yearning heart that week was clear: all one needed to become a "real writer" was a door that locked, a Bic pen, and someone to believe in you.

Thirty-five years later: Thank you to my believers. At Catapult: marketing sorceresses Jenn Kovitz and Elizabeth Ireland, production geniuses Wah-Ming Chang and Jordan Koluch. Nicole Caputo, Sarah Brody, and Sarahmay Wilkinson for the flawless art (and art direction), Katie Boland for the balloons, Jordan and Nicole Jones for catching my mistakes. Stella Cabot Wilson for the extra help sessions, and Megan Fishmann and Alisha Gorder for the good words. Andy Hunter for the faith and the subtitle; Jonathan Lee for the support; Dory Athey for the outreach. And dearest Julie Buntin: you "got" this book from the beginning as an editor and an author, and it is better, broader (bigger!) for your friendship and your guidance.

There aren't a lot of agents out there who can coolly give notes to an author who is writing hard truths about "the biz," but Rebecca Gradinger is one of them. Thank you for your humor, your willingness to experiment, and for your perennially long view. Veronica Goldstein, Elizabeth Resnick, and Vanessa Freifeld, for never letting anything fall through any crack. And thank you to Sally Kim, who gave me my big break and continues to teach me so much about the innate joy and hopefulness of publishing something new.

Benjamin Woodard and Jen Cote, thank you for the brainstorming session, and Amy Kurzweil, you semiotic superstar, thank you for bringing pizzazz and coherence to my Tenure Tower map.

Thank you to all the editors who ever took a chance on me, especially Benjamin Samuel, Halimah Marcus, and Lance Cleland, who let me write funny things about the writing life well before I'd ever published a book. And thank you Diego Ongaro, the most patient, large-hearted, and supportive artist outside of publishing.

But thank you most of all to our contributors: these writers, editors, agents, and industry professionals who took time to be candid with me about what's gone right (and wrong) in their careers; to admit what they would have done differently, and share what they'd still like to do. Catapult, Fletcher & Co., and I have made a donation to Girls Write Now on your behalf. And to the published, to the unpublished, to everyone with an idea that keeps them tethered to the trying: protect your magic and write on.

Resources and references

References

Alam, Rumaan. 2016. "Becoming a Parent Didn't Stop Me from Being a Writer." *BuzzFeed*. www.buzzfeed.com/rumaan/a-writer-and-a -father.

———. 2016. "Can a Male Novelist Really Write, and Get, Women?" Elle.com. www.elle.com/culture/books/a36642/man-writing-novel -about-women.

Alter, Alexandra. 2017. "Boom Times for the New Dystopians." *The New York Times*. www.nytimes.com/2017/03/30/books/boom -times-for-the-new-dystopians.html.

Anker, Patty Chang. 2011. "Why This Chinese Mother Chose to Evolve." *HuffPost*. www.huffingtonpost.com/patty-chang-anker /chinese-mother-evolve_b_807332.html.

Apatoff, Ben. 2014. "The Eleven Best Metal Songs About Literature." *Electric Literature*. electricliterature.com/the-eleven-best-metal-songs -about-literature-da84abb92925.

Attenberg, Jami. 2012. "Debuting again: A good day for Brooklyn novelist Jami Attenberg and 'The Middlesteins.'" *Politico*. www .politico.com/states/new-york/albany/story/2012/10/debuting

-again-a-good-day-for-brooklyn-novelist-jami-attenberg-and-the
-middlesteins-067223.

Baker, Jenn. 2018. "Interview with Morgan Jerkins." *Minorities in Publishing*, podcast. minoritiesinpublishing.libsyn.com/episode-71
-interview-with-morgan-jerkins.

Baker, Jenn. 2018. "Interview with James Han Mattson." *Minorities in Publishing*, podcast. player.fm/series/minorities-in-publishing
/episode-75-interview-with-james-han-mattson.

Benjamin, Chloe. 2017. "Selling Your Second Book." *Poets & Writers*. static1.squarespace.com/static/58af6321725e252c24326cc2/t
/5a09c897e2c483d6cbaf0624/1510590652287/Poets+and+Writers
+-+Benjamin.pdf.

Biedenharn, Isabella. 2016. "Debut Novels: Why New Authors Are Making Millions." *Entertainment Weekly*. ew.com/article/2016/05
/02/debut-novel-millions.

BookBrowse Editorial Staff. 2015. "Librarian Terye Balogh of the Milpitas Library Book Group Shares Some Excellent Advice About Inviting Authors to Your Group, Managing Large Discussions, and Keeping Your Group Engaged." BookBrowse. www.bookbrowse.com/featured-bookclubs/archives/index.cfm
?fuseaction=full&bookclub_number=29I.

Cain, Elna. 2019. "20 Ways to Find Freelance Writing Jobs (as a Beginner)." Elnacain.com. elnacain.com/blog/20-ways-find-freelance
-writing-jobs.

Chee, Alexander. 2018. "On Writing for Love or Money." TinyLetter. newsletter.tinyletter.com/alexanderchee/letters/on-writing-for-love
-or-money.

Coulter, Kristi. 2016. "Enjoli." Medium. medium.com/@kristicoulter
/https-medium-com-kristicoulter-the-24-hour-woman-3425ca
5be19f.

Dykema, Jane. 2017. "What I Don't Tell My Students About 'The Husband Stitch.'" *Electric Literature*. electricliterature.com/what-i-dont-tell-my-students-about-the-husband-stitch-690899157394.

Electric Literature Editorial Staff. 2018. "'Describe Yourself Like a Male Author Would' Is the Most Savage Twitter Thread in Ages." *Electric Literature*. electricliterature.com/describe-yourself-like-a-male-author-would-is-the-most-savage-twitter-thread-in-ages-60d145d638d6.

Electric Literature Editorial Staff. "Financial Management for Freelance Writers." The Authors Guild. www.authorsguild.org/member-services/writers-resource-library/managing-your-finances/financial-management-freelance-writers.

Elkin, Lauren. 2018. "Why All the Books About Motherhood?" *The Paris Review*. www.theparisreview.org/blog/2018/07/17/why-all-the-books-about-motherhood.

Eve, Nomi. 2015. "How One Author Turned the Internet into a Giant Book Club." *Publishers Weekly*. www.publishersweekly.com/pw/by-topic/columns-and-blogs/soapbox/article/68539-how-one-author-turned-the-internet-into-a-giant-book-club.html.

Filgate, Michele. 2017. "What My Mother and I Don't Talk About." Longreads. longreads.com/2017/10/09/what-my-mother-and-i-dont-talk-about.

Flood, Alison. 2015. "Portico Prize Winner Benjamin Myers: 'Why Bother Chasing the Big Publishers?'" *The Guardian*. www.theguardian.com/books/2015/dec/09/portico-prize-winner-benjamin-myers-beastings-why-bother-chasing-the-big-publishers.

Fortin, Jacey. 2017. "Roxane Gay Promotes New Book and Calls Out Podcast for 'Fat-Phobia.'" *The New York Times*. www.nytimes.com/2017/06/13/books/mamamia-roxane-gay-mia-freedman.html.

Gill, John Freeman. 2017. "The Unglamorous Ordeal of Recording Your Own Audiobook." *Literary Hub*. lithub.com/the-unglamorous -ordeal-of-recording-your-own-audiobook.

Gross, Anisse. 2016. "L.A-Based Indie Press Scores with First Title." *Publishers Weekly*. www.publishersweekly.com/pw/by-topic /industry-news/publisher-news/article/70457-we-heard-you-like -books-scores-with-first-title.html.

Hessler, Alissa. 2017. *Ditch the City and Go Country*. Salem, Massachusetts: Page Street Publishing.

Ireland, Justina. 2018. "Goodbye, Sensitivity Readers Database." Medium. medium.com/@justinaireland/goodbye-sensitivity-readers -database-e1cbc53044a9.

Irwin, Neil. 2017. "Under the Trump Tax Plan, We Might All Want to Become Corporations." *The New York Times*. www.nytimes.com /2017/04/28/upshot/under-the-trump-tax-plan-we-might-all -want-to-become-corporations.html.

Islam, Tanwi Nandini. 2016. "On Touring." *Catapult*. catapult.co /stories/on-touring.

Jacob, Mira. 2015. "I Gave a Speech About Race to the Publishing Industry and No One Heard Me." *BuzzFeed*. www.buzzfeed.com /mirajacob/you-will-ignore-us-at-your-own-peril.

———. 2016. "Here's What I'm Telling My Brown Son About Trump's America." *BuzzFeed*. www.buzzfeed.com/mirajacob/a-letter-to-my -brown-son-about-trumps-america.

Jarrell, Andrea. 2017. "Can *The New York Times*' Modern Love Column Change a Writer's Life?" *Literary Hub*. lithub.com/can-the-new -york-times-modern-love-column-change-a-writers-life.

Kachka, Boris. 2018. "Audiobooks Are the New Ebooks, Except They Might Keep Growing." *Vulture*. www.vulture.com/amp/2018/09 /audiobooks-are-booming-but-how-long-will-that-last.html.

Kelsky, Karen. 2015. *The Professor Is In*. New York: Three Rivers Press.

Khakpour, Porochista. 2017. "How to Write Iranian America, or the Last Essay." *Catapult*. catapult.co/stories/how-to-write-iranian-america.

Laity, Paul. 2016. "Maggie Nelson Interview: 'People Write to Me to Let Me Know That, in Case I Missed It, There Are Only Two Genders.'" *The Guardian*. www.theguardian.com/books/2016/apr/02 /books-interview-maggie-nelson-genders.

LaSota, Catherine. 2017. "Two Freelance Artists and a Baby." *Catapult*. catapult.co/stories/two-freelance-artists-and-a-baby.

Lee, Oliver. 2015. "I Have One of the Best Jobs in Academia. Here's Why I'm Walking Away." *Vox*. www.vox.com/2015/9/8/9261531 /professor-quitting-job.

Marzano-Lesnevich, Alexandria. 2011. "A Twist of Fate." *The New York Times*. www.nytimes.com/2011/11/13/fashion/a-twist-of-fate -modern-love.html.

Maum, Courtney. 2012. "Super Sad True Habits of Highly Effective Writers: Part 1." *Tin House*. tinhouse.com/super-sad-true-habits -of-highly-effective-writers-part-1.

McAllister, Tom. 2018. "Who Will Buy Your Book?" *The Millions*. the millions.com/2018/05/will-buy-book.html.

Meyer, Michael. 2009. "About that Book Advance . . ." *The New York Times Book Review*. www.nytimes.com/2009/04/12/books/review /Meyer-t.html.

Munro, Lisa L. 2017. "Stories of Failure: Academic Job Market Edition." Lisamunro.net. www.lisamunro.net/blog-1/2017/12/11 /failing-on-the-academic-job-market.

Nightingale, Rob. 2014. "8 Things Most People Don't Know About Amazon's Bestsellers Rank." MakeUseOf. www.makeuseof.com /tag/8-things-people-dont-know-amazons-bestsellers-rank-sales -rank.

Patrick, Bethanne. 2016. "I Will Always Be Depressed, and I'm OK with That." *Elle*. www.elle.com/life-love/a39440/double-depression.

Popkey, Miranda. 2012. "Debuting, Again: A Good Day for Brooklyn Novelist Jami Attenberg and *The Middlesteins*." *Politico*. www.politico.com/states/new-york/albany/story/2012/10/debuting-again-a-good-day-for-brooklyn-novelist-jami-attenberg-and-the-middlesteins-067223.

Riederer, Rachel. 2014. "The Teaching Class." *Guernica*. www.guernicamag.com/the-teaching-class.

Rose, M. J. and Randy Susan Meyers. 2012. *What to Do Before Your Book Launch*. Evil Eye Concepts, Incorporated.

Sacks, Sam. 2012. "Against Acknowledgements." *The New Yorker*. www.newyorker.com/books/page-turner/against-acknowledgments.

Schuman, Rebecca. 2014. "Why Your Cousin with a Ph.D. Is a Basket Case." *Slate*. www.slate.com/articles/life/education/2014/09/how_do_professors_get_hired_the_academic_job_search_explained.html.

Sehgal, Parul. 2018. "In a Raft of New Books, Motherhood from (Almost) Every Angle." *The New York Times*. www.nytimes.com/2018/04/24/books/review-mothers-jacqueline-rose.html.

Seltzer, Sarah. 2017. "The Sweetest Debut: Liso Ko on Adoption, *The Wire*, and Believing You Deserve the Time to Write." *Flavorwire*. flavorwire.com/604893/the-sweetest-debut-lisa-ko-on-adoption-the-wire-and-believing-you-deserve-to-have-the-time-to-write.

Smith, Christa. 2015. "3 Ways to Outsmart Your Inner Critic." *Psychology Today*. www.psychologytoday.com/us/blog/shift/201504/3-ways-outsmart-your-inner-critic.

Spors, Kelly. 2019. "Traditional IRA vs. Roth IRA." RothIRA.com. www.rothira.com/traditional-ira-vs-roth-ira.

Tartakovsky, Margarita. 2018. "What to Do When You Can't Afford Talk Therapy." *Psych Central*. psychcentral.com/blog/what-to-do-when-you-cant-afford-therapy.

Tishgart, Sierra. 2017. "Author Alissa Nutting Prefers Two Hot Dogs on One Bun." *Grub Street*. www.grubstreet.com/2017/08/alissa-nutting-grub-street-diet.html.

Wade, Carrie. 2016. " 'You're Carrie, Y'Know?' 7 Ways My Non-disabled Friends Get It Right." *Autostraddle*. www.autostraddle.com/youre-carrie-yknow-7-ways-my-nondisabled-friends-get-it-right-339012/.

Watkins, Claire Vaye. 2015. "On Pandering." *Tin House*. tinhouse.com/on-pandering.

Westervelt, Amy. 2018. "Is Motherhood the Unfinished Work of Feminism?" *The Guardian*. www.theguardian.com/commentisfree/2018/may/26/is-motherhood-the-unfinished-work-of-feminism.

Wendig, Chuck. 2017. "Is It Time, Dear Writer, to Ditch Your Literary Agent?" Terrible Minds. terribleminds.com/ramble/2017/02/14/is-it-time-dear-writer-to-ditch-your-literary-agent.

Williams, John. 2014. "PEN Announce Shortlists for 2014 Book Prizes." *The New York Times*. artsbeat.blogs.nytimes.com/2014/06/18/pen-announces-shortlists-for-2014-book-prizes/.

Young, Stella. 2014. "I'm Not Your Inspiration, Thank You Very Much." TEDxSydney. www.ted.com/talks/stella_young_i_m_not_your_inspiration_thank_you_very_much.

Zhang, Jenny. 2017. "Your Best American Girl." *The New York Times Magazine*. www.nytimes.com/interactive/2017/03/09/magazine/25-songs-that-tell-us-where-music-is-going.html?_r=0#/mitski-your-best-american-girl.

Resources

....

0s&1s, Thick Skin Interview Series: www.0s-1s.com/thick-skin-xi

24|Seven Talent: www.24seventalent.com/en-us/home

AgentQuery.com: www.agentquery.com

Alaina Leary: alainaleary.com

Alliance of Artists Communities: www.artistcommunities.org
/residencies/directory

Alyson Sinclair, Nectar Literary PR: www.alysonsinclairpr.com

American Booksellers Association, Winter Institute: www.bookweb
.org/wi2019/winter-institute-2019

Artisan Creative: www.artisancreative.com

Association of Writers & Writing Programs: www.awpwriter.org

Association of Writers & Writing Programs Conference: www.awp
writer.org/awp_conference

Astro Poets: twitter.com/poetastrologers

Autostraddle: www.autostraddle.com

AWP, *The Writer's Chronicle*: www.awpwriter.org/magazine_media
/writers_chronicle_overview

BookExpo: www.bookexpoamerica.com

Books Are Magic: www.booksaremagic.net

BookSparks: gobooksparks.com

Catapult Classes, the Online Novel Generator: catapult.co/classes/the
-online-novel-generator-twelve-weeks-to-a-full-draft-189-2018-08-14

CBC Diversity Initiative: www.cbcdiversity.com

ChronicleVitae: chroniclevitae.com

Conal Conference Alerts: conferencealerts.com

Creative Compass, Artists with Disabilities Access Program: mycreative
compass.org/Money/Grants/Artists-with-Disabilities-Access
-Program

Crit Works Writing Workshop: crit.works

Disabled Writers: www.disabledwriters.com

Duotrope: duotrope.com

Dzanc Books Prizes: dzancbooks.submittable.com/submit

EMT Agency: www.emtagency.net

Freedom Web-Blocking App: freedom.to/freedom-for-writers

Freelancers Union: www.freelancersunion.org

Futurepoem: www.futurepoem.com

GoGrad Fellowship Opportunities: www.gograd.org/financial-aid /scholarships/fellowships

Go Overseas: www.gooverseas.com

Goodreads: www.goodreads.com

GrubStreet Novel Incubator Course: grubstreet.org/programs/intensives /incubators-labs/novel-incubator

Hi Wildflower Beauty & Fragrance: hiwildflower.com

Holy Cross Monastery: holycrossmonastery.com

Horses Atelier: www.horsesatelier.com

Inside Higher Ed: www.insidehighered.com

Jack Jones Literary Arts: www.jackjonesliteraryarts.com

Jane Friedman: www.janefriedman.com

Jewish Book Council: www.jewishbookcouncil.org

The Kenyon Review, the Writers Workshop: www.kenyonreview.org/writers

LibraryThing: www.librarything.com

LinkedIn: www.linkedin.com

Lyceum: www.lyceumagency.com

Matt Bell's Submission Tracker: www.mattbell.com/post/37081194562 /submission-tracker-spreadsheet/

Meetup: www.meetup.com

Middlebury Bread Loaf Writers' Conferences: www.middlebury.edu /bread-loaf-conferences/bl_writers/node/176531

Minorities in Publishing Podcast: www.jennifernbaker.com/podcast

Modern Language Association: www.mla.org/Convention/MLA-2019

Modern Loss: modernloss.com

Monstering: Disabled Women and Nonbinary People Celebrating Monsterhood:
www.monsteringmag.com

National Novel Writing Month: nanowrimo.org

National Writers Union: nwu.org

NOLO, Business Formation: LLCs and Corporations: www.nolo.com
/legal-encyclopedia/llc-corporations-partnerships

OnlineBookClub: onlinebookclub.org

Orcas Islands Lit Fest: oilf.org

PaperCrowd: www.papercrowd.com

PEN America, Health Insurance for Writers: pen.org/health-insurance
-for-writers

Poets & Writers, Conferences and Residencies Database: www.pw.org
/conferences_and_residencies

Poets & Writers, First Book Awards: www.pw.org/tags/markets/book
_awards/first_book_awards

Poets & Writers, Literary Agent Database: www.pw.org/literary_agents

Poets & Writers, Writing Contests, Grants, and Awards: www.pw.org
/grants

Porches Writing Retreat: www.porcheswritingretreat.com

ProFellow: www.profellow.com

Psychology Today, Therapists Database: www.psychologytoday.com
/us/therapists

QueryTracker: querytracker.net

Rebecca Schuman: www.slate.com/authors.rebecca_schuman.html

Sackett Street Writers Workshop: www.sackettworkshop.com

SAG-AFTRA, Audiobooks: www.sagaftra.org/audiobooks

Shaw Guides Guide to Writers Conferences and Writing Workshops:
  writing.shawguides.com

Sick Burns: The Best of Kirkus Reviews Worst: bestbadreviews.tumblr
  .com

Sierra Club Honors and Awards: www.sierraclub.org/awards

Slushpile Hell: slushpilehell.tumblr.com

Speak OUT Boston: www.speakoutboston.org/testamonials

Spruceton Inn Artist Residency: www.sprucetoninn.com/artist
  -residency

Story Studio Chicago, Novel in a Year: www.storystudiochicago.com
  /product/novel-in-a-year-revise-and-launch-with-abby-geni-about

Streak: www.streak.com

Submittable: www.submittable.com/discover

Talk Space: www.talkspace.com

Teach Away: www.teachaway.com

The Authors Guild: www.authorsguild.org

The Book Club Cookbook: www.bookclubcookbook.com

The Cabins Retreat: www.thecabinsretreat.com

The Future Bookshelf: thefuturebookshelf.co.uk

The International Women's Writing Guild: www.iwwg.org

The University of Texas at Austin, Literature by the Pen-City Writers:
  sites.utexas.edu/lsjcs/2018/10/20/literature-by-the-pen-city
  -writers

The Voices of Our Nations Art Foundation: vonavoices.org

The Write Life: thewritelife.com

The Writer's Center: www.writer.org/workshops/calendar

The Writer Contests: www.writermag.com/writing-resources/contests

Vision of Peace Hermitages: vophermitages.org

Volume Writing Workshops: volumeworkshops.com/new-index

We Need Diverse Books, Resources for Writers: diversebooks.org
/resources/resources-for-writers/

Williams & Harricks: www.and.co/williams-harricks

World Teachers: www.worldteachers.net

Write in the Margins: writeinthemargins.org/sensitivity-readers

Interviews and quotations

Cara Blue Adams

Beth Ain

Brianna Albers

Rosa Alcalá

Kathleen Alcott

Henry Alford

Elissa Altman

Allison Amend

Nicole Aragi

Jami Attenberg

Ramona Ausubel

Jay Babcock

Claudia Ballard

Leigh Bardugo

Aaron Belz

Chloe Benjamin

Miranda Beverly-Whittemore

Emily Rapp Black

Jessica Anya Blau

Amy Bloom

Bryan Borland

Michael Bourne

Sarah Bowlin

Amy Brill

Regina Brooks

Julie Buntin

Tara Isabella Burton

Chloe Caldwell

Britt Canty

Tobias Carroll

Patty Chang Anker

Alexander Chee

Alana Chernila

Masie Cochran

Iris Martin Cohen

Yvonne Conza

Patty Yumi Cottrell

Kristi Coulter

Elizabeth Crane

Jennifer Croft

Stephanie Danler

Wendy de Jong

Annie DeWitt	Emily Griffin
Cameron Dezen Hammon	Lauren Groff
Alex Dimitrov	Jimin Han
William Dobbins	Liberty Hardy
Ted Dodson	Leslie Harrison
Anthony Doerr	Marie-Helene Bertino
Polly Dugan	Nathan Hill
Andrea Dunlop	Joanna Hoffman
Elizabeth Ellen	Elliott Holt
Morgan Entrekin	Michelle Hoover
Dave Essinger	Caitlin Horrocks
Sarah Rose Etter	Dave Housley
Melissa Febos	Samantha Hunt
Michael A. Ferro	Lindsay Hunter
Julia Fierro	Yahdon Israel
Michele Filgate	Mitchell S. Jackson
Charles Finch	Mira Jacob
D. Foy	Kristopher Jansma
John Freeman Gill	Morgan Jerkins
Jane Friedman	Barbara Jones
Roxane Gay	Daniel Jones
Sarah Gerard	Saeed Jones
Ellen Gerstein	Tayari Jones
Mollie Glick	Dorian Karchmar
Luke B. Goebel	Porochista Khakpour
Anna Goldfarb	Rachel Khong
Veronica Goldstein	Angie Kim
Hallie Goodman	Lisa Ko
Rebecca Gradinger	Jarett Kobek
Garth Greenwell	Rosalie Knecht

Michelle Kroes

Akil Kumarasamy

Jean Kwok

R. O. Kwon

Jessica Lamb-Shapiro

Jane Larkworthy

Dorothea Lasky

Catherine LaSota

Alaina Leary

Vivian Lee

Kara Leighann

Edan Lepucki

Jonathan Lethem

Lillian Li

Lara Lillibridge

Tara Lindis-Corbell

Kelly Luce

Mike Magnuson

Rebecca Makkai

Halimah Marcus

Juan Martinez

Alex Marzano-Lesnevich

Brendan Matthews

Ryan D. Matthews

Priyanka Mattoo

Lincoln Michel

Haley Mlotek

Wayétu Moore

Paul W. Morris

Ottessa Moshfegh

Eileen Myles

Maggie Nelson

Kevin Nguyen

Monica Odom

Bethanne Patrick

Benjamin Percy

H. W. Peterson

Mira Ptacin

Kristen Radtke

Joanna Rakoff

Nelly Reifler

Elizabeth Rosner

Jess Row

Sarah Ruhl

Etaf Rum

Karen Russell

Jill Santopolo

Saïd Sayrafiezadeh

Mike Scalise

Mark Scarbrough

Robin Beth Schaer

Elisabeth Schmitz

Emily Schultz

Maggie Shipstead

Jim Shepard

Karen Shepard

Leslie Shipman

Alyson Sinclair

Emma Smith-Stevens

Rebecca Soffer

Gina Sorell

Amber Sparks

Emma Straub

Cheryl Strayed

Matt Sumell

Jesica Sweedler DeHart

Tanaïs

Donna Tartt

Justin Taylor

Matthew Thomas

Tony Thompson

Tony Tulathimutte

Deb Olin Unferth

Laura van den Berg

Carrie Wade

Daniel Wallace

Jess Walter

Weike Wang

Claire Vaye Watkins

Teddy Wayne

Bruce Weinstein

Andrew Wetzel

Jen Wilde

Stella Cabot Wilson

Simon Winchester

De'Shawn Charles Winslow

Cathrin Wirtz

Elisa Wouk Almino

Nancy Wu

Vonetta Young

Rolf Yngve

Alexi Zentner

Jess Zimmerman

Tom Zoellner

© Colin Lane

COURTNEY MAUM is the author of the novels *Costalegre*, *Touch*, *I Am Having So Much Fun Here Without You*, and the chapbook *Notes from Mexico*. Her writing has been widely published in such outlets as *BuzzFeed*, *The New York Times*, *O, The Oprah Magazine*, and *Poets & Writers*. She is the founder of the learning collaborative The Cabins, and she also runs a service called The Query Doula where she helps writers prepare their manuscripts and query letters for an agent's eyes. She's very glad you're here.